PERMANENT STATES OF EMERGENCY AND THE RULE OF LAW

Permanent States of Emergency and the Rule of Law explores the impact that oxymoronic 'permanent' states of emergency have on the validity and effectiveness of constitutional norms and, ultimately, constituent power. It challenges the idea that many constitutional orders are facing permanent states of emergency due to the 'objective nature' of threats facing modern states today, arguing instead that the nature of a threat depends upon the subjective assessment of the decision-maker. In light of this, it further argues that robust judicial scrutiny and review of these decisions is required to ensure that the temporariness of the emergency is a legal question and that the validity of constitutional norms is not undermined by their perpetual suspension. It does this by way of a narrower conception of the rule of law than standard accounts in favour of judicial review of emergency powers in the literature, which tend to be based on the normative value of human rights. In so doing it seeks to refute the fundamental constitutional challenge posed by Carl Schmitt: that all state power cannot be constrained by law.

Volume 3 in Hart Studies in Security and Justice

Hart Studies in Security and Justice
Series editor: Liora Lazarus

The interplay between security and justice has always featured prominently in legal scholarship, but it has taken on a particular urgency since the new Millennium. The new scholarly questions that arise are theoretical, doctrinal and empirical, cutting across a range of traditional sub-disciplines within the legal academy. They address some of the most pressing legal issues of our time, such as the legal status of the 'the war on terror', the nature of states of exception, targeted killing, preventive pre-trial detention, mass surveillance and the numerous other threats that security poses to human rights, the rule of law and liberal democracy.

The purpose of this series is to engage with security and justice scholarship broadly conceived, and to promote a sophisticated and complex understanding of the important challenges it faces. The series is inclusive, promoting new and established scholars from a range of disciplines. It covers doctrinal, empirical, historical and theoretical work, as well as studies which focus on domestic, comparative and international dimensions of emerging security and justice fields. The series also strives to promote the most inclusive range of politics and methodologies, scrutinizing received wisdom and established paradigmatic approaches, and promoting an intellectual dialogue between its authors and the wider field of law as a whole.

Recent titles in this series:

Surveillance, Privacy and Trans-Atlantic Relations
Edited by David Cole, Federico Fabbrini and Stephen Schulhofer

Parliament's Secret War
Veronika Fikfak and Hayley J Hooper

Permanent States of Emergency and the Rule of Law

Constitutions in an Age of Crisis

Alan Greene

•HART•
OXFORD • LONDON • NEW YORK • NEW DELHI • SYDNEY

HART PUBLISHING
Bloomsbury Publishing Plc
Kemp House, Chawley Park, Cumnor Hill, Oxford, OX2 9PH, UK

First published in Great Britain 2018

A catalogue record for this book is available from the British Library.

Library of Congress Cataloging-in-Publication data

Names: Greene, Alan (Law teacher) author.

Title: Permanent states of emergency and the rule of law : constitutions in an age of crisis / Alan Greene.

Description: Oxford [UK] ; Portland, Oregon : Hart Publishing, 2018. | Series: Hart studies in security and justice | Includes bibliographical references and index.

Identifiers: LCCN 2017053245 (print) | LCCN 2017055288 (ebook) | ISBN 9781509906161 (Epub) | ISBN 9781509906154 (hardback : alk. paper)

Subjects: LCSH: War and emergency powers. | Rule of law. | Effectiveness and validity of law. | Constituent power. | Emergency management. | Crisis management in government. | Constitutional law.

Classification: LCC K4700 (ebook) | LCC K4700 .G74 2018 (print) | DDC 342/.0628—dc23

LC record available at https://lccn.loc.gov/2017053245

ISBN: HB: 978-1-50990-615-4
ePDF: 978-1-50990-617-8
ePub: 978-1-50990-616-1

Typeset by Compuscript Ltd, Shannon

i ndilchuimhne ar m'athair Alan

ACKNOWLEDGEMENTS

This book started life as my PhD thesis awarded by UCD School of Law in 2014. I am eternally indebted to my supervisor Professor Fiona de Londras whose LLM module on counter-terrorism first awakened my interest in this topic and whose advice and supervision throughout the PhD process and my career has been invaluable. Fiona is responsible for a large part of my academic and career trajectory and this is something I am eternally grateful for. Thanks also to Dr Thomas Mohr for acting as secondary supervisor, and to Dr Eoin Daly and Professor Fionnuala Ní Aoláin for examining my thesis and their helpful comments and feedback that arose from my viva. I am also grateful to UCD School of Law for awarding me a Doctoral Scholarship and for the Irish Research Council for awarding me a postgraduate scholarship and an IRCHSS New Ideas Award.

Thanks to Durham Law School for the period of research leave which allowed me to complete this monograph. I am very grateful to my colleagues and friends who have read and provided feedback on extracts of this work along the way: to Aoife, Roger, Se-shauna, Natasa, Ntina, Ruth, and Kanstantsin. Thanks must also go to the team at Hart Publishing for their effort in bringing this book to publication.

Thanks also to all my friends and family for their support. Special mention goes to Elizabeth, Damien, Liam, Dermot, Ann, and Niall. Thanks also to my Aunt Eileen, my Aunt Louise and my brothers Darragh, Ronan, and, of course, my twin Francis. Thanks also to the late Fergus Callan for his support. Most importantly, I am forever grateful to my mum Sheila who has been an invaluable source of support throughout my life and for encouraging and helping me each step along the way. Finally, this book is dedicated to my late father Alan. Ar dheis Dé go raibh a anam.

CONTENTS

INTRODUCTION

Law and crises are indelibly linked. For Niccolò Machiavelli, the true law-makers of a state are not its legislature, judiciary or, indeed, any other organ of the state, but the extraordinary events i faces; for it is out of these events that many legal provisions are born as the state endeavours to react to the threat at hand.[1] Crises thus create conditions for the inception of new law. However, the necessity for novel legal norms to respond to a crisis also implies that the existing legal powers and legal order are insufficient to deal with the events at hand. Crises therefore also expose the limits of law.

In such extreme conditions, states that espouse their commitment to democracy, human rights and fidelity to the rule of law may, nevertheless, jettison these normative values. These antithetical measures are, however, supposedly justified as necessary to the threat to the state with a view to neutralising it. Such sacrifices are ostensibly justified by the belief that they are merely a temporary aberration from the norm; once the crisis is over, these values are then reinstated and 'normalcy' is restored. States of emergencies, therefore, ought to be 'self-neutralising', restoring the conditions necessary for their cessation by negating the crisis that justified them in the first instance.

Since the twentieth century, however, and particularly since the so-called 'war on terror' in the aftermath 11 September 2001 (9/11),[2] there has been a fundamental rethink of the manner in which states approach crises; most notably, whether such emergency responses are merely temporary derogations from the status quo or whether they are a permanent necessity. This challenge goes to the very heart of the 'emergency paradigm', calling its continued relevance and application into question. It is this oxymoronic permanent state of emergency that is the focus of this book.

The question that I seek to answer in this book is what controls—legal, or political, or both—are necessary on the entity declaring a state of emergency in order to ensure that such a declaration is prescribed by law. To do so, I explore the theoretical underpinnings and practical implications of applying legal as distinct from

[1] Niccolò Machiavelli, *The Discourses* [1531], ed Bernard Crick, trans Leslie J Walker (Penguin, 1998). Oren Gross and Fionnuala Ní Aoláin, *Law in Times of Crisis: Emergency Powers in Theory and Practice* (Cambridge University Press, 2006) .

[2] See National Commission on Terrorist Attacks Upon the United States, *The 9/11 Commission Report: Final Report of the National Commission on Terrorist Attacks Upon the United States* (22 July 2004) <https://9-11commission.gov/report/> accessed 25 August 2017.

purely political controls on decisions to declare a state of emergency contained in a state's constitution. Using a construction of the rule of law that is not dependent upon the normative value of human rights or other substantive values but instead, a 'thinner', formalist version, based on Hans Kelsen's 'Identity Thesis' and the relationship between validity and effectiveness of legal norms, I argue that a permanent state of emergency may qualify as a proxy-constitutional amendment that can only be explained as a claim for the 'constituent power' that is responsible for the foundation of the constitution. Consequently, I contend that judicial review of the decision to declare a state of emergency is necessary to resist this claim for the constituent power, notwithstanding legitimate concerns that exist about the efficacy and institutional suitability of such a control mechanism and, conversely, the potential damage that over-deferential review can do to human rights norms. In so doing, I seek to provide an answer to the challenge posed by Carl Schmitt: that all state power cannot be exercised through law.

The Structure of this Argument

In order to do this, a detailed understanding of the 'state of emergency' is firstly required. This book commences, therefore, with a historical and cross-jurisdictional analysis of emergency regimes in order to attain an accurate understanding of what is termed the 'ideal' state of emergency. The Roman dictatorship is presented as the classical prototypical emergency response mechanism that had a clear demarcation between normalcy and emergency—a fundamental component of what will be termed 'the emergency paradigm'. Building upon this understanding gleaned from the Roman dictatorship, modern manifestations of emergency powers utilised by states and international law are then discussed. From this, the key factors that make up this ideal-type emergency paradigm are extrapolated and a state of emergency is descriptively (as distinct from prescriptively) defined as:

> A crisis identified and labelled by a state to be of such magnitude that it is deemed to cross a threat severity threshold, necessitating urgent, exceptional and, consequently, temporary actions by the state not permissible when normal conditions exist.

This discussion of the emergency paradigm is extrapolated under 'laboratory conditions', focusing on how a state of emergency is envisaged as ideally operating, rather than on how it actually operates. Chapter two takes this ideal-type state of emergency and explores whether the 'emergency paradigm' corroborates with reality. The key argument increasingly prevalent in the literature is the contention that it is now no longer possible to separate normalcy from emergency and that many states are, instead, in a permanent emergency. Chapter two counters this assertion by arguing that the difficulty lies not in the factually evident nature of modern threats to the state as more 'permanent', but with the decision-maker's subjective assessment as to the existence of a state of emergency. Applying the emergency paradigm to deal with increasingly mundane phenomena such as upsurges in criminality, certain manifestations of terrorism, or even economic crises erodes the 'threat severity threshold' that facilitates the distinction between normalcy and emergency. Furthermore, the assessment as to the existence of a state of emergency is fundamentally linked to the subjective assessment of the initial decision-maker. Factors other than an objective assessment of reality—such as heuristics, other mental 'shortcuts' and the role of political rhetoric in shaping the debate—play an important role in the decision-making process. I contend, therefore, that scrutiny should be focused on the decision-makers who declare and review the existence of state of emergency. Moreover, the decision as to the continued necessity of emergency powers must also be scrutinised, as it is the decision-makers' assessment that an emergency still exists and that emergency powers are still necessary that leads to the 'entrenchment' of emergency powers into the ordinary legal order.

In light of this renewed focus on the initial decision-maker, chapter three presents an argument in favour of judicial review of the decision to declare a state of emergency that is contained in a state's constitution. Using Hans Kelsen's Identity Thesis—that the state is identical to the legal order—and his conceptualisation of the relationship between validity and effectiveness of legal norms,[3] I contend that a permanent state of emergency may qualify as an unconstitutional, or an 'illegitimate proxy-constitutional amendment' that impacts upon the 'constituent power' of the people; a conclusion which would present a theory of the state that is more accurately described by Carl Schmitt's theory of sovereignty—that sovereign is he who decides on the exception and that this decision cannot be bound by law—than Kelsen's Identity Thesis. [4] The choice of Kelsen and Schmitt is not an arbitrary one. Rather, Schmitt is considered to be one of the most influential jurists to have written on emergency powers and, what he terms, the state of exception (*Ausnahmezustand*). Schmitt's work is also considered to be a reaction to Kelsen's pure theory of law.[5] Therefore, in order to truly understand Schmitt, one must look at Kelsen and vice versa.

As a result of this dialectic between Kelsen and Schmitt, I conclude that only if judicial review of the decision to declare a state of emergency is available can a declaration of emergency be considered temporary from the perspective of law and can all state power be conceptualised as being constrained and exercised through law. In this manner, I seek to preserve Kelsen's Identity Thesis and ensure that the decision to declare a state of emergency is a legal one. I reach these conclusions without claiming that human rights will prima facie be better protected

[3] See generally Hans Kelsen, *Pure Theory of Law* (University of California Press, 1967), and Hans Kelsen, *General Theory of Law and State* (Harvard University Press, 1949).

[4] See generally Carl Schmitt, *The Concept of the Political*, trans G Schwab (University of Chicago Press, 2007); and Carl Schmitt, *Political Theology: Four Chapters on the Concept of Sovereignty*, trans G Schwab (University of Chicago Press, 2005).

[5] See generally, David Dyzenhaus, *The Constitution of Law: Legality in a Time of Emergency* (Cambridge University Press, 2006).

when judicial review of the existence of an emergency is available. My normative preference for judicial review, therefore, rests not on the better advancement of human rights, but on the integrity of a formalist conception of the rule of law by ensuring all state power is derived from law. In so doing, I seek to insulate the legitimacy of judicial review from critiques that conceptualise judicial decision-making as simply politics by other means and therefore advocate for the resolution of such questions in the political branches of government.

Nevertheless, to argue for judicial review of matters such as national security is to push the judiciary into subject matter that they lack both the expertise and democratic legitimacy to decide. Chapter four therefore addresses these concerns by demonstrating the unique constitutional implications of contending that a state of emergency is a non-justiciable or political question. Such issues are often conceptualised as 'legal black holes'—zones of decision-making created by law but within which decision-makers are more or less free to act according to their discretion. So long as the decision-maker stays within the bounds of their discretion, judicial review is effectively ousted. Chapter four, however, will demonstrate that permanent states of emergency amount not to the creation of a legal black hole but of a 'zone beyond law' as the power revealed is not one created or exercised through law but exists *beyond* law. It is, as established in chapter three, a claim for the constituent power. As a result, such a claim should be rejected and the justiciability of the decision to declare a state of emergency established.

Establishing the importance of judicial review of the decision to declare a state of emergency does not necessarily ensure, however, that this review will be exercised robustly. Chapter five therefore engages with what David Dyzenhaus terms 'legal grey holes': zones of legal decision-making where the justiciability of the decision is established; however, the review exercised is so deferential that it only serves to legitimise the initial decision rather than act as any meaningful check on power. Consequently, Dyzenhaus asserts that legal grey holes are more dangerous than legal black holes.[6] Chapter five confronts this argument by challenging the contention made by Dyzenhaus that a more substantive conception of the rule of law is required in order to confront the Schmittian Challenge. It will be demonstrated that a human rights approach often leads to questions of proportionality being addressed, rather than the 'hyperopic' question regarding the existence of a state of emergency. Consequently, while Dyzenhaus is critical of Cass Sunstein's 'minimalist' approach to constitutional questions, a substantive conception of the rule of law may also lead to this approach.[7] Moreover, an overreliance on human rights norms can ignore the impact permanent states of emergency can have on other constitutional norms that may be equally affected. Consequently, by invoking the concept of constituent power, this book seeks to establish the importance of judicial review of the decision to declare a state of emergency and, in so doing,

[6] ibid, 41–43.

[7] See Cass Sunstein, 'Minimalism at War' [2004] *Supreme Court Review*.

give the judiciary solid constitutional foundations and legitimacy to conduct this task.

In providing for a state of emergency, constitutions expressly concede that there may be certain situations in which the norms it espouses may not be applicable. This admission may itself be seen as a capitulation to Schmitt. Chapter six therefore addresses these arguments, confronting alternatives to dealing with states of emergency through constitutional provisions. It will be shown that constitutions that do not provide for emergency powers may, nevertheless, find that they are reinterpreted so as to permit an exceptional response. However, such constitutions lack the 'shielding effect' of emergency powers that constitutional emergency provisions benefit from, namely quarantining exceptional measures to exceptional situations. In addition, accommodating emergencies through legislation rather than constitutional mechanisms may make such exceptional measures seem more 'banal' and side-step the hyperopic lens that a constitutional declaration of a state of emergency requires. Chapter six will also deal with constitutional orders that vindicate the sovereignty of parliament with a view to assessing how the argument pertaining to judicial review and constituent power established in chapter three is applicable to these constitutions. Chapter six then concludes with an assessment of what Oren Gross terms the extra-legal measures model as a means of confronting states of emergency. I will argue, however, that this model is inconsistent as to the nature of the power legitimating the extra-legal measure and, moreover, this model cannot displace the need for a legal emergency regime, be it constitutional or legislative.

In light of this continued relevance of the emergency paradigm, chapter seven concludes this book with an examination of constitutional mechanisms designed to control and constrain states of emergency. It will be shown, however, that while many of these measures are laudable, they cannot oust the importance of judicial review of the decision to declare a state of emergency. Finally, I emphasise the transformative nature of permanent states of emergency, arguing that it is often their banality that is their most dangerous property.

The Scope of this Book and its Claims

I do not claim in this book that the judiciary is best placed to make assessments regarding all issues of national security. Nor is the claim made that the judiciary should ex ante make the decision to declare a state of emergency. Rather, I contend that this decision should be made by one of the political branches, due to their expeditious decision-making capabilities and expertise on matters of national security, but that such a decision ought to be amenable to judicial review. In this manner, many of the practical problems that would arise were the judiciary empowered to make an ex-ante decision as to the existence of an emergency are acknowledged and addressed—in particular, the slow speed at which judicial systems operate. However, such criticisms pertaining to efficacy are no longer applicable once a state of emergency has been declared and its continued existence is questionable. In such conditions, the state of emergency *is* the status quo and delay during its assessment does not put the emergency powers that are available at risk.

Jurisdictions

Much of the literature referred to will draw from common law jurisdictions, in particular, the US and the UK. Ireland will also be referred to as its entrenched state of emergency from 1939 to 1995 provides an excellent illustration of many of the key questions posed by emergency powers. However, this is not to say that the arguments contained in this book should be exclusively limited to common law jurisdictions. India will also be referred to in chapter three with regards to its theory pertaining to unconstitutional constitutional amendments, as will Weimar Germany and debates regarding the supremacy of the constitution over legislation and the role of judicial review in this supremacy. The infamous use of Article 48 will also be referred to throughout this book but particularly in chapter five pertaining to substantive limits on emergency powers. Moreover, chapters one and two of this book draw upon a wide array of different constitutional backgrounds to establish the emergency paradigm and to illustrate examples of permanent states of emergency. Chapters six and seven will also discuss the states of emergency declared by France in 2015 and Turkey in 2016. In addition, much of the literature on constituent power draws upon French revolutionary thinkers and, indeed, modern applications of these theories, for example, in South America.[8] While international humanitarian law will be referred to, particularly in chapter two, an in-depth focus on this branch of law would, it is submitted ignore the use of emergency powers to deal with natural disasters or economic crises. Instead, I give greater focus to international human rights law given the more malleable emergencies it is applicable to. In particular, I will focus on the challenges facing the European Court of Human Rights (ECtHR) in reviewing the decision to declare a state of emergency under Article 15 ECHR. Despite the vast array of different constitutional and legal traditions of the 47 members of the Council of Europe, it will be shown that the ECtHR's approach to emergencies is remarkably consistent with that of the contracting particles. Consequently, I will contend that the assumptions—and challenges to these assumptions—of the emergency paradigm therefore are almost universal. In turn, the relative weakness of the judiciary in the British 'political constitution' relative to the legislature and executive makes the UK an excellent jurisdiction in which to stress-test much of these arguments

[8] See, for example, Joel L Colón-Ríos, *Weak Constitutionalism: Democratic Legitimacy and the Question of Constituent Power* (Routledge, 2012).

regarding judicial review and the political branches in a state of emergency. Thus, while this book does not seek to explore the nature of states of emergency and constituent power in every constitutional order, the diverse constitutional arrangements which I do draw upon should, it is submitted, compensate for this.

A Brief Note on Terminology

The term 'emergency' is used in this book precisely because of its amorphous nature. Emergency powers are known by a number of different synonyms—martial law, state of siege, state of defence, state of urgency, state of exception, and constitutional dictatorship to name but a select few. However, these synonyms are often legally defined in various jurisdictions in a variety of different ways referring to specific conditions at the exclusion of others, and hence are too narrow for the purposes of this book. Relatedly the use of the term 'state of exception' is also problematic. While defined and utilised by Giorgio Agamben[9] and Carl Schmitt[10] (albeit with important differences between them),[11] 'state of exception' is a potentially loaded term indicative of a response that may or may not be authorised by law. It is this very issue that is the subject of this book. Moreover, 'exception' does not give any indicator to the reader as to what conditions or phenomenon may require or trigger such a response. While it is conceded that 'exception to the rule' is a component of a 'state of emergency', the term connotes none of the notions of threat, urgency, catastrophe and temporariness that are evoked by the term 'emergency'. Similarly, Clinton Rossiter's use of the term 'constitutional dictatorship', while evocative of the consolidation of power in the executive branch of government that is a key indicator of an emergency response, also sheds no light on the phenomenon or crisis that triggers such a response.[12] By utilising the term 'emergency' in this book, I seek to maintain the link between phenomenon and response while accurately describing them both. Nevertheless, 'state of exception' will often be used in this book, particularly in the context of chapter three when discussing the theory of Carl Schmitt. This is done in order to ensure fidelity to Schmitt's conception and avoid oscillating between exception and emergency which may cause confusion. However, to reiterate 'emergency' is ultimately to be preferred over 'exception' where possible, precisely because of its link to the response taken.

'Emergency' has the added advantage that its antonym is 'normalcy'. A fundamental distinction between normalcy and emergency, therefore, is clearly evoked by the term emergency. If one were to utilise the term 'state of exception' one

[9] See generally, Giorgio Agamben, *State of Exception* (University of Chicago Press, 2005).

[10] Schmitt, *Political Theology* (n 4).

[11] See Jef Huysmans, 'The Jargon of Exception—On Schmitt, Agamben and the Absence of Political Society' (2008) 2 *Journal of Political Sociology*.

[12] Clinton Rossiter, *Constitutional Dictatorship: Crisis Government in the Modern Democracies* (Transaction Publishers, 2002).

immediately asks 'exception to what?' It is not clear that what is meant is exception to normalcy. As I will argue, the rules and constraints on power in normalcy are often conceptualised as impeding the necessary emergency measures and hence it is these rules to which an exception is made. In using the term 'emergency', this book avails of the flexibility and scope of its usage, while at the same time acknowledging that it is this very flexibility that can lead to abuse of its application, confusion as to its parameters, and questions as to its legitimacy as a foundation for a legal or political doctrine. It is therefore imperative that the parameters of emergency are explored and defined in sufficient detail so that confusion and abuse of the term is mitigated and its flexibility is curtailed by a solid grounding in a theoretical and factual framework. So let us begin by exploring this very point.

1

The Ideal State of Emergency

Introduction

Crises of various magnitude and urgency are a human universal. It is upon these two variables—magnitude and urgency—that responses are prioritised, with exceptional events at the extreme ends of these scales requiring immediate action. In a similar manner, states concentrate resources and government energy to deal with what are perceived to be the most urgent issues of the day. Emergency services and other response systems, for example, must be coordinated in order to mitigate the potentially harmful effects of the crisis at hand. At its most basic denotation, therefore, the term 'emergency' refers to crises at the extreme end of this matrix of magnitude and urgency.[1] In such emergency situations, a response must be coordinated; consequently, lexicological definitions of emergency define not merely the events and consequences of such an event but also envisage a response to such an event.[2] Similarly, regulations pertaining to emergency responders such as paramedics, firefighters and local law-enforcement agencies outline definitions of emergency not only to identify and describe crises most in need of a response but also to facilitate this response.[3] The term 'emergency' therefore is not merely concerned with describing the phenomena that produce crises; it is also intimately linked to the response itself.

Yet even in this most basic descriptive account of 'emergency' a paradox is revealed: emergencies are simultaneously a universal, inevitable reality but also unforeseen, exceptional events invariably requiring equally exceptional responses.

[1] The *Oxford English Dictionary* (Oxford University Press, 2010) defines an emergency as 'a serious, unexpected, and often dangerous situation requiring immediate action'. The *Cambridge Advanced Learner's Dictionary* (Cambridge University Press, 2010) defines an emergency as 'something dangerous or serious, such as an accident, which happens suddenly or unexpectedly and needs fast action in order to avoid harmful results'. *Merriam-Webster* defines an emergency as (1) 'an unforeseen combination of circumstances or the resulting state that calls for immediate action or (2) an urgent need for assistance or relief'. 'Emergency' (*Merriam-Webster*) <www.merriam-webster.com/dictionary/emergency> accessed 7 August 2017.

[2] See dictionaries, ibid. The second definition proffered by *Merriam-Webster* (an urgent need for assistance or relief) refers only to the response element of emergency with no mention of what sort of phenomenon would induce such a need.

[3] Clifford Oliver, *Catastrophic Disaster Planning and Response* (CRC Press, 2011) 4–8.

They are unseen and exceptional yet, nevertheless, they must somehow be prepared for. It is this paradox that is the subject of this book: the inevitability of exceptional events and how constitutions should confront them. In this regard, 'emergency' tends to be defined in broad brushstrokes. 'Emergency' refers not to a single phenomenon and subsequent response but a range of such conditions; it is an 'umbrella term' indicative of a group or set of shared conditions. When dealing with such an ambiguous term, therefore, a problem of certainty arises as to whether a particular crisis amounts to an emergency or not. There will, of course, be severe instances where the existence of an emergency is undisputed. In these 'core', paradigmatic cases, the crossing of the severity threshold triggering an emergency should be clearly and objectively identifiable. However, the majority of crises may reside instead in the penumbra—where the lines of demarcation between normalcy and emergency are less clear as the key coefficients of magnitude and urgency are incapable of precise scientific measurement.[4] Here the identification relies more on the decision-maker's subjective assessment of the situation than objective fact.

The 'Ideal' Emergency

To assist with this identification, definitions of emergency frequently assert that the severity threshold is only crossed when normal responses to the threat are ineffectual. 'Emergency' therefore is envisaged as an event beyond the status quo; an outlier from the ordinary operation of society. Declaring a state of emergency enables a response that would not be possible were normal conditions to prevail. It is thus not merely the crisis or phenomenon but also the response that is beyond the norm. To reveal the characteristic features of the state of emergency, this chapter will explore the 'ideal' state of emergency. 'Ideal' refers not to the fact that an emergency is desired but of the concept of the 'ideal-type' as defined by Max Weber. The ideal state of emergency is not one that exists in reality; nor is it merely a hypothesis. Instead, it assists with the creation of a hypothesis: the 'emergency paradigm'. Ideal types are formed by

> [t]he one-sided accentuation of one or more points of view and by the synthesis of a great many diffuse, discrete, more or less present and occasionally absent concrete individual phenomena which are arranged according to those one-sidedly emphasised viewpoints into a unified thought construct. In its conceptual purity, this mental construct cannot be found empirically anywhere in reality. It is a utopia.[5]

[4] HLA Hart, 'Positivism and the Separation of Law and Morals' (1958) 71 *Harvard Law Review* 593, 607.

[5] Max Weber, *The Methodology of the Social Sciences*, trans Edward Shils and Henry Finch (Free Press of Glencoe, 1949) 90.

Ideal types are constructed inductively, through observations of reality and extrapolating the key characteristics that the observer identifies as indicative of the phenomenon being observed. Constructing the ideal state of emergency should therefore strive to be an objective exercise; although the extent to which this is possible in the social sciences—and even in the natural sciences—is, to put it mildly, a subject of disagreement.[6] For example, the selection of sources in constructing the ideal type can potentially amount to an avenue whereby subjectivity and, in turn, normativity can seep into the account. Weber's account of the social sciences stresses this dichotomy between the descriptive and prescriptive, noting that invariably the descriptive explanation of social phenomena is sought precisely in order to construct policy responses to these, ie to illuminate what *should* be done.[7] Thus, being acutely aware of the penchant for the descriptive to stray into the realm of the normative, this chapter will construct the ideal type emergency by analysing contemporary legal sources and the historical office of the Roman dictatorship—considered by many to be the archetypal emergency response upon which modern approaches are based.[8] This broad historical and contemporary array of jurisdictions referred to should allay concerns as to subjectivity distorting the ideal state of emergency. These assumptions will then be stress-tested in the following chapter, by analysing the degree to which this ideal type state of emergency is realised today.

The Dictatorship of the Roman Republic

The 'ideal' state of emergency is epitomised by the extraordinary constitutional office of the dictatorship of the Roman Republic.[9] When analysing such an ancient institution, conflicting sources of questionable credibility invariably arise. Ronald T Ridley stresses that the Roman sources written about the dictatorship were

[6] Thomas Kuhn, for example, famously stressed that even paradigms in the natural sciences do not necessarily change in the face of objective evidence. Rather, powerful subjective forces mean that the refuted dominant paradigm will be clung on to until the 'crisis' in the field can only be resolved by a 'scientific revolution'. See Thomas Kuhn, *The Structure of Scientific Revolutions*, 4th edn (University of Chicago Press, 2012).

[7] Weber (n 5) 51–54.

[8] See Oren Gross and Fionnuala Ní Aoláin, *Law in Times of Crisis: Emergency Powers in Theory and Practice* (Cambridge University Press, 2006) 17–26; Clinton Rossiter, *Constitutional Dictatorship: Crisis Government in the Modern Democracies* (Princeton University Press, 1948) 15–28; Nomi Claire Lazar, *States of Emergency in Liberal Democracies* (Cambridge University Press, 2009) ch 5; John Ferejohn and Pasquale Pasquino, 'The Law of the Exception: A Typology of Emergency Powers' (2004) 2 *International Journal of Constitutional Law* 210; Niccolò Machiavelli, *The Discourses* [1531], ed Bernard Crick, trans Leslie J Walker (Penguin, 1998); Jean-Jacques Rousseau, *The Social Contract and Discourses* [1762] (Everyman, 1993) 294.

[9] Gross and Ní Aoláin (n 8) 17–26; Rossiter (n 8) ch 2; Lazar (n 8) 113–35.

recorded at a time when the dictatorship no longer functioned.[10] Moreover, they were often written by historians with contemporary political agendas. Benjamin Straumann thus questions whether one can call many of the sources documenting the use of the dictatorship in the early period of the Republic 'historical'.[11] Sources were not necessarily constructing a descriptive account of the Roman dictatorship but were instead emphasising, embellishing or perhaps even fabricating particular aspects of the office to justify approaches to the contemporary political challenges at the time of their writing.[12] The oldest accounts of the Roman dictatorship that do exist therefore are arguably ideal types in and of themselves; however, they are ideal types potentially contaminated by the subjective ulterior motives of their authors. Furthermore, one must also bear in mind that the Roman dictatorship existed for over three hundred years and to portray the operation of such an institution as static would be misleading.[13] However, so too would according overemphasis to discrepancies from the proper function of the office that occurred in the later periods of the dictatorship's existence when, for example, the dictator was relegated to conducting elections.[14]

The Function and Powers of the Dictator

The perceived necessity of a constitutional office such as the Roman dictatorship was dependent upon the ordinary constitutional order of the Roman Republic. The Republic was founded in the aftermath of the tyrannical reign of the king Tarquinius Superbus and his subsequent deposition and expulsion.[15] Tarquinius' rule became symbolic of the tyranny of monarchy, with his overthrow becoming a 'foundational myth' for the new Republic.[16] Unification of power in one individual was seen by the Republic as indicative of the expelled monarchy and the resultant constitutional order was a complex system of checks and balances striving to ensure that this was improbable.[17]

The separation of powers in the Roman Republic, much like modern states today, divided power amongst different institutions which checked and balanced

[10] Ronald T Ridley, 'The Origins of the Roman Dictatorship: An Overlooked Opinion' (1979) 122 *Rheinisches Museum für Philologie* 303, 304. See also Carl Schmitt, *Dictatorship*, trans Michael Hoelzl and Graham Ward (Polity Press, 2014) 2–4.

[11] Benjamin Straumann, *Crisis and Constitutionalism: Roman Political Thought from the Fall of the Republic to the Age of Revolution* (Oxford University Press, 2016) 65.

[12] ibid.

[13] Ferejohn and Pasquino (n 8) 226.

[14] What Kaplan refers to as *Dictator comitiorum habendorum causa*. Arthur Kaplan, 'Religious Dictators of the Roman Republic' (1973–74) 67 *Classical World* 172, 172.

[15] Hans Julius Wolff, *Roman Law: An Historical Introduction* (University of Oklahoma Press, 1964) 24–26.

[16] Andreas Kalyvas, 'The Tyranny of Dictatorship: When the Greek Tyrant Met the Roman Dictator' (2007) 35 *Political Theory* 412, 428.

[17] Wolff (n 15) 27.

each other: the Senate, the magistrates, and the people through elected officials called tribunes. This 'separation of powers', however, is not synonymous with the three branches of legislature, executive and judiciary seen in modern states today. Rather, the Roman Republic, according to Cicero, was more an embodiment of Plato's republic, where the three forms of government of the ancient world—monarchy, oligarchy and democracy—existed simultaneously, thus preventing one form decaying into another.[18] Also like modern states, Rome recognised three kinds of power: *auctoritas*, *potestas* and *imperium*; although, again, these three powers do not correlate with the modern powers of legislative, executive and judicial.[19] *Auctoritas* was essentially advisory power and was the primary manner through which the Senate exercised its influence. Magistrates were thus free to reject this advice but, over time, through practice and respect for the Senate's opinion (the Senate being composed of wealthy, high-ranked individuals who themselves were often the class from which magistrates were elected) such advice became de facto binding.[20] As a result, the Senate eventually emerged as the chief governing force of the Republic.[21] *Potestas* was that which give one the authority and capacity to exercise legally bestowed duty. Thus, lower magistrates within the narrow, legally defined jurisdiction bestowed upon them had the authority (*potestas*) to issue and enforce fines according to their discretion.[22]

The ultimate form of *potestas* was *imperium*, or supreme coercive and administrative power, and was exercised by the most important magistrates. *Imperium* often had a distinct military aspect to its nature and thus was closely linked to the idea of a 'command' and the authority to order an individual to act in a certain way. This power was, however, subject to the veto of tribunes—officials elected by the plebeian class—who also had the power to summon the Senate and submit proposals before it.[23] The consuls were the supreme magistrates and were effectively the successors of the kings, possessing the highest *imperium* and the body that most closely resembles the modern-day executive. Two consuls of equal authority sat at any one time, each with a veto over the other's commands.[24] They were elected for a year-long term of office and their primary task was political leadership and command of the army.

[18] Jed W Atkins, *Cicero on Politics and the Limits of Reason: The Republic and Laws* (Cambridge University Press, 2013) ch 3; Andrew Lintott, *The Constitution of the Roman Republic* (Oxford University Press, 1999) ch 12.

[19] Nomi Claire Lazar, 'Making Emergencies Safe for Democracy: The Roman Dictatorship and the Rule of Law in the Study of Crisis Government' (2006) 13 *Constellations* 506, 510.

[20] The word Senate is derived from *senatus*, itself linked to *senex* or 'old man'. The Senate was originally composed of elder statesmen who had above a certain minimum threshold of wealth, with some arguing that it was the successor of the advisory council of the expelled king. See RF Pennell, *History of Rome from the Earliest Times to 476AD* (Echo Library, 1890) 9–10.

[21] See Herbert Felix Jolowicz, *Historical Introduction to the Study of Roman Law* (Cambridge University Press, 1965) ch 2.

[22] Lintott (n 18) 95–97.

[23] ibid, 122–24.

[24] Wolff (n 15) 32–33; Jolowicz (n 21) 53.

In the Roman Republic, therefore, powerful institutions and individuals were deliberately juxtaposed against equally powerful institutions. Rather than dividing powers and institutions into separate jurisdictions, the Roman Republic's system arranged institutions both internally and externally in conflict with each other.[25] It was this continuous interaction and conflict between the relevant bodies that was supposed to prevent the abuse of power and avoid the tyranny of monarchy that the Republic ousted. Yet these checks and balances were arguably too successful, meaning that decision-making was cumbersome and slow.[26] In particular, the effect of consular collegiality and veto over each other's commands could render this office impotent and incapable of expedient decision-making in times of crisis. Consequently, in such situations, a dictator would be appointed. Provided for within the framework of the Roman constitution, yet antithetical to the very foundational myth of the Republic itself, the dictatorship was a formidable tool for dealing with emergencies.[27]

The Roman dictatorship was a constitutional office that only existed in times of emergency, when the normal constitutional structures were considered unable to deal with a crisis in a satisfactory manner. There are several different theories regarding the origins of the Roman dictatorship. In pre-Roman times, the population in the Italian peninsula was organised by social groups known *gentes.*[28] Due to a lack of sources, the structure of a *gens* is impossible to discern; however, Frezza argues that a *gens* was a loose association of families which chose a common leader only when confronted with an emergency.[29] By uniting around a single leader, the tribes of the Italian peninsula recognised the utility of expedient, decisive leadership in times of crisis. Similarly, at the time of the Roman Republic, some neighbouring Latin states also had an institution similar to the Roman dictator but it is unclear as to whether the Roman dictatorship was inspired by these.[30] A final theory is that the Roman dictatorship amounted to a temporary restoration of monarchical rule. It was designed to combat the unique problems and threats that faced the Republic by sacrificing the very checks on power that were in place to prevent the tyranny of the earlier monarchy and resulted in the establishment of the Roman Republic in the first instance.[31]

A dictator was appointed *rei gerundae causa*—to get things done.[32] Ordained to complete a specific task, the dictator is described as having the authority to do

[25] See Robert J Bonner, 'Emergency Government in Rome and Athens' (1922) 18 *Classical Journal* 144.

[26] Jolowicz (n 21) 53; Rossiter (n 8) 19.

[27] Keyes Clinton Walker, 'The Constitutional Position of the Roman Dictatorship' (1917) 14 *Studies in Philology* 298.

[28] Wolff suggests that *gentes* derives from *gens* which translates as clan: Wolff (n 15) 23–24.

[29] ibid.

[30] RT Ridley 'The Origin of the Roman Dictatorship: An Overlooked Opinion', (1979) 304 <www.rhm.uni-koeln.de/122/Ridley.pdf> accessed 7 August 2017.

[31] ibid.

[32] Rossiter (n 8) 21.

anything considered necessary to further this objective. Freed from the collegiality that constrained the consuls, the superior *imperium* (*imperium maius*)[33] of the dictator created what Clinton Rossiter describes as 'as absolute a ruler as could well be imagined'.[34] Machiavelli states that he could act without consultation and punish without appeal but that he could not change existing institutions.[35] Rousseau too stresses this point, arguing that he could do anything except make laws,[36] and Carl Schmitt states that the dictator had freedom from legal controls and unlimited power over life and death.[37] Livy's account of the Roman dictatorship places particular emphasis on the dictator's freedom from the fundamental constitutional right of appeal (*provocatio*) which, in ordinary times guaranteed that a Roman citizen could not be executed without trial.[38] The Roman republican conception of liberty consisted, first and foremost, of this right of appeal.[39] Thus the Senate's execution of leading suspects in the Second Cataline Conspiracy without an appeal was subsequently used by Publius Clodius Pulcher to justify the exile of Cicero, who was Consul at the time of the executions, and led the Senate against the conspirators.[40] While a dictator was often appointed to deal with military threats, a fundamental task in this regard was adequate financing and mustering of an army. Dictators therefore were frequently tasked with imposing levies on the plebs and were often appointed at times when imposition of such a levy would have been difficult when debt was high and the plebs had a right to appeal.[41]

Controls on the Roman Dictatorship

The tension between the normal constitutional order of the Roman Republic and the exceptional office of the Roman dictatorship, with its autocratic design and evocation of the spectre of monarchy, meant that strict controls on this office were necessary in order to protect the Republic from the very institution it resorted to in a time of crisis. The most striking of these was the strict limitation on the duration of the dictatorship. This was closely linked to the militaristic nature of the threats facing the Republic and also illustrates that the dictatorship was primarily a defensive mechanism.[42] As military campaigns in the time of the Republic tended

[33] See Victor Ehrenberg, 'Imperium Maius in the Roman Republic' (1953) 74 *American Journal of Philology* 113.
[34] Rossiter (n 8) 23.
[35] Machiavelli (n 8) 94.
[36] Rousseau (n 8) 294.
[37] Lazar (n 19) 510; see also Schmitt (n 10) 2.
[38] Straumann (n 11) 65.
[39] ibid, 70.
[40] Oren Gross uses this episode as an illustrative example of the extra-legal measures model. Oren Gross, 'Extra-Legality and the Ethic of Political Responsibility' in Victor V Ramraj, *Emergencies and the Limits of Legality* (Cambridge University Press, 2008) 69–71. See also text to n 176 in ch 6 of this book.
[41] Straumann (n 11) 65–69.
[42] Gross and Ní Aoláin (n 8) 23.

to occur only in the summer months, the dictator's term of office was limited to six months only, or until the consuls that appointed him stepped down at the end of their term, whichever came first.[43] This time limit could not be extended by the dictator, nor could he appoint his own successor or be reappointed himself.[44] As the dictator was, 'ideally', appointed *rei gerundae causa*, once his purpose was completed, it was common for him to step down.[45] The sooner a dictator stepped down, the higher the regard in which he was held by the people. The most famous example of this is the legendary dictatorship of Cincinnatus who, after only fifteen days as dictator, stepped down having defeated the Aequi in the Battle of Mons Algidus.[46] By temporally limiting the dictator's power, the office was designed to ensure that the legal order prior to the dictator's appointment was preserved and all traces of his reign erased once he abdicated. Once the dictator relinquished his position he could not be held retrospectively to account for transgressions during his period in office.[47]

An additional key control on the appointment of a dictator was that of heteroinvestiture: that he who decided that a dictator should be appointed could not himself become a dictator.[48] The appointment procedure involved both the Senate and the consuls, with the Senate deciding whether an emergency necessitated a dictator and the consuls choosing the individual to be appointed.[49] The consuls could also propose that a dictator be appointed but this resolution required affirmation by the Senate.[50] A consul was debarred from selecting himself as dictator; however, due to the reverence of the office they held, the dictator was often a former consul.[51] Although the Senate had no authority to name who should be appointed dictator, as its power grew, an informal custom arose whereby the Senate's favourite was usually selected.[52] Eventually, this authority evolved to such an extent that Cicero regarded the nomination of dictator as depending positively upon the Senate.[53] In essence, the two separate decisions of whether a dictator was needed and who should be dictator were merged into one decision, thus weakening this control of heteroinvestiture.

On the appointment of a dictator, the consuls and Senate continued to perform their constitutional functions.[54] This resulted in the ordinary constitutional order

[43] Rossiter (n 8) 23–26; Wolff (n 15) 36; Machiavelli (n 8) 194; Gross and Ní Aoláin (n 8) 22; Rousseau (n 8) 296.
[44] Rossiter (n 8) 23.
[45] ibid.
[46] ibid, 24; Gross and Ní Aoláin (n 8) 25.
[47] ibid.
[48] Ferejohn and Pasquino (n 8) 218.
[49] ibid; Rossiter (n 8) 20–21; Gross and Ní Aoláin (n 8) 23–24.
[50] Rossiter (n 8) 20–21.
[51] ibid.
[52] ibid; Wolff (n 15) 36–37.
[53] Rossiter (n 8) 20.
[54] Gross and Ní Aoláin (n 8) 23. Schmitt notes, however, that there are diverging opinions as to whether the power of existing magistrates came to an end upon the appointment of a dictator: Schmitt (n 10) 2.

acting as a guide to the dictator, ensuring he stuck to the noble path.[55] However, as the dictator occupied the highest office in the land, possessed *imperium maius* and was empowered to do anything required to complete his task, his appointment would invariably impact upon the operation and functions of the normal constitutional order. As a result, those who declared an emergency and appointed a dictator had nothing to gain directly; their powers would not be enlarged and might, in fact, be functionally undermined by the dictator's *imperium maius*. In this regard, the Republic was structured to ensure that the declaration of a state of emergency and the appointment of a dictator was a decision of bona fide concern for the survival of the Republic.

Given the spectre of monarchical tyranny evoked by the dictatorship, a dictator, once appointed, had himself to appoint a *magister equitium* (master of the horse). Nomi Claire Lazar thus questions Rossiter's description of a man who could not even mount a horse without permission as 'as absolute a ruler as could well be imagined'.[56] Coupled with the dictator's financial dependence on the Senate, whose opinion was rarely rejected, Lazar portrays the dictator as an office more enmeshed with the normal system of governance and less an exception to the normal constitutional order.[57] This requirement that a dictator seek permission before he mounts his horse,[58] and the appointment of a junior colleague as the *magister equitum*,[59] may, however, be similar to the ban on touching iron to which the dictator was also subject, owing to the ancient nature of the office, dating from a time when the horse was taboo because of its late introduction to Europe and its even later adoption for riding.[60] Both of these taboos would have the effect of diminishing the inner personal power (*mana*) of the dictator.[61] The ban on riding a horse therefore may be indicative of the immense *mana* and, hence, respect and authority the dictator possessed, rather than an attempt to lessen his *imperium*. Levi's account of the appointment of the *magister equitum* as a means to curtail the dictator's power is corroborated to some extent by Staveley, who suggests that it was an attempt at reconciling a return to monarchical-like control with the principle of collegiality that was indicative of the Roman Republic.[62] However, Staveley also rejects the contention that it was of any practical significance; it did not in any way lessen his authority. In essence, it was merely a legal fiction; an homage to the constitutional principles that were essentially being abandoned.[63]

[55] Gross and Ní Aoláin (n 8) 23.
[56] Lazar (n 8) 510.
[57] Rossiter (n 8) 24.
[58] Lazar (n 8) 126–28.
[59] Rossiter (n 8) 26; Gross and Ní Aoláin (n 8) 21.
[60] D Cohen, 'The Origin of Roman Dictatorship' (1957) 10 *Mnemosyne* 300, 314.
[61] Ibid, 315.
[62] E Stuart Staveley, 'The Constitution of the Roman Republic 1940–1954' (1956) 5 *Historia: Zeitschrift fur Alte Geschichte* 74, 103.
[63] ibid; 'legal fiction' is a term defined by Lon Fuller as essentially amounting to a 'fact' assumed or created and then used in order to apply a legal rule and reach a desired outcome, even though the 'fact' may not necessarily exist in reality. See generally, Lon Fuller, *Legal Fictions* (Stanford University Press, 1967).

Unleashing the Tyranny of Dictatorship

Before the revival of the office by Sulla in 82 BC, the last dictator was allegedly appointed in 202 BC.[64] However, the office's position as an extraordinary institution of the Republic's constitution had begun to wane long before this. Once the army evolved from a defensive tool to an offensive one and campaigns lasted beyond six months, the dictator was no longer a viable option. Furthermore, Bonner notes that the dictatorship faced considerable opposition from the anti-aristocratic popular party (*populares*) who feared its role in the hands of a conservative Senate to suppress liberty, particularly in light of the dictator being free from *provocatio*.[65] It was also the Senate's own suspicion of the office that eventually led to it acquiring its influential role in the nomination process of the dictator, especially in the latter stages of the Republic when the *auctoritas* of the Senate essentially became binding.[66] The 'exceptionality' of the Roman dictatorship, therefore, was slowly eroded over time, embedding it within controls and checks on its powers from which it was originally designed to escape. The ultimate demise of the dictatorship, however, came not from this seepage of normalcy into this office, but from the abuse of its exceptionality.

The dictatorship lay neglected for over 100 years from 202 BC until 82 BC. Following his capture of Rome and defeat of the Consul Gaius Marius the Younger, Sulla was appointed dictator *legibus faciendis et rei publicae constituendae* (dictator for the enactment of such laws as he might deem best and for the regulation of the commonwealth).[67] The very raison d'être of his appointment therefore was to effect permanent change to the pre-existing legal order—something the dictatorship was principally designed to avoid. The changes that Sulla wrought to the Republic's Constitution under his dictatorship were ultimately a major factor in the Republic's tumultuous metamorphosis into Empire. For example, his decoupling of the loyalty of legions to their commander rather than to Rome itself further increased the importance of *imperium* and, by extension, the political power of magistrates and military generals who possessed it.[68] According to Machiavelli, however, the most fundamental change to the dictatorship precipitated by Sulla was the departure from the traditional six-month time limit.[69] With no time limit on his office, he would hold such a position until his task was completed; however, the terms of reference of his office were so vague that no one but him

[64] Staveley (n 62) 475.

[65] Bonner (n 25) 146

[66] ibid; Jolowicz (n 21); Rousseau (n 8) 295; Wolff (n 15) 43–44.

[67] Ehrenberg (n 33) 123; Straumann (n 11) 75.

[68] Lintott (n 18) 210–13.

[69] The *Decemviri* or 'the ten citizens' were those who, according to Machiavelli, were entrusted by the Roman people to make laws for Rome in the latter years of the Republic. Unlike the Roman dictator, they were not appointed for a limited period of time. Also, unlike the dictatorship, the tribunes, senate and consuls were not contemporaneously operating and so provided no check on their power. See Machiavelli (n 8) 194. Straumann (n 11) 77, however, casts doubt as to the existence of the *Decemviri*, arguing instead that what is key is the meaning attributed to them in the late Republic.

could ascertain when he had completed his objective.[70] Consequently, this was no real control on his power in the same way the dictator *rei gerunda causa* was restricted to a maximum of six months. Sulla thus had the potential to remain in office for life but abdicated after one year which, nevertheless, was twice the length of time a dictator was supposed to remain in office. In turn, this created the precedent for Gaius Julius Caesar to appoint himself dictator for life.[71] In so doing, Caesar unleashed the monarchical tyranny that was always latent within the dictatorship but was held in check by the constitutional controls on the office.[72] Following Caesar's assassination, Marcus Antonius abolished the dictatorship in 44 BC 'to ban kingly power for good'.[73] Cicero proclaimed this to be his greatest achievement; however, many considered this to be mere gamesmanship aimed at appeasing the Senate, with Antonius' main goal being vested with *imperium* to command the Macedonian forces.[74] Ultimately, this was proved to be the case with Sulla's constitutional reforms pertaining to *imperium* and the loyalty of military legions, again, a major factor in this course of events. The dictatorship therefore played a pivotal role in the transformation of the Republic into an autocratic regime, ultimately resulting in the Roman Empire under Caesar Augustus—the very antithesis of the foundational myth of the Republic.

Despite the ultimate decline and abuse of the Roman dictatorship, the fundamental assumptions made by the Roman Republic in providing for such an office—temporariness, exceptionality, expediency and the controls on these powers—are worthy of study today. These parameters may still be seen today in modern attempts to respond to emergencies. Furthermore, Machiavelli argues that it is imperative that republics have access to an institution akin to the Roman dictatorship lest they face ruin.[75] These parameters evident in the Roman dictatorship are ultimately what construct the 'ideal type' emergency paradigm. In turn, the propensity of exceptional powers to be abused and the exceptional to become permanent is a valuable parable to take from the Roman dictatorship.

The 'Ideal' Emergency in Legal Systems Today

Provisions for states of emergency are seen in numerous states, transcending civil and common law jurisdictions, Islamic constitutions, and international law.[76]

[70] Machiavelli (n 8) 194.

[71] ibid; see also Miriam Pucci Ben Zeev, 'When Was the Title "Dictator Perpetuus" Given to Caesar?' (1996) 65 *L'Antiquité Classique* 251.

[72] Kalyvas (n 16). This was also the view of Dionysius who considered the potential for tyranny inherently linked to its power to override the right to appeal: Straumann (n 11) 74.

[73] Straumann (n 11) 64–65.

[74] ibid, 74.

[75] Machiavelli (n 8) 193.

[76] For an example of a study analysing the emergency powers contained in various constitutions from different legal backgrounds, see LC Keith and SC Poe, 'Are Constitutional States of Emergency Clauses Effective? An Empirical Exploration' (2004) 26 *Human Rights Quarterly* 1071.

They are provided for and defined by constitutions, legislation, executive orders and international treaties. Equally diverse are the names ascribed to these emergency regimes. A comprehensive empirical study of all of these constitutional and legislative provisions relating to emergency, while valuable, would have been inefficient for the purposes of this book. Sources were therefore chosen on the grounds that they are illustrative of the key components of emergency. That conceded, an eclectic mix of sources from a variety of legal and political backgrounds is necessary given the universal nature of emergency powers and to avoid injecting subjectivity into the creation of the ideal type. Thus, while the following is not a comprehensive analysis of emergency definitions derived from all constitutions, the sources considered are, it is submitted, an accurate and fair representation of the concept of emergency as they are realised today.[77] While diverse, all these emergency provisions nevertheless contain two key elements: the phenomenon that triggers the state of emergency; and the response permitted in lieu of such a declaration.

Defining the Phenomenon

International Human Rights Law

International human rights treaties that give effect to civil and political rights make accommodation for emergencies. Article 4 of the International Covenant on Civil and Political Rights (ICCPR) provides that:

> In time of public emergency which threatens the life of the nation ... States Parties to the present Covenant may take measures derogating from their obligations under the present Covenant.[78]

Mirroring this closely, Article 15 of the European Convention on Human Rights (ECHR) states that:

> [I]n time of war or other public emergency threatening the life of the nation any High Contracting Party may take measures derogating from its obligations under this convention to the extent strictly required by the exigencies of the situation.[79]

Finally, Article 27 of the American Convention on Human Rights (ACHR) provides that:

> [I]n time of war, public danger, or other emergency that threatens the independence or security of a State Party, it may take measures derogating from its obligations under the present Convention.[80]

[77] ibid.

[78] International Covenant on Civil and Political Rights (adopted 16 December 1966, entered into force 23 March 1976) 999 UNTS 171 (ICCPR).

[79] Convention for the Protection of Human Rights and Fundamental Freedoms (European Convention on Human Rights, as amended).

[80] American Convention on Human Rights (adopted 26 June 1981).

The similar wording of these treaties is of no coincidence given the interrelated nature of the UN and regional human rights regimes, their recognition of similar norms, and the persuasive authority each system has on the other.[81] Notably, the African Charter on Human and Peoples' Rights contains no derogation clause, resulting in the African Commission concluding that no derogation is possible.[82] The principal difference between the ICCPR, ECHR and ACHR is that Article 4 ICCPR does not mention 'war'. The reason for this, however, is not that a state cannot derogate from the ICCPR in a time of war but that:

> While it was recognised that one of the most important public emergencies was the outbreak of war, it was felt that the covenant should not envisage, even by implication the possibility of war, as the United Nations was established with the object of preventing war.[83]

Consequently, the key term in Article 4 of the ICCPR is the description of a public emergency as a condition which 'threatens the life of the nation'. The United National Economic and Social Council (UNESC) has attempted to shed some light on the meaning of this phrase, stating in the Siracusa Principles on the Limitation and Derogation Provisions in the ICCPR (the 'Siracusa Principles') that in order for conditions to amount to a threat to the life of the nation, they must constitute a situation of 'exceptional and actual or imminent danger'.[84] Similarly, the International Law Association in their Paris Minimum Standards of Human Rights Norms in a State of Emergency outlines that:

> [T]he expression 'public emergency' means an exceptional situation of crisis or public danger, actual or imminent, which affects the whole population or the whole population of the area to which the declaration applies and constitutes a threat to the organized life of the community of which the state is composed.[85]

The United Nations Human Rights Committee (UNHRC) has stated that not every disturbance or catastrophe qualifies as a public emergency which threatens the life of the nation; rather the situation must reach a certain tipping point (the threat-severity threshold) to qualify as an emergency.[86]

[81] Dinah Shelton, *Regional Protection of Human Rights* (Oxford University Press, 2008) 17.

[82] African Charter on Human and Peoples' Rights (adopted 27 June 1981, entered into force 21 October 1986) (1982) 21 ILM 58 (African Charter); 9th Annual Activity Report of the African Commission (1995–96) (Comm 74/92); Christof Heyns, 'The African Regional Human Rights System: The African Charter' (2003–04) 108 Penn State Law Review 679, 693. Heyns, however, considers the lack of a derogation clause in the African Charter to be unfortunate as in real emergencies the provisions of the Charter will simply be ignored.

[83] 'Travaux Préparatoires to the European Convention on Human Rights', DH(56)4 CDH(77)5, Appendix I, 14 [39] <www.echr.coe.int/LibraryDocs/Travaux/ECHRTravaux-ART15-DH(56)4-EN1675477.pdf> accessed 23 March 2017.

[84] 'The Siracusa Principles on the Limitation and Derogation Provisions in the International Covenant on Civil and Political Rights' (1985) 7 *Human Rights Quarterly* 3, 7.

[85] Richard B Lillich, 'The Paris Minimum Standards of Human Rights Norms in a State of Emergency' (1985) 79 *American Journal of International Law* 1072, 1073.

[86] United Nations Human Rights Committee, 'General Comment No 29: States of Emergency (Article 4)' (31 August 2001) CCPR/C/21/Rev.1/Add.11, para 3.

A similar understanding of what amounts to an emergency 'threatening the life of the nation' under Article 15 of the ECHR can be seen in the early jurisprudence of the European Court of Human Rights (ECtHR) on this issue. In *Lawless v Ireland*, an emergency was defined as

> [a] situation of exceptional and imminent danger or crisis affecting the general public as distinct from particular groups and constitution a threat to the organised life of the community which composes the state in question.[87]

The minority in the Commission stage sought a more rigorous definition of emergency, tantamount to war, that could only be said to exist when the constitutional order has broken down, but did not succeed in having this higher threshold accepted by the Court.[88] Nevertheless, a lay reading of the preferred interpretation would suggest a threat would have to meet a significant threshold of severity in order to justify a state derogating its human rights obligations using Article 15. This expectation of a significant threshold is also complemented by the Commission in a case involving Greece, where it laid down the following characteristics that a public emergency threatening the life of the nation should have:

i. It must be actual or imminent.
ii. Its effects must involve the whole nation.
iii. The continuance of organised life of the community must be threatened.
iv. The crisis or danger must be exceptional, in that the normal measures or restrictions, permitted by the Convention for the maintenance of public safety, health and order, are plainly inadequate.[89]

As we shall see in chapter five, however, scrutiny of this threat severity threshold has been almost non-existent by the Court and so does not match the understanding of a state of emergency that a lay reading of Article 15 would suggest.[90]

International human rights law thus makes no differentiation between the phenomena that causes the emergency; instead, the definitions are primarily concerned with the effect of the phenomenon—that it constitutes a threat to the life of the nation—to identify the severity threshold rather than whether the trigger is, for example, armed conflict or natural disaster. That stated, the Siracusa Principles boldly assert that 'economic difficulties per se cannot justify derogation measures'.[91] The absence of a derogation clause from the International Covenant on Economic Social and Cultural Rights (ICESCR) would also suggest that economic crises should not justify infringements on human rights; however, there is evidence that the UN Committee on Economic Social and

[87] 3 ECHR (Ser.A) (1960–61).

[88] Gross and Ní Aoláin (n 8) 269–73.

[89] *Denmark, Norway, Sweden and the Netherlands v Greece* App No 3221.67 European Commission of Human Rights, 5 November 1969, 70, [113].

[90] See text to nn 29–54 in ch 5.

[91] Siracusa Principles (n 84) [41].

Cultural Rights is shifting its approach towards a model that satisfies several conditions of the emergency paradigm.[92]

Constitutional Definitions

Like international human rights treaties, the constitutions of many states define the phenomena that trigger emergencies in very broad terms. Indeed, some constitutions, such as those of Cyprus, Namibia and South Africa, mirror the phase 'threat to the life of the nation'.[93] The French Constitution also focuses on the effects of a crisis, providing for a state of emergency when

> the institutions of the Republic, the independence of the Nation, the integrity of its territory or the fulfilment of its international commitments are under serious and immediate threat, and where the proper functioning of the constitutional public authorities is interrupted.[94]

Such broad definitions of states of emergency are often accompanied with illustrative examples of phenomena that can potentially give rise to an emergency. War, armed rebellion or invasions are core examples frequently given. Article 37(1) of the South African Constitution, for example, permits an emergency to be declared when (a) the life of the nation is threatened by war, invasion, general insurrection, disorder, natural disaster or other public emergency; and (b) the declaration is necessary to restore peace and order.[95] Similarly section 305(3) of the Nigerian Constitution permits the president to declare a state of emergency when (a) the Federation is at war or (b) the Federation is in imminent danger of invasion or involvement in a state of war.[96] The French Constitution also provides for the declaration of a state of siege, although it gives no further details as to what conditions may warrant such a declaration.[97] Historical experience, however, would

[92] See Ben Warwick, 'Socio-Economic Rights During Economic Crises: A Changed Approach to Non-Retrogression' (2016) 65 *ICLQ* 249.

[93] See, for example, Art 37.1 Constitution of South Africa; Art 183, Constitution of the Republic of Cyprus; Art 23.1, Constitution of Lesotho; Art 26.1 Constitution of Namibia.

[94] Following an attack on Paris on 13 November 2015 that killed 130 people, France declared a state of emergency to confront the perceived terrorist threat. 'Paris Attacks: What Happened on the Night', *BBC News*, 9 December 2015, www.bbc.co.uk/news/world-europe-34818994, accessed 11 August 2017. See text to nn 78–82 in ch 6 for further discussion of France's 2015 state of emergency.

[95] Art 37(1) Constitution of South Africa, entered into force 1996.

[96] It then continues by expanding the concept to cover instances where (c) there is actual breakdown of public order and public safety in the Federation or any part thereof to such extent as to require extraordinary measures to restore peace and security; (d) there is a clear and present danger of an actual breakdown of public order and public safety in the Federation or any part thereof requiring extraordinary measures to avert such danger; (e) there is an occurrence or imminent danger, or the occurrence of any disaster or natural calamity, affecting the community or a section of the community in the Federation; (f) there is any other public danger which clearly constitutes a threat to the existence of the Federation. Finally, it permits a state of emergency where (g) the President receives a request to do so by the governor of a state when a motion is passed by two thirds of the state assembly.

[97] Art 36 Constitution of France.

suggest that it would be triggered in the event of an emergency that is militaristic in nature and thus powers ordinarily exercised by the police are transferred to the military.[98] Similarly, the Greek Constitution permits the introduction of a state of siege 'in case of war or mobilization owing to external dangers or an imminent threat against national security, as well as in case of an armed coup aiming to overthrow the democratic regime'.[99] States of siege are a common recurrence in a number of different states' constitutions, particularly former French, Portuguese and Spanish colonies.[100] Argentina, for example, describes a foreign invasion or internal disorder as a trigger event, although the latter enables less drastic powers than the former.[101] The Chilean Constitution also identifies 'internal war or grave internal commotion' as grounds for declaring a state of siege.[102]

Some constitutions provide for a variety of different states of emergency, the key variables of which are either the gravity of the situation or the nature of the threat. In addition to providing for a state of siege, Article 19 of the Portuguese Constitution enables the declaration of a state of emergency 'where the circumstances … are less serious [than those warranting a declaration of a state of siege]'.[103] When deciding whether to declare a state of emergency or state of siege the principle of proportionality is to be applied with consideration for the duration of the powers to be utilised and the extent to what is strictly necessary.[104] The Chilean Constitution also differentiates between types of states of emergency according to the nature of the crisis. As mentioned above, a state of siege refers to 'war or internal commotion',[105] whereas a state of emergency correlates to an 'event of serious disturbance of public order, harm or danger to the national security, resulting from causes of either internal or external origin'.[106] Finally a state of catastrophe may be declared in instances of 'public disaster'.[107]

The Polish Constitution allows for three different kinds of emergency—martial law, a state of emergency or a state of natural disaster—depending upon the phenomenon. In a similar vein, the Basic Law of Germany (*Grundgesetz*) provides for three distinct emergency situations: state of defence,[108] state of tension[109] and

[98] Rossiter (n 8) chs 6–7.
[99] Art 48 Constitution of Greece.
[100] See, for example: Art 58 Constitution of Burkina Faso; Art 9.1 Constitution of Cameroon; Art 58 Constitution of the Central African Republic; Art 121 Constitution of Chad; Art 49 Constitution of Morocco.
[101] Art 16 Constitution of Argentina.
[102] Art 40 Constitution of Chile.
[103] Art 19(3). The conditions for a state of siege are set out in Article 19(1) and are defined as only in cases of 'actual or imminent aggression by foreign forces, serious threat to or disturbance of the democratic constitutional order, or public calamity'.
[104] Art 19(4) Constitution of Portugal.
[105] Art 40.2 Constitution of Chile, approved 21 October 1980.
[106] Art 40.3 Constitution of Chile.
[107] Art 40.4 Constitution of Chile.
[108] Art 115(a) of the Basic Law of Germany. This article and the subsequent articles mentioned here regarding emergency powers were added to the Basic Law by the German Emergency Acts passed on 30 May 1968. For a critical discussion of these amendments, see Wolf-Dieter Narr, Marc Silberman and Dave Harris, 'Threats to Constitutional Freedoms in West Germany' (1976) 8 *New German Critique* 20.
[109] Art 80(a) Basic Law of Germany.

internal state of emergency.[110] The distinctions between the states depend on the phenomenon that creates the threat to the nation. A state of emergency exists when the state is under attack or imminent attack by an armed force.[111] A state of tension covers the period leading up to a state of defence allowing for the efficient mobilisation of defensive forces. 'Internal state of emergency' refers to natural disasters or man-made phenomena that may threaten the free democratic order or pose a danger to public security or order.[112]

Article 119 of the Turkish Constitution provides for the declaration of a state of emergency in the event of natural disaster, dangerous epidemic diseases or a serious economic crisis;[113] meanwhile, Article 120 enables the declaration of an emergency 'in the event of serious indications of widespread acts of violence aimed at the destruction of the free democratic order established by the Constitution or of fundamental rights and freedoms, or serious deterioration of public order because of acts of violence'.[114] Article 122 further provides for a period of martial law, mobilisation and state of war

> in the event of widespread acts of violence which are aimed at the destruction of the free democratic order or the fundamental rights and freedoms embodied in the Constitution and more dangerous than the cases necessitating a state of emergency; or in the event of war, the emergence of a situation necessitating war, an uprising, or the spread of violent and strong rebellious actions against the motherland and the Republic, or widespread acts of violence of internal or external origin threatening the indivisibility of the country and the nation.[115]

From the above examples, it is clear that many constitutions use 'emergency' as an umbrella term, covering a multitude of phenomena. Core crises such as 'war' or 'natural disasters' are expressly provided for; these are then followed by abstract terminology such as 'threat', 'urgency' or 'crisis'. While the orthodox understanding is that economic crises cannot justify a state of emergency in international human rights law, a number of constitutions take the opposite approach, with economic states of emergency expressly accommodated in the constitutions of South Korea,[116] Taiwan,[117] Venezuela[118] and Turkey[119] to name but a few. This potentially gives rise to a tension between their domestic constitutions and the international legal order; however, much would depend upon the nature of the measures enacted. Thus, it may not be the case that a government considers it

[110] Art 91 Basic Law of Germany.

[111] See European Commission for Democracy through Law, *Emergency Powers*, CDL-STD (1995) <www.venice.coe.int/docs/1995/cdl-std(1995)012-e.asp> accessed 7 August 2017.

[112] ibid.

[113] Art 119 Constitution of Turkey. See text to nn 56–60 in ch 7 for a discussion of Turkey's declaration of a state of emergency in July 2017.

[114] Art 120 Constitution of Turkey.

[115] Art 122 Constitution of Turkey.

[116] Art 89.5 Constitution of South Korea.

[117] Art 43 Constitution of Taiwan.

[118] Art 338 Constitution of Venezuela.

[119] Art 119 Constitution of Turkey.

necessary to suspend certain civil and political rights during an economic crisis. Rather, such constitutional provisions often empower the executive to take expedient decisions, circumventing the ordinary ex ante checks of the legislature.[120]

The ultimate result is that constitutions conceptualise 'emergency' as an amorphous concept, covering a multitude of distinct phenomena or events. Its boundaries must, axiomatically, be nebulous due to the unpredictability of crises, and an over-rigid definition of emergency may prevent the deployment of emergency powers in a crisis the nature of which was unforeseen. At the extreme end of these amorphous provisions are the constitutions that offer little guidance whatsoever on the conditions that justify a state of emergency. For example, Article 51(2) of the Slovak Constitution merely states that: '[T]he conditions and scope of limitations of the basic rights and freedoms during war, under the state of war, martial state and state of emergency shall be laid down by the constitutional law.'[121] Article 154 of the Egyptian Constitution goes further, stating that: '[T]he President of the Republic declares, after consultation with the Cabinet, a state of emergency in the manner regulated by law.' No more detail is given.[122]

Ultimately, the utility of a typology of emergency powers based on the phenomenon that initially triggers it is questionable due to the fluid nature of crises.[123] A natural disaster, for example, could give rise to dire economic consequences which could itself precipitate civil unrest. Constitutions, therefore, that compartmentalise emergencies according to the phenomena that trigger them may, invariably, require simultaneous declarations of emergency.[124] Moreover, constitutions that delineate in broad terms what constitutes a state of emergency may also result in these powers being used to tackle phenomena that may not align with the paradigmatic understanding of what triggers an emergency. Italy is an illustrative example of this trend. Article 78 of the Italian Constitution allows parliament to declare a state of war and invest the necessary powers in the executive.[125] Similarly, Article 77 allows the Italian parliament to pass an enabling act 'in case of necessity and urgency' which gives a government decree the force of law. Article 77 also permits the government to adopt temporary measures in cases of necessity and urgency provided they are retrospectively validated by the legislature within five days.[126] Finally, Article 76 allows legislative functions to be delegated to the executive for limited periods for 'specified purposes'.[127] These three articles taken together therefore invest extensive emergency powers in the

[120] Alan Greene, 'Questioning Executive Supremacy in an Economic State of Emergency' (2015) 35 *Legal Studies* 594, 617–20; see also text to nn 159–79 in ch 2 of this book.

[121] See also European Commission for Democracy through Law (n 111).

[122] See text to nn 85–89 in ch 2 for a discussion of Egypt's experience of emergency powers.

[123] Greene (n 120) 609.

[124] Thus Art 40.5 of the Chilean Constitution allows the declaration of more than one type of emergency at any one time.

[125] Art 78 Constitution of Italy.

[126] Art 77 Constitution of Italy.

[127] Art 76 Constitution of Italy.

Italian executive and have been utilised, particularly in the area of economic management.[128] In a similar manner, Article 48 of the German Weimar Constitution was infamously used repeatedly to enable exceptional powers to be utilised by the German government to tackle rampant hyper-inflation and economic collapse in the face of a divided parliament rendered impotent by ardent opposition to the existing constitutional order by communists and national socialists. This use of Article 48 ultimately paved the way for Adolf Hitler's ascent to power and the conversion of the constitutional democracy of Weimar Germany into the fascist dictatorship of the Third Reich.[129]

The Emergency Response

Despite the variations in the phenomena that can trigger a state of emergency, emergency provisions all agree on the apparent necessity of the response. The entire purpose of declaring a state of emergency is to enable powers not ordinarily permissible under the constraints of the constitution. It is this necessity of exceptionality that identifies when a phenomenon crosses the 'threat severity threshold', thus warranting the declaration of a state of emergency.

In international human rights law, once a notice of derogation pursuant to an emergency is lodged with the requisite treaty body, a state is absolved from its obligations to protect and vindicate certain human rights to their fullest degree. International human rights treaties thus recognise scenarios whereby the very norms they seek to entrench and protect may be sacrificed. This sacrifice, however, is justified on the grounds that it is merely temporary. International human rights treaties thus conceptualise emergencies as a sword and a shield from a human rights perspective: as the former, they allow a state to breach civil rights and the rule of law that ordinarily constrain them; yet also, by outlining when such measures may be undertaken, they shield and protect human rights in times when conditions do not equate to an emergency.[130] A state of emergency thus expands a state's power, permitting it to take actions that it would otherwise be unable to do, albeit within certain limits. In this way, international human rights treaties are evocative of the manner in which the Roman right of *provocatio*—the bulwark of liberty against tyranny—was sacrificed upon the appointment of a dictator in order to preserve the very Republic itself.[131]

Human rights entrenched in constitutions are also frequently curtailed following the declaration of a state of emergency. Some states' constitutions mirror

[128] See Giorgio Agamben, *State of Exception*, trans Kevin Attell (University of Chicago Press, 2005) 16–18.

[129] ibid, 14–16. See text to nn 158–69 in ch 5 for a further discussion of Art 48.

[130] Alan Greene, 'Shielding the State of Emergency: Organised Crime in Ireland and the State's Response' (2011) 62 *Northern Ireland Legal Quarterly* 249, 250.

[131] Text to n 38 above.

international human rights law and only allow emergency measures taken that are 'to the extent strictly required by the exigencies of the situation'.[132] While the Turkish Constitution does contain such a requirement of proportionality, Article 148 further states that 'no action can be brought before the Constitutional Court alleging unconstitutionality as to the form or substance of decrees having the force of law issued during a state of emergency, martial law or in time of war'.[133] A 2016 judgment of the Turkish Constitutional Court declared that this provision meant that it had no jurisdiction to review whether such emergency measures were required by the exigencies of the situation.[134] Article 148 therefore empties the Article 15 requirement of proportionality of any real meaning.

Another common approach is to delineate specific rights or constitutional provisions that may be suspended, rather than theoretically subjecting every article of the constitution to suspension.[135] Article 28.3.3° of the Irish Constitution, for example, contains an extremely broad declaration that nothing in the Constitution, save Article 15.5.2° (the prohibition on the death penalty), may invalidate any act taken by the state in time of emergency.[136] James Casey notes that the Oireachtas (the Irish Parliament) is essentially given carte blanche not only to suspend basic fundamental rights but also, theoretically, to revise the separation-of-powers doctrine and in essence rewrite the Constitution.[137] A number of constitutions explicitly prevent this by prohibiting their amendment during an emergency.[138]

Human rights are not, however, the only constitutional norms vulnerable in a state of emergency. Due to the perceived necessity of a swift, decisive response, constitutional provisions regarding legislative procedures may be swept aside for a more expedient system. The executive is seen as the body most capable of acting quickly and decisively given the general consensus of opinion at cabinet or the absence of formal procedures that may slow down such decision-making. In contrast, slow legislative procedures are seen as dangerous, hampering a swift, decisive response necessary to dispose of the threat.[139] Thus in Austria, the president may enact law-amending ordinances in instances when the parliament is not assembled or if it cannot do so. Similar clauses also exist

[132] eg Art 15 Turkish Constitution and Art 53 Romanian Constitution (Constitution of Romania 1991 (as amended to 2003)).

[133] Art 148 Constitution of Turkey; Başak Bağlayan, 'The Turkish State of Emergency under Turkish Constitutional Law and International Human Rights Law' (2017) 21 *ASIL Insights* <www.asil.org/insights/volume/21/issue/1/turkish-state-emergency-under-turkish-constitutional-law-and#_edn5> accessed 7 August 2017.

[134] ibid.

[135] See Art 44 Constitution of Uganda 1995 (as amended to 2005)).

[136] Art 28.3.3° Constitution of Ireland.

[137] James Casey, *Constitutional Law in Ireland*, 3rd edn (Roundhall Sweet & Maxwell, 2000) 181.

[138] Eg Art 60.3 §1° of the Constitution of Brazil 1988 (as amended to 2015); Art 81.4 German Basic Law.

[139] Eric A Posner and Adrian Vermeule, *Terror in the Balance: Security, Liberty and the Courts* (Oxford University Press, 2007) 41–42.

in Denmark[140] and Italy.[141] Even in states where there are no formal protocols for the transfer of power to the executive in a period of emergency, serious crises may provide a catalyst for the expedition of executive policy by encouraging the legislature and judiciary to defer to executive assessment regarding what response ought to be taken.[142]

Emergencies may, therefore, confer on the executive broad powers to enact decrees that would, in a period of normalcy, be exclusively within the competence of the legislature and thus contrary to the principle of non-delegation of the legislative function as recognised by many constitutions.[143] This abdication or circumvention of the legislative function thus illustrates how emergencies today can have a damaging effect on democratic values. In turn, this broad delegation of power to the executive or other administrators can have a detrimental effect on the rule of law, specifically, the principle of legality which requires that laws be enunciated clearly so as to ensure certainty as to a law's scope and application.[144] States of emergency therefore today mirror many of the aspects of the Roman dictatorship, or at least, an idealised notion of how the Roman dictatorship was envisaged to operate. Elements of necessity, exceptionalism, expediency, and, most importantly, a fundamental tension between emergency powers and the ordinary constitutional order are present in constitutions that provide for emergency powers.

The Ideal Type Emergency Paradigm

As outlined above, the declaration of a state of emergency has potentially wide-ranging ramifications for individual rights, separation of powers, law-making processes and, ultimately, the constitutional order itself. However, if the link between the phenomenon and the necessity of the response is maintained, then such a response theoretically remains an essential and consequently understandable power available to the state. The question then becomes how to quarantine that response to situations in which it is actually required. A first step is to identify core elements of the emergency paradigm against which declarations of an emergency can be assessed. The historical, regulatory and contemporary legal approaches outlined here indicate the core elements that can be identified. The extent to which these are actually realised in practice will be considered in chapter two.

140 Section 23 Constitution of Denmark, adopted 5 June 1953.

141 Art 77 Constitution of Italy, pronounced 27 December 1947; text to nn 125–28 above.

142 See Fiona de Londras and Fergal Davis, 'Controlling the Executive in Times of Terrorism: Competing Perspectives on Effective Oversight Mechanisms' (2010) 30 *OJLS* 19. See also text to nn 2–25 in ch 6 of this book.

143 See Eoin Carolan, 'Democratic Accountability and the Non-Delegation Doctrine' (2011) 33 *Dublin University Law Journal* 220.

144 See text to nn 21–29 in ch 4 of this book for a discussion of clarity and certainty as values inherent in the rule of law.

The Existence of a Serious Threat to the State Recognised by an Organ of the State

The Roman dictator clearly satisfied this criterion. Such a threat was recognised by the Senate, which delegated to the consuls to appoint a dictator. Rousseau notes that recourse to the dictatorship was common in the early periods of the Republic as the state had not yet a firm enough basis to maintain itself.[145] The dictatorship was therefore required to preserve the very existence of the state, and the principle of heteroinvestiture attempted to ensure that this labelling was not motivated by a personal desire for power by the assessor. Indeed, Rousseau argues that such recourse should only be permitted when the threat is of such severity as to undermine the very existence of the state: 'None but the greatest dangers can counterbalance that of changing the public order, and the sacred power of the laws should never be arrested save when the existence of the country is at stake.'[146] This is clearly reflected in modern definitions of emergency as 'threats to the life of the nation'.

Relatedly, threats of a serious military nature, such as those that faced that Roman dictatorship, are also accommodated in modern manifestations of the emergency paradigm. As noted above, many constitutions and international human rights treaties refer explicitly to war or armed conflict and outline clauses relating to the mobilisation of the military and the imposition of martial law, etc. Threats of this nature are thus contained within the core concept of emergency: they clearly cross the threat-severity threshold and consequently their existence should, ideally, be unequivocal. Relatedly, there may be more contested threats to the security of the state—namely threats labelled as terrorism—that nevertheless may be deemed to cross this threat-severity threshold and justify the declaration of a state of emergency. These threats can be considered to lie within the 'penumbra' of the term 'emergency' and thus are potentially more subjective than the core instances.[147] Consequently, the labelling of such threats as 'emergencies' should be subject to scrutiny.[148]

In later periods of the Roman Republic, however, dictators were also appointed to quell internal strife between the patricians and the plebs.[149] Use of the dictatorship for political gain in such instances inherently weakened the office as plebeian suspicion grew and the spectre of tyrannical monarchy manifested itself. Rousseau also notes that the cheapening of the office in later periods to conduct elections weakened its function and role in the Roman Republic.[150] Such an office

145 Rousseau (n 8) 294.
146 ibid, 293–94.
147 Hart (n 4) 607–08.
148 See ch 2 for a more detailed discussion of the application of the emergency paradigm to deal with threats such as terrorism or other phenomena that may lie within the penumbra of 'emergency'.
149 Rossiter (n 8) 21–22.
150 ibid.

possessing the highest *imperium* should only be utilised when an emergency threatens the very existence of the state. Again, many sources of emergency powers today recognise internal strife and conflict as constituting a threat that may in certain instances justify emergency powers.[151] Such threats may originate from a multitude of different sources, however, with different constitutions recognising phenomena ranging from civil war to industrial disputes, strikes and even economic crises.[152] In such instances, whether such conditions cross the threat-severity threshold may be less clear. Conditions in these instances also occupy the penumbra of the emergency paradigm and tend to be predominantly dependent upon the subjective assessment of the person or body entrusted to decide upon and declare the existence of an emergency.

There is also evidence of dictators being appointed to confront natural disasters such as plagues.[153] In the case of disease, it was a Roman custom to hammer a nail into a tree in order to quell the evil power within that was believed to be the source of the disease or the harm.[154] Cohen suggests that the dictator was entrusted with this solemn task as it was he who possessed the *imperium maius* in the Roman Republic.[155] It was this power and internal *mana*, equivalent to that of the kings of old, that qualified the dictator to perform the function. Today, natural disasters are still a concern for states and thus modern constitutions anticipate and deal with them in a variety of ways. They may be explicitly accommodated by a specific type of state of emergency outlined to deal with them,[156] or come under a more general ambit as long as they meet the requisite threat-severity threshold. Indeed, as mentioned previously, what is key to understanding the ideal emergency is not the nature of the origin of the threat to the state but the conditions that it creates and the response it necessitates.

A Reactive or Defensive Mechanism

As a threat must exist to warrant the declaration of an emergency, resort to emergency powers like the Roman dictatorship constituted a defensive measure.[157] The dictator, appointed *rei gerundae causa* ('to get things done'), could not be chosen until there was something for him to tackle. Unless an emergency was declared, the ordinary constitutional order functioned. A dictator was only appointed at the stage when either the consuls or the Senate recognised the existence of a threat that required the appointment of a dictator. The ideal-type emergency therefore is not declared pre-emptively and should not be an offensive act. The Roman

151 See text to n 95–115 above.
152 See text to nn 116–19 above.
153 Cohen (n 60) 305.
154 ibid.
155 ibid, 306–07.
156 See text to nn 121–29 above.
157 Gross and Ní Aoláin (n 8) 22.

constitutional order recognised this and according to John Ferejohn and Pasquale Pasquino, no dictator ever led armies out of Italy until the Second Punic War from 218 to 201 BC dragged on.[158]

Modern definitions of emergency also envisage the existence of an event or series of events that must be dealt with in an extraordinary way. Derogations consequently are reactive measures as emphasised by the Siracusa Principles.[159] A declaration of an emergency should not, *ideally*, be pre-emptive although the ECtHR has stressed that emergencies must be 'actual or imminent'.[160] This allowance for 'imminence' suggests some relaxation of the defensive nature of emergencies. The declaration of an emergency should, moreover, be based on an objective analysis of the facts as they exist at the time when the emergency is declared, at least to the extent to which this is possible.[161] It should be, like the Roman dictatorship, a reactive mechanism. That conceded, it may be possible to argue that the UK's declaration of a state of emergency and derogation from the ECHR in the aftermath of the terrorist attacks in the United States on 11 September 2001 could be construed as a 'pre-emptive' declaration of a state of emergency. It should be noted, however, that this declaration took place *after* the attack on the United States and therefore it can be argued that it was still reactive in nature.

The Consolidation of Powers in a Branch/Office of Government

Rossiter's use of the term 'constitutional dictatorship' to describe an emergency response is reflective of the consolidation of power in the executive during periods of emergency in constitutions today and the parallels he draws with the Roman dictatorship.[162] Allowing one person almost absolute power was completely counter to the underlying ideology of the Roman Republic, redolent of the very monarchy that the Republic ousted.[163] Yet such recourse was chosen when the exigencies of the situation required it. These emergency measures, reflecting autocracy, the abandonment of collegiality, the potential for tyranny, the absence of *provocatio*, and lack of ex post facto accountability for the dictator's actions, in office are repugnant to the very nature of the constitutional order it was designed to protect. Machiavelli notes, however, that the only way a Republic may survive is if it contemplates and accommodates every probable scenario that may confront it.[164] The dictator's extreme powers were, ideally, proportionate in magnitude to

[158] See Ferejohn and Pasquino (n 8).
[159] See 'Siracusa Principles' (n 84).
[160] ibid, 8. Again, however, it must be stressed that this chapter is an exploration of an ideal-type emergency.
[161] See text to nn 116–39 in ch 2 for a more detailed discussion on subjective factors that influence the decision to declare a state of emergency.
[162] See text to n 12 in the Introduction of this book.
[163] Jolowicz (n 21) 53.
[164] Machiavelli (n 8) 195.

the threat he was appointed to confront. Free from appeal and accountability he could focus solely on the task before him. It was his superior *imperium maius* that made the institution effective.[165] Yet it is also in this superiority that the potential for tyranny lay.[166]

As the executive is afforded a level of secrecy, it is considered to be the body best situated to deal with emergencies, particularly those pertaining to matters of national security, today.[167] Similarly, the executive is the body most capable of acting quickly and decisively given the general consensus of opinion at cabinet or the absence of formal procedures that may slow down such decision-making. In contrast, slow legislative procedure is seen as dangerous, hampering the swift, decisive response necessary to confront the threat.[168] The judiciary are often conceptualised as being particularly inept at assessing the existence of a state of emergency and what response ought to be taken. Both domestic and international courts thus generally defer to the initial decision-maker's assessment of the situation.[169] In this manner, states of emergency operate to result in a consolidation of powers in a branch of government—usually the executive—similar to how power was consolidated in the Roman dictator.[170]

The Enactment of Exceptional Measures that would not have been Permitted in a State of Normalcy

As noted above, the purpose of declaring a state of emergency in international human rights law is to allow a state to derogate from the very human rights obligations these treaties were drafted to protect. Similarly, a dictator was appointed in order to allow the state to act in a manner that was otherwise prohibited under the Roman Republic's ordinary separation of powers. Measures, often draconian in nature that would otherwise be prohibited, are thus allowed. Emergency provisions in constitutions operate similarly, allowing a state to pursue measures that would, but for a declaration of emergency, be deemed inconsistent with the provisions contained in the constitution. Emergency measures may suspend constitutional rights and ordinary constitutional procedure in favour of a more securitised state of affairs.[171] Synonymous with 'state of emergency', the

[165] See ES Staveley, 'The "Fasces" and "Imperium Maius"' (1963) 12 *Historia: Zeitschrift für Alte Geschichte* 458.

[166] Kalyvas (n 16).

[167] Gross and Ní Aoláin (n 8) 65.

[168] See Posner and Vermeule (n 139); text to n 142 above.

[169] David Dyzenhaus, *The Constitution of Law: Legality in a Time of Emergency* (Cambridge University Press, 2006) 176–81.

[170] Rossiter (n 8) 23–24.

[171] Jules Lobel, 'Emergency Power and the Decline of Liberalism' (1989) 98 *Yale Law Journal* 1387, 1387–92.

phrase 'state of exception' focuses on this criterion of the emergency paradigm.[172] States of emergency, therefore, put under pressure the very norms that give a constitutional order its identity.

The Necessity of the Measures Enacted

Ideally, a dictator was appointed only when it was considered absolutely necessary for the survival of the Roman Republic to do so. The inability of the normal institutions of Rome to provide an effective emergency response meant a novel exceptional office was required. The dictatorship was the lesser of two evils—a temporary resort to autocracy as opposed to maintaining the constitutional status quo and the ultimate fall of the Republic. However, the strict time limit and other controls on the office ensured restoration of this status quo ex ante.

The frequency with which dictators were appointed in the early days of Rome, when its foundations were vulnerable, is a key indicator of its function as a tool of necessity. In the later years of the Republic, as Rome's borders were well protected and wars conducted further from the epicentre of Roman power became the standard, the office of dictator declined in use and morphed into a more ceremonial role.[173] The diminution of the status of the dictatorship can be seen by the increasing frequency with which a dictator was appointed in the later days of its existence to deal with mundane procedures such as the conducting of elections as opposed to it being a necessary requirement for the preservation of the state.[174]

As explored earlier, it is the framework of decision-making in normalcy that makes a declaration of emergency necessary. Thus, in modernity, emergency powers may be necessitated by the need for swift, decisive action that cannot be achieved by the operation of the normal separation-of-powers doctrine. Similarly, certain human rights obligations may effectively hinder a response to an emergency. The ECHR and ICCPR recognise necessity as the ground for permitting derogations from treaty provisions. However, they also use necessity as a control on the state's powers, allowing derogations only in proportion to the exigencies of the situation. Again, consequentialist notions of the lesser of two evils are prevalent. This is perhaps best captured by Abraham Lincoln's famous plea upon the

[172] Indeed, Carl Schmitt argues that this propensity of a liberal democratic order to relax or abandon the rule of law in a period of crisis is proof that the state is not synonymous with the legal order and that power of the state, and the state itself, exist prior to the legal order. Carl Schmitt, *Political Theology* (MIT Press, 1985) 12. See generally Agamben (n 128) 32–36; Charles E Frye, 'Carl Schmitt's Concept of the Political' (1966) 28 *Journal of Politics* 818, 825; Oren Gross, 'The Normless and Exceptionless Exception: Carl Schmitt's Theory of Emergency Powers and the "Norm–Exception" Dichotomy' (2000) 21 *Cardozo Law Review* 1825, 1840.

[173] Jolowicz (n 21) 53; Rossiter (n 8) 22–23; Rousseau (n 36) 295; Lazar (n 8) 512.

[174] Rousseau (n 8) 22–23.

outbreak of the US Civil War: 'Are all the laws but one to go unexecuted and the government itself go to pieces lest that one [habeas corpus] be violated?'[175]

The Separation of Normalcy and Emergency

The Roman dictatorship was both inherently constitutional and, at the same time, exceptional to the ordinary workings of the system. It was an office that existed only when an emergency was declared and ceased to function once the time limit had expired or the threat was neutralised, whichever came first. The dictatorship is thus a manifestation of the Romans' recognition of a separation between normalcy and emergency.[176] In the Roman Republic, emergency and normalcy were mutually exclusive conditions; only one state could exist at any one moment in time. Yet they are also inherently linked, considered in terms of a dichotomised dialectic.[177] Thus when normalcy was considered no longer to exist, an emergency was declared and vice versa. There was no middle ground; no grey area. Emergency was the exception, an outlier, an empirical irregularity, recognisable only against a background of normalcy.[178] Indeed, it was this background of normalcy and its inability to make quick decisions that warranted a dictatorship.

The dictator had immense powers; however, he could not legislate, introduce any permanent laws or change the fundamental constitutional order. His powers were 'quarantined' to the exceptional period of his office. When he resigned, the constitutional order reverted to normalcy, identical to that which existed before the declaration of emergency. No trace of the dictator's autocratic power remained, only the results: the successful defence of the Republic. It is this that made Sulla's appointment as dictator *legibus faciendis et rei publicae constituendae* so striking. Sulla was appointed precisely to make changes to the status quo ex ante rather than simply defend it. His dictatorship was not designed to protect the prior constitutional order in its entirety as it was, according to him, the very facets of this constitutional order that gave rise to the emergency in the first instance. It was only by fundamentally altering these prior existing norms that Sulla felt that his goal could be accomplished and the emergency negated. Sulla's dictatorship was therefore not to protect normalcy; it was to change normalcy through exceptional measures.

[175] Abraham Lincoln, 'Special Session Message' (4 July 1861) available at *The American Presidency Project* <www.presidency.ucsb.edu/ws/?pid=69802> accessed 25 August 2017.

[176] Oren Gross, 'Chaos and Rules: Should Responses to Violent Crises Always Be Constitutional?' (2000) 112 *Yale Law Journal* 1011, 1069.

[177] Oren Gross, '"Once More Unto the Breach": The Systematic Failure of Applying the European Convention on Human Rights to Entrenched Emergencies' (1998) 23 *Yale International Law Journal* 437.

[178] ibid.

Modern states of emergency, like the Roman dictatorship as it operated before Sulla, still make this fundamental assumption that emergency can be separated from normalcy.[179] Indeed, this is the most fundamental aspect of the emergency paradigm. In international human rights law, derogation clauses axiomatically consider that treaty-based rights should normally be applied and respected.[180] The ICCPR's General Comment on Article 4 states that the purpose of a derogation under Article 4 and hence its justification is the restoration of a state of normalcy where full respect for the covenant can again be secured.[181] Consequently, such measures must be of an exceptional and temporary nature. Emergencies constitute outliers from the status quo. Juxtaposed against this status quo, a declaration of emergency creates the anomalous situation whereby these rights are no longer enforceable against the state as it struggles against a threat to the life of the nation. The phenomenon triggering the emergency is portrayed as an outlier, which the mechanisms of normalcy are not equipped to deal with.[182] These derogations are only justified to deal with the threat, and once this threat is defeated, the measures should be repealed and normalcy restored.[183] Without this goal, derogation clauses would fundamentally undermine the goal of the treaties that contain them. The same is true for constitutional norms.

The phenomenon that produces the threat to the life of the nation is itself representative of this fundamental separation between normalcy and emergency. The crisis is considered to be a temporary phenomenon. Thus, the invading armies that threatened the Roman Republic would cease to exist once they were defeated and the emergency declared over. This is also true today, with the enemy neutralised and no longer existing once the emergency is over. Thus, like the emergency response the phenomenon itself is an outlier.

The separation of normalcy from emergency is often facilitated by the use of time limits and the belief that emergencies are only temporary.[184] As stated previously, emergencies in the Roman Republic were temporally limited to a maximum of six months—the length of the Dictator's office. They existed for only a short period of time as an exception to the norm. Once they were successfully dealt with by the dictator, the emergency was deemed to have ended.

Today, the Paris Minimum Standards[185] stress that the declaration of a state of emergency shall never exceed the period strictly required to restore normal conditions. Similarly, the Siracusa Principles state that a derogation made under Article 4 of the ICCPR shall terminate in the shortest time required to bring to

[179] ibid, 454.

[180] ibid.

[181] ICCPR, General Comment No. 29: States of Emergency (Article 4), 31 August 2001, c/21/Rev.1/Add.11.

[182] Ferejohn and Pasquino (n 8) 221.

[183] ICCPR, General Comment No. 29: States of Emergency (Article 4), 31 August 2001, c/21/Rev.1/Add.11.

[184] Gross (n 177) 1073.

[185] ibid.

an end the public emergency that threatens the life of the nation.[186] The Inter-American Court has also considered Article 27 to assume that derogations are only temporary for 'the period of time strictly required by the exigencies of the situation'.[187]

Many constitutional emergency provisions also contain an expressly defined time limit.[188] In Poland, a state of emergency declared by the president may only be introduced for a maximum of three months and extended only once.[189] In Chile, a state of siege and state of emergency may last ninety days but can be subject to renewal. In contrast, a state of catastrophe enacted pursuant to a natural disaster is subject to no time limit. In a worldwide study conducted in 2004, of 2,552 cases of emergency rule, 627 were subject to an express time limit provision and 214 subject to a qualified time limit provision. Consequently, the cases not subject to a time limit of any sort amounted to 1,711.[190] Nevertheless often sources that do not include express time limits do envisage the temporal nature of emergency powers.

As stated previously, this chapter is an attempt to discern the key ideal parameters of a state of emergency. As the term emergency is necessarily vague to accommodate the various manifestations of emergency that may occur, these parameters may vary from case to case. However, if challenges to a certain parameter occur in reality with sufficient frequency, then this may undermine whether a given condition is indeed a parameter at all. In this regard, the temporary nature of emergencies is under particularly intense scrutiny. Thus, in *A v UK*[191] the ECtHR held that emergencies under Article 15 can be perpetual. Similarly, the treatment of terrorism as a temporary phenomenon or outlier from the status quo does not conform to observations in certain jurisdictions such as Northern Ireland where the shadow of terrorism was an everyday experience for almost thirty years in the late twentieth century. That conceded, the separation of normalcy and emergency is a key theoretical underpinning of the state of emergency. It is this separation that makes certain responses palatable and confers legitimacy upon human rights derogations. It is this separation that ensured the Roman Republic was indeed a Republic and not a permanent dictatorship. Machiavelli stresses that it was the erosion of the time limit of the dictator's office that lead to the end of the Republic

[186] Siracusa Principles (n 84) 8.

[187] Shelton (n 81) 421.

[188] Malta has an express time limit of 14 days, Greece 15 days, Cyprus, Lithuania and Turkey 2 months. See European Commission for Democracy through Law (n 111).

[189] Art 250(1). In Poland, a state of emergency declared by the president may only be introduced for a maximum of three months and extended only once: Constitution of Poland, entry into force, 17 October 1997, Ch XI, Art 230.

[190] Keith and Poe (n 76) 1090.

[191] *A v Secretary of State for the Home Department* [2005] 2 WLR 87; *A and Others v United Kingdom*, Judgment of 19 February 2009, [2009] ECHR 3455/05. See text to nn 44–54 in ch 5 for a further discussion of this judgment.

and the tyranny of the *Decemviri*. Finally, it is this separation that distinguishes emergency measures from other forms of governance and coercion.[192]

Conclusion

The aim of this chapter was not to present a concise, juridical definition of an emergency capable of being applied and adapted into a legal norm. The dangers and inherent contradiction of such a definition have been alluded to. However, these dangers and contradictions do not apply to a definition utilised by the legal scientist.[193] The legal scientist's definition is merely descriptive rather than prescriptive, akin to theory formulated by the natural scientist based on observations in her data. In light of this clarification, this book conceptualises a state of emergency as:

> A crisis identified and labelled by a state to be of such magnitude that it is deemed to cross a threat severity threshold, necessitating urgent, exceptional, and, consequently, temporary actions by the state not permissible when normal conditions exist.

Firstly, this definition recognises the connection between phenomenon and response which is key to the understanding of a state of emergency. By conceding that an emergency is 'identified and labelled by a state' it also reflects a certain level of subjectivity in ascertaining whether the phenomenon has crossed the severity threshold and warrants an emergency response. That conceded, however, such labelling is open to scrutiny and critique by the legal scientist. Therefore, one can challenge whether what was identified by the state as an emergency crosses the severity threshold. Indeed, the legal scientist may challenge when a phenomenon is not identified as crossing the severity threshold.

The response envisaged is one explained by the necessity of the actions required. Again, there may be the possibility of a level of subjectivity in ascertaining what is necessary, notwithstanding the claim to objectivity that invoking necessity makes. Such a response should be urgent and, more importantly, exceptional; it should be one that cannot be permissible under normal conditions. Often, this exceptionality is the very antithesis of the values vindicated in normalcy, leading to their restriction and even suspension. Consequently, this definition of a state of

[192] For a discussion of models of responding to crises that do not utilise this separation between normalcy and emergency, see Gross and Ní Aoláin (n 8) 86–05; Ian Zuckerman, 'One Law for War and Peace? Judicial Review and Emergency Powers between the Norm and the Exception' (2006) 13 *Constellations* 522, 524.

[193] This in effect mirrors Hans Kelsen's distinction between the legal scientist and a law-making authority. The legal scientist can only describe, not prescribe which is the function of a law-making authority such as a legislature. Thus, a descriptive definition of emergency avoids the pitfalls that a rigid prescriptive definition may incur as the descriptive definition is not a source of coercion. See MDA Freeman, *Lloyd's Introduction to Jurisprudence*, 7th edn (Sweet & Maxwell, 2001) 260.

emergency envisages normalcy and emergency as mutually exclusive conditions. The separation is facilitated by the additional component to the definition that as the measures are exceptional they should be temporary. Normalcy is therefore presumed to be the status quo, with a state of emergency constituting an outlier to the proper functioning of the constitutional order.

While this is submitted to be a wholly accurate definition of a 'state of emergency', it still suffers from a level of vagueness. Phenomena that may induce emergencies are defined as crises, an incredibly broad term, again subject to subjective interpretation. However, vagueness is itself a constituent of the emergency paradigm, as emergency must remain a term devoid of concrete parameters.

The discussion of the emergency paradigm undertaken in this chapter is designed to show how it *ought* to operate. In reality, however, there is often a gap between theory and practice. The elasticity of these parameters around emergency powers puts emphasis on the individual or institution entrusted to assess the existence of a state of emergency. While briefly mentioned in this chapter, this role of decision-maker requires further investigation. The following chapter will discuss challenges to the emergency paradigm, namely that we are no longer able to separate normalcy from emergency but are instead living in a period of permanent emergency. If this is accurate, then the emergency paradigm is obsolete. It is within this context of how the emergency paradigm operates today that the role of the decision-maker will be explored.

2

The Permanent State of Emergency

Introduction

In chapter one, I defined a state of emergency as:

> A crisis identified and labelled by a state to be of such magnitude that it is deemed to cross a threat severity threshold, necessitating urgent, exceptional, and, consequently, temporary actions by the state not permissible when normal conditions exist.

To recount, this definition was delineated under 'laboratory conditions' by examining historical and contemporary manifestations of emergency powers and the fundamental assumptions that underlie their formulation; it was a discussion of the 'ideal type' emergency as it ought to operate. Of course, theory may diverge dramatically from reality. This chapter therefore 'stress-tests' this ideal emergency paradigm, evaluating how its fundamental assumptions function in practice and exploring the challenges to, and refutation of, these assumptions. In particular, the fundamental hypothesis that normalcy can be separated from emergency will be examined as it is this assumption that has come under the most intense scrutiny. Events of the twentieth and early twenty-first centuries, particularly the aftermath of 11 September 2001, have led to arguments that it is no longer possible to separate normalcy from emergency.[1] The result is a permanent state of emergency where so-called temporary powers are perpetuated, entrenched and eventually normalised.[2] This oxymoronic permanent state of emergency should be fatal to the emergency paradigm as the raison d'être of states of emergency is to restore the status quo ex ante that existed prior to the declaration of a state of emergency.

In response to this oxymoronic and, indeed, constitutionally transformative permanent state of emergency, some theorists have jettisoned the emergency paradigm, focusing instead on alternative models of crisis accommodation. These models attempt to avoid constitutionally entrenching this apparently flawed normalcy–emergency dichotomy, instead striving to protect the existing

[1] See Oren Gross, 'Chaos and Rules: Should Responses to Violent Crises always be Constitutional?' (2003) 112 *Yale Law Journal* 1011, 1089–95.

[2] ibid, 1089–94; Giorgio Agamben, *State of Exception*, trans Kevin Attell (University of Chicago Press, 2005) 4.

constitutional order while at the same time allowing a state to respond to the threat accordingly.[3] We will return to these models in chapter six; rather, the focus of this chapter is to interrogate whether the emergency paradigm is actually obsolete.[4] While the nature of threats faced by the modern state are appreciably different from those faced by the Roman Republic, for example, to place the blame of permanent emergencies on the objective conditions that the state faces today is to ignore the key role of the decision-maker and the requisite subjective factors that may impact upon their decision to declare a state of emergency.

Consequently, I contend that a key driver of permanent states of emergency is that the application of the emergency paradigm has broadened considerably, being applied to increasingly 'mundane' and therefore more regular crises. These 'quotidian' emergencies are not necessarily evoked by legal terminology such as 'a threat to the life of the nation'. In light of this, focus must be concentrated on the more overtly political factors affecting the decision-maker's assessment of the existence of a state of emergency. Moreover, how this initial declaration frames the course of the debate, with subsequent scrutiny of this decision weighing heavy on the reviewers, be they democratically elected or otherwise, will also play a role. Insights from fields such as psychology and concepts of heuristics, biases and risk assessment further illuminate the importance of the role of the decision-maker in assessing the existence of a state of emergency. Consequently, it is rash to declare the emergency paradigm obsolete; rather it is misapplied or inherently linked to the subjective assessment of the decision-maker.

The Permanent State of Emergency: Separating Normalcy from Emergency

Constitutional emergency provisions are an admission that there are situations that the ordinary constitutional order cannot, or should not, accommodate. Thus, the Roman dictator, as discussed in chapter one, was appointed in order to circumvent the inter-consular veto which could delay effective decision-making, and a citizen's right of appeal (*provocatio*) that was fundamental for the protection of liberty. At the same time, however, the ordinary constitutional order remained intact, preventing such powers that were antagonistic to the Republic's values from becoming permanent. It was also noted in Chapter 1 how values respected by the archetypal constitutional order today, such as human rights, democratic processes

[3] For examples of an extra-legal approach, see Gross (n 1) 1096; Mark Tushnet, 'Defending Korematsu? Reflections on Civil Liberties in Wartime' [2003] *Wisconsin Law Review* 273, 304–07. See also Nomi Claire Lazar's rejection of the state of exception discourse in Nomi Claire Lazar, *States of Emergencies in Liberal Democracies* (Cambridge University Press, 2009).

[4] Text to nn 173–92 in ch 6 of this book.

and the rule of law, may too be adjusted or suspended in a period of emergency in favour of the security concerns of the state. Once the threat is neutralised and normalcy restored, the emergency measures that were deployed should, ideally, also disappear. Much criticism of the emergency paradigm today, however, stems from the notion that the phenomena that now trigger a state of emergency are often incapable of separation from normalcy. The result is an entrenched, perpetual and, ultimately, permanent state of emergency.[5] This argument contends that the normalcy–emergency dichotomy is no longer possible as the distinct 'degrees' of separation that facilitate this distinction—individual, temporal and geographical—are outmoded.[6] It is to these degrees of separation to which we now turn.

Individual Separation: Distinguishing Friend from Enemy

As noted in Chapter 1, the archetypal 'core' example of a state of emergency is war. War, as classically understood, not only threatens the loss of military and civilian life but also has the potential to overthrow the state itself.[7] War requires an identifiable threat—namely an opposing military force—and a state or army should be able to identify clearly this military force and its members from the ordinary population, non-participants and allies.[8] The enemy personifies the threat to the security of the state and thus the duration of the emergency indelibly linked its existence. Traditional approaches to responding to militaristic threats to the state rely upon this clear distinction between 'friend' and 'enemy'. International humanitarian law, for example, specifies that combatants should distinguish themselves from the general population by bearing arms openly, wearing uniforms and displaying clear, identifiable symbols.[9] Such caveats would not have been necessary prior to the invention of long-range weapons, given the close hand-to-hand nature of combat and battle tactics based on troop formations. Soldiers would have had no choice but to cluster together and distinguish themselves as an army in order engage in hostilities in the first instance. Consequently, the point at which this threat was neutralised was clearly identifiable: when the enemy either surrendered or was annihilated. The Roman dictatorship was specifically designed to accommodate this kind of military threat with the maximum six-month duration of the office corresponding to the working year of the army.[10]

[5] See Oren Gross and Fionnuala Ní Aoláin, *Law in Times of Crisis: Emergency Powers in Theory and in Practice* (Cambridge University Press, 2006) ch 4.

[6] Gross (n 1).

[7] Carl Schmitt, *Theory of the Partisan*, trans GL Ulmen (Telos Press Publishing 2007) 11.

[8] See Toni Pfanner, 'Military Uniforms and the Law of War' (2004) 86 *International Review of the Red Cross* 93.

[9] Geneva Convention, Art 4(a) 2.

[10] Text to n 43 in ch 1.

Military combat changed radically, however, with the invention of firearms and other modern weapons capable of being operated at a distance. Of course, clandestine methods of political violence have always existed; however, ranged weapons amplified their effects and importance considerably. In this context, the first example of the figure known as the 'partisan' appeared in the Napoleonic Wars during France's invasion of Spain, engaging in guerrilla-style warfare against the invading French.[11] The partisan had a tactical interest in not distinguishing himself from the ordinary civilian so wore no uniform to differentiate themselves clearly from the local population.[12] This allowed them to utilise hit-and-run tactics and blend seamlessly into the background.[13] The partisan's tactics correlated closely with ordinary criminal activity and also helped distinguish him from the classical personification of military force.[14] However, although the modus operandi of the partisan was similar to that of the ordinary criminal, the intense political nature of the partisan's goal—the defeat of the invading enemy and defence of his homeland as opposed to personal financial reward or other motive—demarcated him.[15] The partisan thus presented a novel challenge to the laws of war, which at the time resembled, and, indeed, continue to resemble, the intricate rules of duelling between gentlemen.[16] The partisan instead blurred this distinction between friend and enemy, making it extremely difficult to apply a set of norms to him, and, in turn, difficult to recognise when such a threat ceased to exist.[17]

To say that international law is still playing catch-up with the demands of modern warfare or conflict is somewhat of an understatement, particularly when the figure known as the terrorist is added to the equation. Although 'terrorist' and 'partisan' are certainly not synonymous, GL Ulmen, in his introductory remarks to his translation of Carl Schmitt's work, argues that the *Theory of the Partisan* contains an implicit theory of the terrorist.[18] Like the partisan, the perpetrators of modern terrorist acts wear no identifiable uniform in order to blur the distinction between friend and enemy, making the identification of who is responsible for an attack and likely to carry out future attacks difficult to discern.[19] The enemy terrorist is thus a paradox in the sense that they are presented simultaneously as being both 'one of us' yet somehow different or 'other' to us.[20] The result

[11] Schmitt (n 7) 4.
[12] ibid.
[13] ibid, 17–18.
[14] ibid, 16.
[15] ibid, 14.
[16] ibid, 23–26.
[17] ibid, 89–95.
[18] GL Ulmen, 'Translator's Introduction', in Schmitt (n 7) xvi.
[19] Gross (n 1) 1089–95.
[20] See Stanley Cohen, *Folk Devils and Moral Panic: The Creation of the Mods and Rockers*, 3rd edn (Routledge, 2002) 10–11; Fiona de Londras, *Detention in the War on Terror: Can Human Rights Fight Back?* (Cambridge University Press, 2011) 75–82; Jock Young, *The Vertigo of Late Modernity* (Sage, 2007) ch 8.

of this paradox is that incredibly broad stereotypes may be constructed in order to identify an individual as correlating to a possible terrorist threat. These stereotypes emphasise race, religion, nationality and skin-tone in order to construct this image of the 'other'.[21] Since 9/11, this 'othering' has had a disproportionate impact on Muslim communities in many states.[22] This reaction is not, however, novel or unique to the recent 'war on terror' as is evidenced by the US mass detention of Japanese citizens during World War II;[23] so too the UK's introduction of internment in Northern Ireland, which in the majority of cases was deployed against the mostly Catholic Irish nationalist community, rather than the mostly Protestant Unionist community.[24] Indeed, Schmitt states that the lack of identification of the partisan can result in non-conformists being labelled partisans without any consideration as to whether they would actually take up arms or not.[25]

A further key distinction between the terrorist and the partisan is their target. While both terrorists and partisans often have similar modi operandi, Schmitt considered the partisan's target to be exclusively the enemy military. Terrorism today often targets civilians, with the result being that attacks often occur in populated areas of 'everyday life' as distinct from a clearly demarcated battlefield. Thus, while the partisan challenged this idea of 'individual separation', terrorism shattered it.

Geographical Separation

The principal difference, however, between the partisan and the terrorist is, according to Ulman, the 'telluric' nature of the partisan.[26] The partisan is a figure

[21] Kevin R Johnson, 'Racial Profiling after September 11: The Department of Justice's 2003 Guidelines' (2004) 50 *Loyola Law Review* 67, 77–79.

[22] ibid; Javaid Rehman, 'Religion, Minority Rights and Muslims in the United Kingdom' in Javaid Rehman and Susan Breau (eds) *Religion, Human Rights and International Law* (Martinus Nijhoff, 2007) 521; Chris Allen, 'Fear and Loathing: The Political Discourse in relation to Muslims and Islam in the Contemporary British Setting' (2010) 4 *Politics and Religion* 221; Sam Howell and Andrew Shryock, 'Cracking Down on Diaspora: Arab Detroit and America's "War on Terror"' (2003) 76 *Anthropological Quarterly* 443; Reem Bahdi, 'No Exit: Racial Profiling and Canada's War against Terrorism' (2003) 41 *Osgoode Hall Law Journal* 294.

[23] *Korematsu v United States* (1933) 323 US 214. For a detailed discussion of *Korematsu* from the perspective of emergency power regimes, see Mark Tushnet, 'Defending *Korematsu*? Reflections on Civil Liberties in Wartime' [2003] *Wisconsin Law Review* 273; see also text to n 14 in ch 6 of this book.

[24] Brice Dickson, *The European Convention on Human Rights and the Conflict in Northern Ireland* (Oxford University Press, 2010) 53–61; Fergal F Davis, 'Internment Without Trial; The Lessons from the United States, Northern Ireland & Israel' (August 2004) available at SSRN: <http://ssrn.com/abstract=575481> 15–16. Fionnuala Ní Aoláin attributes the subsequent increase in violence in Northern Ireland to the introduction of internment and its detrimental perception amongst Catholics: Fionnuala Ní Aoláin, *The Politics of Force: Conflict Management and State Violence in Northern Ireland* (Blackstaff, Press 2000) 41.

[25] Scchmitt (n 7) 17–18.

[26] Ulmen (n 7) xvii.

that has a connection with a regular base and limits his operations to a specified geographic area. In this regard, Ulman's interpretation of Schmitt almost evokes a romantic image of the partisan, similar to that captured by Leonard Cohen's 'The Partisan'.[27] In contrast, the terrorist lacks this telluric relationship and is free to transcend geographical borders, and attack on land and at sea.[28] The partisan therefore is a defensive figure, whereas the terrorist is an offensive one.[29] Both the partisan and the terrorist operate contrary to law, but it is this offensive character of the terrorist, denying him a frame of reference (geographical or historical), that makes his illegality illegitimate.[30] Schmitt therefore draws a clear distinction between terrorist and freedom fighter. Modern manifestations of the phenomenon known as terrorism are also conceptualised as lacking this telluric restraint, transcending the globe and making the defeat of such an organisation incredibly difficult to ascertain. Thus, the killing of al-Qaeda founder and leader Osama bin Laden in May 2011 could simultaneously be heralded as a watershed moment in the 'war on terror' and as an event that may trigger reprisal attacks.[31] Bin Laden's death did not lead to an end to US overseas military operations against suspected terrorist groups or the repeal of domestic counter-terrorist legislation passed following 9/11.[32] Rather, the splintered command structure that al-Qaeda operates under renders it impossible to discern when, if ever, it is completely defeated. [33]

This international dimension of terrorism also poses challenges for states seeking to derogate from international human rights treaties for the purposes of overseas military actions against suspected terrorist targets. While no state has ever derogated from an international human rights treaty on these grounds, in 2016 the then UK government intimated that it may seek to derogate from the ECHR in future for its armed forces overseas.[34] As noted in Chapter 1, to declare a state of

[27] See Leonard Cohen, 'The Partisan' (1969). Cohen's version is a translation of Emmanuel d'Astier de la Vigerie's 'La Complaint du Partisan', which was written about the French Resistance in World War II.

[28] Ulmen (n 7) xvii.

[29] ibid.

[30] ibid.

[31] R Booth and R Norton Taylor, 'Osama Bin Laden Death Prompts Worldwide Security Alert' *The Guardian* (2 May 2011) <www.guardian.co.uk/world/2011/may/02/osama-bin-laden-death-security-alert> accessed 7 August 2017.

[32] As described by UN Secretary General Ban Kai Moon: 'Bin Laden Death Is "Watershed Moment" Says Ban Ki Moon' *BBC News* (2 May 2011) <www.bbc.co.uk/news/world-us-canada-13260609> accessed 7 August 2017.

[33] Al-Qaeda has been described loosely as merely constituting a shared ideology as opposed to an organisation. See Jason Burke, 'Think Again: Al Qaeda' [1 May 2004] *Foreign Policy* 18. Moisé Naím considers al-Qaeda to be a 'loose network of individuals united by a shared passion for a single cause' similar to NGOs. See Moisés Naím, 'Missing Links: Al Qaeda, the NGO' [1 March 2002] *Foreign Policy* 100. The general consensus appears to be that al-Qaeda, particularly in the aftermath of 9/11, operates as a loose network of independent cells, with a diminished centralised command structure. Robert Chesney and Jack Goldsmith, 'Terrorism and the Convergence of Criminal and Military Detention Models' (2007–08) 60 *Stanford Law Review* 1079, 1094.

[34] Peter Walker and Owen Bowcott, 'Plan for UK Military to Opt Out of European Convention on Human Rights' *The Guardian* (4 October 2016) <www.theguardian.com/uk-news/2016/oct/03/plan-uk-military-opt-out-european-convention-human-rights> accessed 28 August 2017.

emergency under Article 15 ECHR, there must exist a 'war or other public emergency threatening the life of the nation'. To date, the Court has not been required to adjudicate upon the meaning of 'war' under Article 15.[35] Moreover, the UK does not generally declare war in the deployment of armed forces overseas. Indeed, the very phrase 'war' is problematic given that it has fallen out of use in international law with the terms 'international armed conflict' or 'non-international armed conflict' being preferred. War is, therefore, a somewhat archaic term. Nevertheless, war still remains the core, paradigmatic example of a crisis that justifies declaring a state of emergency.[36] Despite this, Marko Milanovic has argued that 'war' in Article 15 should be parsed from the phrase 'threatening the life of the nation', to incorporate armed conflicts that do not meet this threshold.[37] Similar contentions have been made by the right-wing think-tank Policy Exchange, arguing that war 'should not be read down to apply only to wars in which the national survival of the UK is at stake'.[38]

These arguments, however, fundamentally misinterpret Article 15 ECHR and the purpose of declaring a state of emergency. The Council of Europe's own guide to Article 15 conceptualises war at the upper end of the scale of what constitutes a state of emergency with 'any substantial violence or unrest short of war ... likely to fall within the scope of the second limb or Article 15.1, a "public emergency threatening the life of the nation"'.[39] This interpretation is in line with other international human rights treaties.[40] Under this understanding of Article 15, a 'war' or armed conflict can only justify a derogation under Article 15 if it 'threatened the life of the nation'.[41] To parse 'war' from 'public emergency threatening the life of the nation' would be a fundamental misinterpretation of Article 15. 'War' is not just an illustrative example of a public emergency threatening the life of the nation; it is a 'core' or paradigmatic example of this. 'Public emergency threating the life of the nation' is a phrase that expands Article 15 to conditions falling short of this. To interpret war as amounting to a phenomenon that falls short of this requirement is to flip this on its head, making 'war' the term in Article 15 that expands its application and the phrase 'public emergency threatening the life of the nation' its limiting aspect.

[35] European Court of Human Rights, 'Guidance on Article 15 of the European Convention on Human Rights' (31 August 2016) <www.echr.coe.int/Documents/Guide_Art_15_ENG.pdf> 6 para 6.

[36] Text to n 115 in ch 1 of this book.

[37] Marko Milanovic, 'Extraterritorial Derogations from Human Rights Treaties in Armed Conflict' in Nehal Bhuta (ed), *The Frontiers of Human Rights: Extraterritoriality and its Challenges* (Oxford University Press, 2014) 55, 68–69.

[38] Jonathan Morgan, Richard Ekins and Guglielmo Verdirame, 'Derogation from the European Convention on Human Rights in Armed Conflict: Submission to the Joint Committee on Human Rights (7 April 2017) 2, <http://judicialpowerproject.org.uk/wp-content/uploads/2017/04/JPP-JCHR-submission-on-ECHR-derogation.pdf> accessed 4 August 2017.

[39] ibid.

[40] Text to n 78 in ch 1.

[41] ibid.

While the war on terror and international terrorism has demonstrated the difficulty in geographically demarcating emergency from normalcy, the weakness of boundaries, however, is already evident even from the ideal-type emergency response of the Roman dictatorship. Although the enemy may have remained outside the walls of Rome, the dictator's *imperium maius* operated inside the city itself and over the whole of Roman life.[42] As noted in Chapter 1, the dictator's appointment was often necessary in order to circumvent the right of appeal and pass a levy on Roman citizens to raise the necessary resources required to wage war[43] The separation between military and civilian was thus a thin line in the Roman Republic, ie the appointment of a dictator turned all of Rome into a military camp.

Even attempting to draw parameters around natural disaster emergencies is problematic. The US Federal Emergency Management Agency (FEMA), for example, uses the geographical impact of an emergency to categorise disaster events.[44] There is an obvious underlying assumption here that one can clearly discern between areas unaffected by the disaster, and areas affected; between zones of emergency and zones of normalcy.[45] This, for example, would be clear in the aftermath of a natural disaster such as an earthquake, flood, hurricane, etc. In these emergencies, the extent of the damage to property and life would be unmistakable. However, FEMA also implicitly acknowledges the weakness in attempting to contain emergencies via geographical distinctions, as effects, other than physical damage to property and lives, may permeate beyond 'Ground Zero'. FEMA therefore also looks at the financial response that may be necessary to combat the crisis, adjudging whether federal as opposed to merely local resources from directly affected states may be necessary.[46]

It is not merely the economic cost or indeed the emotional distress caused by a disaster that can permeate beyond the scene of the crisis. Like the Roman Republic, particularly where the threat is that of war or armed insurrection, the emergency response may envelop the entire state and beyond. In the aftermath of 9/11, the UN Security Council passed Resolution 1368 requiring all Member States to pass laws dealing with terrorism.[47] In essence, the world was plunged into an emergency. Canada, sharing a border with the US, responded with new counter-terrorist legislation; so too did Australia.[48] The UK, thousands of miles away from 'Ground Zero', lodged a derogation notice under Article 15 ECHR in response to

[42] Clinton Clinton Rossiter, *Constitutional Dictatorship: Crisis Government in the Modern Democracies* (Princeton University Press, 1948) 21.

[43] See text to n 41 in ch 1.

[44] Clifford Oliver, *Catastrophic Disaster Planning and Response* (CRC Press, 2011) 4–8.

[45] ibid.

[46] ibid.

[47] Security Council Resolution 1368 (2001).

[48] See Andrew Goldsmith, 'The Governance of Terror: Precautionary Logic and Counterterrorist Law Reform after September 11' (2008) 30 *Law and Policy* 141.

the apparent threat posed to it by al-Qaeda.[49] The modern terrorist therefore blurs the line between domestic and international issues. The increasingly globalised nature of the world, coupled with the exponential growth of connectivity and the speed and quantity of information being shared, fuels this indistinction further, meaning the impact of domestic crises can reverberate around the globe.[50] Terrorism blurs this distinction so dramatically that international law is finding it increasingly difficult to distinguish international from non-international armed conflicts.[51] Moreover, advances in modern warfare, eg the use of drones, expands the potential for states to confront perceived terrorist threats across geographical borders and legal frameworks.[52]

While terrorism is by no means new, the threat posed by recent manifestations of Islamic extremist terrorism is often conceptualised as presenting a novel challenge to 'Western civilisation' and consequently requiring an unprecedented response.[53] The desired goal of the fundamentalist Islamic terrorist is often represented as the destruction of Western civilisation as a whole.[54] The improbability of this goal, even in the long term, suggests the legal, political and military responses that make up the so-called 'war on terror' are unlikely to end any time soon.[55] The war on terror has instead been equated to an operation more similar to the 'war on drugs' or the 'war on crime' as opposed to a conflict between nation states.[56] Indeed, the apparent perpetual nature of these 'wars' has led to this term falling out of favour. 'War' implies that there is an endpoint in mind. When this endpoint is not achieved, it could be interpreted as a failure of the policies

[49] The validity of this derogation was assessed in *A v Secretary of State for the Home Department* [2005] 2 WLR 87 (2005); *A and Others v United Kingdom* Judgment of 19 February 2009, (2009) 3455 ECHR 5. See also text to n 44–54 in ch 5.

[50] Eg the spike in oil prices as a result of the uprising in Libya in 2011 had a global impact potentially stymieing economic growth in numerous countries. See C Krauss and J Mouawad, 'Uncertainty Drives Up Oil Prices' *New York Times* (1 March 2011) <www.nytimes.com/2011/03/02/business/02oil.html?_r=1> accessed 7 August 2017.

[51] See Markus Gunneflo, *Targeted Killing: A Legal and Political History* (Cambridge University Press, 2016) ch 4.

[52] See Marjorie Cohn (ed), *Drones and Targeted Killing: Legal Moral, and Geopolitical Issues* (Olive View Press, 2015).

[53] Thus, post-9/11, the UK sought to highlight the 'uniqueness' of the threat al-Qaeda posed to the UK, notwithstanding the decades-long conflict in Northern Ireland. See de Londras (n 20) 104.

[54] Burke argues that al-Qaeda seeks not conquest but to beat back Western crusades from Islamic territory. Nevertheless, Wedgwood describes al-Qaeda's methods as shifting from pogrom to extermination of Western peoples. See Burke (n 33). Ruth Wedgwood, 'Al Qaeda, Terrorism, and Military Commissions' (2002) 96 *American Journal of International* Law 328, 357. This is corroborated by the severity of the attacks of 11 September 2001. Indeed, the nature of terrorism, particularly Islamist terrorism, is a highly contested term with Richard Jackson arguing that it is 'profoundly unhelpful' due to its highly politicised, intellectually contestable nature, as well as its counterproductive impact on community relations. See Richard Jackson, 'Constructing Enemies: "Islamic Terrorism" in Political and Academic Discourse' (2007) 42 *Government and Opposition* 394.

[55] See Gilles Andréani, 'The "War on Terror": Good Cause, Wrong Concept' (2004–05) 46 *Survival* 31.

[56] Joan Fitzpatrick, 'Sovereignty, Territoriality, and the Rule of Law' (2001–02) 25 *Hastings International and Comparative Law Review* 303; Jonathan Simon, *Governing Through Crime* (Oxford University Press, 2007) ch 9.

pursued, military stalemate or even defeat. Thus, the Obama administration abandoned the phrase, preferring instead the more banal, bureaucratic-sounding 'overseas contingency operations'.[57]

From 2013 onwards, al-Qaeda was supplanted by the Islamic State (ISIS) as the principal terrorist threat in the 'West', and with it came a revival of a more telluric relationship between the terrorist and the area in which they fought. The legitimacy of ISIS in the eyes of its followers is dependent upon control of territory large enough to enable the declaration of a caliphate.[58] Furthermore, ISIS fighters may demarcate themselves with flags and tend to operate in a more conventional military sense in order to hold this territory.[59] This would thus suggest that regaining control of ISIS-held territory would also result in their defeat, thus again suggesting a resurgence in the idea of drawing a geographical distinction between normalcy and emergency. Despite this, ISIS, nevertheless, undermines the geographical boundaries of emergency zones. Firstly, the fluid and ever-changing territory under the control of ISIS means that its borders, theoretically, pose no limit to its potential expansion—or contraction.[60] Moreover, a major problem that many states are grappling with is the issue of their residents and citizens travelling to areas under the control of ISIS to fight for it.[61] This international dimension has prompted a number of states, such as the UK and Australia, to introduce a range of legal measures to prevent people from travelling there in the first instance and to prevent them from returning, as well as enhancing liberty-restricting measures for such suspected individuals.[62] In turn, while there may

[57] See Lynn M Williams and Susan B Epstein, 'Overseas Contingency Operations Funding', *Congressional Research Service* (7 February 2017) https://fas.org/sgp/crs/natsec/R44519.pdf, accessed 7 August 2017. Mark Tran, 'War on Terror—A Term that No Longer Applies', *The Guardian*, 15 January 2009, www.theguardian.com/news/blog/2009/jan/14/war-on-terror-david-miliband-mumbai, accessed 7 August 2017; Oliver Burkeman, 'Obama Administration Says Goodbye to "War on Terror"', *The Guardian*, 25 March 2009, www.theguardian.com/world/2009/mar/25/obama-war-terror-overseas-contingency-operations, accessed 7 August 2017.

[58] Graeme Wood, 'What ISIS Really Wants', *The Atlantic*, March 2015; Daniel Byman, 'Understanding the Islamic State—A Review Essay' (2016) 40 *International Security* 127, 136–37, 139; Andrew F March and Mara Revkin, 'Caliphate of Law' (2015) 94 *Foreign Affairs* <www.foreignaffairs.com/articles/syria/2015-04-15/caliphate-law> accessed 28 August 2017.

[59] Byman (n 58) 144; Audrey Kurth Cronin, 'ISIS Is Not a Terrorist Group' (2015) 94 *Foreign Affairs* <www.foreignaffairs.com/articles/middle-east/isis-not-terrorist-group> accessed 28 August 2017; Michael Weiss and Hassan Hassan, *ISIS: Inside the Army of Terror* (Regan Arts, 2015) xv.

[60] Lina Khatib, 'The Islamic State's Strategy: Lasting and Expanding' (Carnegie Middle East Centre 2015) <http://carnegieendowment.org/files/islamic_state_strategy.pdf> accessed 28 August 2017, 6–9.

[61] Patrick Wintour, 'Islamic State Fighters Returning to UK "pose huge challenge"' *The Guardian* (9 March 2017) <www.theguardian.com/uk-news/2017/mar/09/islamic-state-fighters-returning-to-uk-pose-huge-challenge> accessed 28 August 2017.

[62] See Counterterrorism Crime and Security Act 2015. Amongst the changes brought in under this Act were the introduction of relocation powers under Terrorism Prevention and Investigation Measures legislation, increased powers to port police to temporarily seize a passport, and putting in place a temporary exclusion order that could prevent a British citizen from returning to the UK for a period of time. Section 119.2 of the Australian Criminal Code Act 1995 empowers the Minister for Foreign Affairs to make it an offence to enter a declared area. On 2 March 2015, the Minister declared the Mosul District in Iraq to be one such zone, thus making it an offence, punishable by 10 years' imprisonment for an Australian citizen to enter or remain in Mosul. See 'Travel Warning: Mosul District, Ninewa Province,

be a more conventional military hierarchy operated by ISIS in the territory that they control, the same cannot be said for terrorist attacks carried out in Western states that are described as 'ISIS inspired' or carried out by 'ISIS sympathisers'. An attack on Paris, France can be linked to one in Orlando, USA, which can, in turn, be linked to one in Berlin, Germany or Manchester, UK.[63] An attack in one state or city is now 'an attack on us all'.[64] Moreover, terrorist organisations, such as ISIS, no longer need command structures or communicative logistics in place to conduct operations or claim responsibility for attacks. Instead, through use of terms such as 'ISIS inspired' or 'ISIS sympathisers', the state, the media and other public discourse framers connect the dots for them, regardless of the degree of interaction or direction (if any) from ISIS commanders in Iraq and Syria.[65]

At first glance, this may all seem paradoxical. ISIS is conceptualised as both a classic state-like entity holding territory, while simultaneously spreading terror across beyond its borders through a loose connection of cells or 'lone wolf' actors influenced and inspired by extremist material read online. In actuality, these two different dimensions of how ISIS is conceptualised are symbiotic. The state-like dimension of ISIS needs radicalised 'lone wolf' attacks to aggrandise the scope and power of ISIS, which, in turn, can act as a recruiting tool for their cause. This is the classic, 'propaganda of the deed' dimension of terrorism.[66] In turn, the 'lone wolf' needs the state dimension of ISIS as his motivation and inspiration for carrying out such attacks. In truth, the lone wolf needs the pack and vice versa. This dual dimension of ISIS is also useful for those who wish to justify confronting its threat through both military force and the criminal justice system.

Legal Manifestations of Geographical Distinctions

Despite this non-telluric aspect, many state responses to terrorism, nevertheless, seek to rely upon a geographical distinction between normalcy and emergency, enabling something permissible in zone X that would be impermissible in zone Y. In this regard, Giorgio Agamben uses the metaphor of 'the camp' to conceptualise the parameters that demarcate the effects of a state of exception. The camp is

> a piece of land placed outside the normal juridical order, but is nevertheless not simply an external space … the camp is thus the structure in which the state of exception is realised normally.[67]

Iraq', Australian Government (3 March 2015) <www.nationalsecurity.gov.au/WhatAustraliaisdoing/Documents/Travelwarning-Mosul-district-Ninewa-province-Iraq.PDF> accessed 17 August 2017.

[63] Byman (n 59) 142; Jason Burke, 'The Myth of the "Lone Wolf" Terroist' *The Guardian* (30 March 2017) <www.theguardian.com/news/2017/mar/30/myth-lone-wolf-terrorist> accessed 28 August 2017.

[64] Donovan Slack, 'Obama: Paris Attack Is an Attack on Us All' *USA Today* (13 November 2015) <www.usatoday.com/story/experience/beach/new-hampshire/2015/11/13/obama-paris-attack-attack-us-all/75735544/> accessed 28 August 2017.

[65] Alan Greene, 'Defining Terrorism: One Size Fits All' (2017) 66 *ICLQ* 411, 436–39.

[66] Sue Mahan and Pamala Griset, *Terrorism in Perspective*, 2nd edn (Sage, 2008) 40.

[67] Giorgio Agamben, *Homo Sacer: Sovereign Power and Bare Life* (Stanford University Press, 1998) 96.

Agamben raises the concentration camps of Nazi Germany as such an example. Inside these camps, Jews and other so-called 'enemies of the state' were stripped, not just of their legal rights, but reduced in law to bare life, *Homo sacer*.[68] Devoid of any recourse to law, they were at the disposal of the sovereign's discretion.[69] The geographical perimeter of the camp thus acts as the separation between normalcy and emergency.[70] It is the 'event-horizon' that marks the boundary between the ordinary zone of law, and the black hole created by the state of exception. The term 'camp' connotes a temporary structure, often militaristic in nature and is hence a useful metaphor when describing the limits of a state of emergency.

At the outset of the 'war on terror' the Bush administration sought to utilise this 'camp' paradigm when detaining individuals. Fiona de Londras summarises the US rationale behind using Guantanamo Bay in Cuba as a detention facility for the following four reasons:

> 1) Cuban law did not apply to Guantanamo Bay on the basis of the terms of the agreement leasing the property to the United States; 2) US federal courts had no jurisdiction and constitutional rights did not apply because it was de jure Cuban territory; 3) US statutes did not apply there unless they expressly provided for extra-territorial application; and 4) unincorporated international human rights law did not apply there because it had neither domestic nor extraterritorial effect.[71]

Guantanamo Bay, therefore, was an attempt to establish a 'camp' and create a zone of little law, through law. It was based on the assumption that emergency or exceptional powers could be used and quarantined within clear demarcated zones. Within these geographical areas, or camps, a state of emergency or exception existed, as distinct from a state of normalcy which existed everywhere else. Ultimately, however, this 'camp' was eroded with the courts gradually asserting through a series of cases, culminating in *Boumediene v Bush*, that detainees in Guantanamo Bay possessed constitutional rights—a point that will be returned to in Chapter 5.[72] Nevertheless, Guantanamo Bay, at the time of writing, remains open.[73]

More banal aspects of this 'camp' metaphor than Guantanamo Bay can also be seen in the counter-terrorist responses taken by states. Section 44 of the Terrorism Act 2000 empowered British police to establish special zones wherein individuals could be stopped and searched without a warrant. Aside from evidence indicating a racial prejudice pertaining to those stopped, the lack of procedural safeguards

[68] ibid.

[69] ibid, 96.

[70] ibid.

[71] Fiona de Londras, 'Guantanamo Bay, the Rise of Courts and the Revenge of Politics' in David Jenkins, Amanda Jacobsen, and Anders Henriksen (eds), *The Long Decade: How 9/11 Has Changed the Law* (Oxford University Press, 2012) 155, 156.

[72] *Boumediene v Bush*, (2008) 553 US 723; de Londras, ibid; text to n 55–59 in ch 5.

[73] Priscilla Alvarez, 'Will Guantanamo Bay's Prison Ever Close?' *The Atlantic* (21 December 2016) <www.theatlantic.com/politics/archive/2016/12/obama-guantanamo-bay/511349/> accessed 7 August 2017.

ultimately led the ECtHR to find a breach of Article 8 (right to privacy) on the grounds that the powers were not sufficiently prescribed by law.[74] Australia, too, can be seen to be embracing the 'camp' with its strict immigration policy of detaining asylum seekers in detention centres, the most high profile of which is on the island of Nauru.[75] The link between these asylum seekers and 'national security' is frequently raised in political discourse defending the system and restrictions of freedom of expression that stem from counter-terrorist legislation applying to individuals visiting these centres.[76] The inclusion of geographical constraints on the scope of counter-terrorist powers is inconsistent, however. Indeed, section 44 of the Terrorism Act 2000 was itself evident of this. Such stop-and-search powers were originally included in counter-terrorism legislation only applicable in Northern Ireland.[77] The 2000 Act, however, made them permanent and applied them to the entirety of the UK.

Evidence would appear to suggest, therefore, that states of emergency can no longer be maintained within geographical borders.[78] However, geographical demarcation of an emergency response has always placed rather weak restraints on emergency powers. What has advanced this capitulation, however, since 9/11 is that the dividing line between domestic and international relations is now blurred.[79] The transnational nature of the terrorist threat posed by 'Islamic extremism' means it challenges approaches favouring accommodation by a criminal justice model or by waging war on the organisation. The response is a hybrid of both with measures taken, not just by the US, but by other countries only remotely affected by the event.

Temporal Separation: The Permanent State of Emergency

The belief that emergencies are only temporary is fundamental to the legitimacy of the normalcy–emergency dichotomy.[80] Positing emergency as the exception and normalcy as the rule conceptualises an emergency as capable of being neutralised and therefore something that necessitates the otherwise illegitimate and

[74] *Gillan and Quinton v United Kingdom* ECtHR 12 January 2010.

[75] See Brian Opeskin and Daniel Ghezelbash, 'Australian Refugee Policy and its Impacts on Pacific Island Countries' (2016) 36 *Journal of Pacific Studies* 73; George Williams, 'Asylum Seekers on Nauru are in a Legal Black Hole' *Sydney Morning Herald* (3 February 2016) <www.smh.com.au/comment/nauru-a-legal-black-hole-for-asylum-seekers-20160203-gmklf8.html> accessed 7 August 2017.

[76] See Gillian Triggs, 'Human Rights and the Overreach of Executive Discretion: Citizenship, Asylum Seekers and Whistleblowers' (20160) 16 *Macquarie Law Journal* 3; Julian Burnside, 'The Leaked Transcript of Turnbull's Call with Trump Shows Him at his Worst' *The Guardian* (4 August 2017) <www.theguardian.com/commentisfree/2017/aug/05/the-leaked-transcript-of-turnbulls-call-with-trump-shows-him-at-his-worst> accessed 28 August 2017.

[77] See text to n 45 in ch 6.

[78] Gross reaches a similar conclusion: see Gross (n 1) 1075–89.

[79] ibid, 1077–82. See also Fitzpatrick (n 57) 317–25.

[80] Gross (n 1) 1073–75.

unlawful response.[81] Regardless of this fundamental rationale, permanent or perpetual states of emergency are commonplace throughout the twentieth and twenty-first centuries. Ireland, for example, was in an official state of emergency from September 1939 until 1995.[82] Egypt, too, existed in a persistent state of emergency from 1981 and for all but four years since 1957.[83] Despite a popular movement that ousted President Hosni Mubarak in February 2011, the state of emergency he declared in 1981 remained in force until 2012.[84] Egypt's experience with emergency powers dates from the British military's use of martial law in the country in the early twentieth century.[85] Subsequently, the newly independent Egypt and the various governmental manifestations that have existed since 1922 have all found emergency powers to be useful in dealing with various threats, be it a response to World War II, the Arab–Israeli War, the Suez War, the Six-Day War, the Yom Kippur War of 1973 or the assassination of President Anwar el-Sadat in 1981. This declaration of a state of emergency remained in force until 31 May 2012 whereupon it was repealed by the democratically elected government of Mohamad Morsi, a year after the ousting of President Mubarak.[86] Morsi was then himself overthrown by a military coup on 3 July 2012, and then acting President Adly Monsur declared a state of emergency on 14 August to enable the military to enforce security measures. Egypt has subsequently experienced a number of intermittent emergencies since with, at the time of writing, the most recent being a three-month emergency declared in April 2017 following the bombing of two Christian churches on Palm Sunday.[87]

Like Egypt, many of the states involved in the 'Arab Spring' made use of permanent states of emergency as a means of exercising political control. On 24 February 2011, Algeria lifted its nineteen-year state of emergency following a period of popular public protest.[88] Likewise, the state of emergency proclaimed in Syria on 9 March 1963, effectuating Legislative Decree No 51 of 22 December 1962, remained in force until President Bashar al-Assad repealed it on 21 April 2011.[89]

[81] Conversely, if a threat is incapable of neutralisation a response is not possible. Hence FEMA's identification of an extinction level event as one to which no effective response is available. Text to n 45 above.

[82] See text to nn 171–74 in ch 3; Alan Greene, 'The Historical Evolution of Article 28.3.3° of the Irish Constitution' (2012) 47 *Irish Jurist* 117, 139.

[83] Sadiq Reza, 'Endless Emergency: The Case of Egypt' (2007) 10 *New Criminal Law Review* 532.

[84] 'Egypt Lifts Unpopular Emergency Law' *CNN* (2 June 2012) <http://edition.cnn.com/2012/05/31/world/africa/egypt-emergency-law/index.html> accessed 28 August 2017.

[85] Reza (n 83) 535–37.

[86] 'Egypt Lifts Unpopular Emergency Law' (n 84).

[87] This was then extended in June 2017. See Amina Ismail, 'Egypt to Extend State of Emergency for Three Months' *Reuters* (22 June 2017) <www.reuters.com/article/us-egypt-security-idUSKBN19D20A> accessed 17 August 2017.

[88] 'Algeria Officially Lifts State of Emergency' *CNN* <http://articles.cnn.com/2011-02-24/world/algeria.emergency_1_islamist-party-algerian-press-service-emergency-declaration?_s=PM:WORLD> accessed 30 June 2011.

[89] B Knight, 'Syria Lifts State of Emergency' *ABC News* (20 April 2011) <www.abc.net.au/news/stories/2011/04/20/3196294.htm> accessed 30 June 2011.

Syria's de jure state of emergency from 1963 to 2011 was the second longest in the world when it ended.[90] Normalcy in any real sense, however, was not restored as Syria was then plunged into civil war which, at the time of writing some five years later, is still ongoing.

In 1987, Turkey declared a state of emergency in the face of escalating terrorist attacks.[91] This remained in force until it was lifted in the last two provinces in November 2002.[92] The State Security Courts, founded under the same law,[93] remained in operation until 2004, although they have been demilitarised in accordance with a judgment of the ECtHR.[94] In July 2016, a new state of emergency was declared in response to a failed army coup aimed at overthrowing President Recep Tayyip Erdoğan. Turkey's constitutional provisions that deal with emergencies permit the initial declaration of a state of emergency to last six months.[95] These may be extended by a period of four months upon a resolution of the Grand Assembly of Turkey.[96] In this time, Turkey has undertaken a widespread purging of the judiciary, military, police, universities and other public institutions. Emergency powers to deal with the attempted coup were almost immediately deployed against Kurdish opposition groups, unconnected to the coup. In addition, following a referendum in April 2017, the Constitution has also been subject to fundamental amendments that strengthen the role of the president.[97]

A final illustration of this phenomenon of permanent emergency is Israel, which has been in a state of emergency since May 1948, ie since its inception as an independent sovereign state.[98] As a state surrounded by hostile neighbours, such as Syria and Lebanon, Israel has partaken in numerous wars during this period. There have also, however, been periods of relative calm.[99] The difficulty this presents to the state is that when an escalation of events occurs, there is no formal heightened threat response mechanism available to distinguish these new events from the background that preceded it. Thus, the so-called 'Second Intifada', which started in October 2000 and led to more than 300 deaths, was met with debate in the Knesset as to whether an emergency coalition government should

[90] ibid.

[91] Ümit Cizre, 'Demythologyzing the National Security Concept: The Case of Turkey' (2003) 57 *Middle East Journal* 213, 220.

[92] ibid.

[93] ibid; see *Sener v Turkey* Application No 26680/95, Judgment of the European Court of Human Rights, 18 June 2000, Available at: http://hudoc.echr.coe.int/sites/eng/pages/search.aspx?i=001-58753 (accessed 22 July 2013), where the presence of a military judge on a State Security Court was found to breach the requirement of impartiality in Art 6.1 ECHR.

[94] ibid, 220.

[95] Art 121 Constitution of Turkey.

[96] ibid.

[97] See text to nn 56–61 in ch 7 for further discussion of Turkey's state of emergency.

[98] See Adam Mizock, 'The Legality of the Fifty-Two Year State of Emergency in Israel' (2001) 7 *University of California, Davis Journal of International Law and Policy* 223; Suzie Navot, *The Constitution of Israel: A Contextual Analysis* (Hart Publishing, 2014) 250–51.

[99] Mizock, ibid.

be formed.[100] In addition, elections were postponed until the emergency was over; not the emergency that stretched back to 1948, but to the new, heightened set of events that existed as a result of the Second Intifada.[101] Thus Israel, while in a permanent state of emergency since 1948, arguably entered into a more heightened, de facto state of 'hyper' emergency in October 2000.[102]

The Fall of the Emergency Paradigm?

It would appear, therefore, that normalcy can no longer be distinguished from emergency. The modern manifestation of terrorism represents the most critical challenge to this separation. The clandestine nature of the terrorist; the transformation of cities and ordinary civilian networks into terrorist targets; the international dimension of this phenomenon, transcending national borders; and the continued perpetuation of emergency powers in numerous states that have utilised them all seem to indicate that we can no longer separate normalcy from emergency. This conclusion, however, is based on the assumption that the above examples are a matter of empirical objective fact and ignores the fundamental importance of the role that decision-makers have in identifying and drawing these lines of demarcation.

Is the Emergency Paradigm Obsolete? Focusing on the Decision-Maker

Attributing the cause of permanent states of emergency to the existence of permanent threats is, however, problematic. This conclusion assumes that the decision taken that an emergency response is necessary is one that is an objective exercise. Gross is himself highly sceptical of this, stating that the flexibility of emergency accommodation models is 'innately susceptible to manipulation'.[103] Giorgio Agamben's influential *State of Exception* takes the opposite view of objective emergencies, stressing the naïvety of assuming necessity is an objective fact.[104] Agamben instead asserts that the concept of necessity is 'an entirely subjective one, relative to the aim that one wants to achieve'.[105] Agamben thus argues that 'not only does necessity come down to a decision, but that on which it decides is, in

[100] ibid 241–42.
[101] ibid.
[102] ibid.
[103] Gross (n 1) 1096.
[104] Giorgio Agamben, *State of Exception*, trans Kevin Attell (University of Chicago Press, 2005) 29–30.
[105] ibid, 30

truth, something undecidable in fact and law'.[106] Agamben in this way puts the decision-maker central to the question of necessity and state of exception. This can be illustrated by the so-called 'migrant crisis' experienced by the EU from the summer of 2015 onwards. This triggered declarations of emergency in Hungary[107] and Macedonia,[108] and rhetoric evocative of emergency in other states and from the EU.[109] This emergency, however, was framed, not in order to enable a response to rescue tens of thousands of desperate people; rather, it was to conceptualise these people *as* the threat and justify exceptional measures such as the closure of borders and erection of fences.[110] However, while Agamben is correct to draw attention to the subjective aspect of 'necessity' and, by proxy, 'emergency', 'necessity' is not, and should not, be conceptualised as 'wholly' subjective. Nor must one concede to this claim fully in order to argue for enhanced scrutiny of the decision-maker declaring the state of emergency.

In this regard, constructivism provides an intermediary between the two extremes of objectivity and subjectivity. Constructivism, like interpretivism, emphasises the role of the observer and his/her perception or categorisation of reality.[111] Constructivists, however, also acknowledge that there is such a thing as an objective reality. Constructivism thus emphasises the determinism of individual actors yet also acknowledges that the social world does tend to obey certain rules. Both the observer and the observed are integral.[112] Constructivism therefore instructs us to focus on the unique specificities of the individual assessing and interpreting reality. Taking this 'constructivist turn', this chapter shall now explore how the threat and conditions of the emergency themselves impact upon the decision-maker's assessment of the situation in ways that distort and hamper an objective assessment. In turn, a further factor to consider is how emergency powers have been utilised to confront an ever-increasing diverse range of phenomena, the severity of which is equally diverse.[113] This 'broadening' of the term emergency to encompass more 'banal' or 'quotidian' crises is a key driver of permanent emergencies. Conversely, the decision not to declare a state of emergency,

[106] ibid, 30–31.

[107] Cassandra Vinograd, 'Europe's Refugee Crisis: Hungary Declares State of Emergency over Migrants' *NBC News* (9 March 2016) <www.nbcnews.com/storyline/europes-border-crisis/europe-s-refugee-crisis-hungary-declares-state-emergency-over-migrants-n534746> accessed 28 July 2017.

[108] 'Macedonia Declares State of Emergency to Tackle Migrant Crisis' *The Guardian* (20 August 2015) <www.theguardian.com/world/2015/aug/20/macedonia-state-of-emergency-migrant-crisis> accessed 28 July 2017.

[109] Philip Sherwell and Nick Squires, '"Migrant Crisis is a Security Crisis" says EU Foreign Policy Chief' *The Telegraph* (11 May 2015) <www.telegraph.co.uk/news/worldnews/europe/eu/11597651/Migrant-crisis-is-a-security-crisis-says-EU-foreign-policy-chief.html> accessed 17 August 2017.

[110] ibid.

[111] Friedrich Kratochwil, 'Constructivism: What it Is (Not) and Why it Matters' in Michael Keating and Donatella Della Porta (eds), *Approaches and Methodologies in the Social Sciences: A Pluralist Perspective* (Cambridge University Press, 2008) 80–99.

[112] ibid, 86–87.

[113] Mark Neocleous, 'The Problem with Normality: Taking Exception to "Permanent Emergency"' (2006) 31 *Alternatives* 191, 197.

but then for the government to act for all intents and purposes as if one exists, in turn raises further challenges to the claim that permanent emergencies are an objective inevitability today.

Framing the Emergency: Focusing on the Decision-Makers

Terms such as 'war' or 'emergency' are loaded with emotion. Given the unseverable link between emergency and response established in Chapter 1, this emotional dimension can be utilised in order to convey a sense of urgency and motivation. In particularly political emergencies, such as in the area of national security, a declaration of an emergency can serve to convey and reassure a fearful public that that the government is 'doing something'. In turn, the initial decision as to the existence of a state of emergency sets out the parameters of this debate and 'frames' the manner in which subsequent decision-makers and reviewers engage with and assess the situation.

Framing refers to the selection of 'some aspects of a perceived reality and make them more salient in a communicating text, in such a way as to promote a particular problem definition, causal interpretation, moral evaluation, and/or treatment recommendation for the item described'.[114] Jim Kuypers defines framing as:

> [A] process whereby communicators, consciously or unconsciously, act to construct a point of view that encourages the facts of a given situation to be interpreted by others in a particular manner. Frames operate in four key ways: they define problems, diagnose causes, make moral judgments, and suggest remedies.[115]

Frames thus affect how individuals perceive and make sense of events. In public discourse, various frames proffered from different sources will compete to become the dominant interpretation of a particular event. Meaning in public discourse is not found or discovered but is instead created by 'rhetors'. Moreover, each rhetor is not on an equal footing to dictate the agenda. Rather, the individual or branch of government that constructs the initial narrative or frame shapes and directs the course of the subsequent debate. For this reason, the US president has been called 'the nation's chief story teller, its Interpreter-in-chief'.[116] The president's power is therefore as much about persuasion as it is about its contours as laid out in the Constitution.[117] With regards to emergencies, if a crisis is identified and labelled

[114] RM Entman, 'Framing: Toward Clarification of a Fractured Paradigm' (1993) 43 *Journal of Communication* 51; Zizi Papacharissi and Maria de Fatima Oliveira, 'News Frames Terrorism: A Comparative Analysis of Frames Employed in Terrorism Coverage in US and UK Newspapers' (2008) 13 *International Journal of Press/Politics* 52, 53.

[115] Jim A Kuypers, *Bush's War: Media Bias and Justifications for War in a Terrorist Age* (Rowman & Littlefield, 2009) 8; Oren Gross and Fionnuala Ní Aoláin, 'The Rhetoric of War: Words, Conflict, and Categorisation Post-9/11' (2014) 24 *Cornell Journal of Law and Public Policy* 241, 247.

[116] Mary E Stuckey, *The President as Interpreter-in-Chief* (CQ Press, 1991) 1.

[117] Richard E. Neustadt, *Presidential Power and the Modern Presidents: The Politics of Leadership from Roosevelt to Reagan* (The Free Press 1991) 11.

as such by the US president, or other initial decision-makers such as the executive in a parliamentary democratic system, framing would suggest that the resultant debate and decisions that flow from this debate would be seen through this frame of emergency. Consequently, decision-makers such as the judiciary when engaging in review may also see the situation as an emergency without actually questioning the frame presented by the executive or legislature.

The importance of framing in constructing narratives around emergencies is further compounded by insights from psychology and other branches of the social sciences regarding how individuals interpret reality. Prospect theory, for example, suggests that how we interpret choices as gains or losses influences how much risk we are willing to take.[118] Framing information in terms of a loss can result in a different decision being taken by an individual than if the flip side of this choice, ie the gain, is emphasised. For example, a public policy may gain more support if the resultant 90 per cent employment rate is emphasised rather than framing the debate in terms of a 10 per cent unemployment rate.[119] Prospect theory further suggests that individuals give greater weighting to the outcome of a particular event than they do to the probability of such an event occurring.[120] As delineated in Chapter 1, if the raison d'être of a state of emergency is restoration of the status quo that existed before the emergency existed, then when an emergency is declared it is reasonable to assume that the decision-maker views the position that they are in to be one of loss relative to the previous status quo.[121] Consequently they may be more inclined to make a decision and enact a response that enhances security.[122]

Additional decision-making biases such as heuristics may also affect individuals when assessing the existence of an emergency and what response ought to be taken. The availability heuristic, for example, is a phenomenon that demonstrates that individuals overestimate risks stemming from vivid, immediate images and accord lesser weight to more abstract or long-term risks.[123] The availability heuristic explains why people feel at greater risk from easily conceivable phenomena such as a violent terrorist act, particularly in the aftermath of one, notwithstanding the fact that the actual risk to their life is much less.[124] In contrast, risks to health

[118] Jonathan Mercer, 'Prospect Theory and Political Science' (2005) 8 *Annual Review of Political Science* 1, 1.

[119] ibid.

[120] Gross (n 1) 1040.

[121] See text to n 184 in ch1.

[122] Thus, Mercer argues that US President George Bush was arguably in a situation of loss after 9/11. See Mercer (n 125) 6–7. Mercer, however, also argues that the support the US government was enjoying after the invasion of Afghanistan may then have put the Bush administration in a situation of gain which they then tried to capitalise upon by invading Iraq. Mercer therefore cautions that: 'Although the validity of prospect theory depends on a correct assessment of an actor's motivation, there is nothing within prospect theory to help with that assessment.'

[123] Cass R Sunstein, *Laws of Fear: Beyond the Precautionary Principle* (Cambridge University Press, 2005) 36–39; John Ip, 'Sunset Clauses and Counterterrorism Legislation' [2013] *Public Law* 74; Christina E Wells, 'Questioning Deference' (2004) 69 *Missouri Law Review* 921, 928.

[124] Sunstein, ibid.

such as heart disease or cancer from smoking, diet or other lifestyle choices are undervalued. The availability heuristic thus suggests that in the aftermath of an emergency, public perceptions would tend to overestimate the actual risk from future, similar phenomena creating pressure on democratic institutions to address these concerns. 'Worst case scenarios have a distorting effect on human judgment, often producing excessive fear about unlikely events.'[125] Television, the internet and other visual media can compound this by broadcasting images of these worst-case scenarios around the globe, far beyond the epicentre of a terrorist attack. Measures may therefore be taken by a state that may impact severely upon human rights, while at the same time not materially improving the security of the citizen as the threat in the first instance was not actual.

Consequently, the subjective lens through which the decision-maker views the phenomenon that triggers the state of emergency is integral to understanding why the decision-maker considered that an exceptional response was necessary in the first instance. Even in constitutional orders where decision-making in an emergency is not exercised exclusively by an initial decision-maker, their original perception and framing of the situation is highly influential upon all subsequent decision-makers, and, indeed, on anyone trying to understand and make sense of the situation.

Democratic Decision-Making and States of Emergency

In Chapter 1 it was noted that the Roman Republic utilised the principle of heteroinvestiture—that he who is empowered to appoint a dictator cannot appoint himself as dictator—in order to ensure that this decision-maker could not themselves profit from the dictatorship.[126] Modern constitutions do not necessarily follow this principle, however, as it is generally either the executive or legislature which declares states of emergency and gains the resultant powers that flow from this declaration. While presidential systems may correlate more closely with this concept of heteroinvestiture, the domination of the legislature by the executive in parliamentary systems means that any separation between the two is weak at best.[127] The democratic branches of government are thus in a position whereby they may increase the scope of their powers through their own declaration of a state of emergency.

Gross has described this relationship between democracy and states of emergency as 'a tension of tragic dimensions'.[128] Democracies are weak at spreading burdens evenly amongst societies, particularly in periods of emergency. Rather, the majoritarian forces tend to exact this burden upon the minority, usually an

[125] ibid, 105.
[126] See text to n 48 in ch 1.
[127] See 'The Decline of Parliament' (1963) 34 *Political Quarterly* 233.
[128] Gross (n 1) 1027.

underrepresented group in the political landscape.[129] Democratic decision-makers may therefore benefit politically from overreacting to, as distinct from underreacting to, an apparent threat in a manner that an unelected judiciary, for example, may not be susceptible to. De Londras argues that this is driven by a fear generated from both the top down and the bottom up.[130] 'Bottom-up' panic stems from the public's desire for greater security due to their fear of not only terrorist attacks, but of crime in general. David Garland, for example describes this panic generation as part of a 'culture of control' that has developed in Western states such as the US and UK.[131] This demand by the public for 'tough measures' to combat crime has resulted in the left and right of the political spectrum converging on penal policy with a view to capitalising on this trend.[132] The othering of the terrorist, and, indeed, the criminal in general, is inextricably linked to a rhetoric of fear surrounding this 'other'. This rhetoric may, in turn, be driven from the 'top down' by politicians, the media and other rhetors in a position to shape and frame public debate. By declaring war on crime,[133] war on drugs, or war on terrorism, a common enemy is created in the eyes of the public. This may then create a 'rally around the flag effect' that bolsters support for the emergency response taken.[134] The powerful emasculation a state feels in the aftermath of a terrorist attack is therefore combated with a proactive declaration that helps unite society against the perceived threat of the terrorist who, although perhaps a citizen of the state, is nonetheless perceived as an other.[135] It is of no coincidence, therefore, that it is often weak governments that make declarations of wars on crime or other phenomena in an attempt to consolidate public disaffection and anger against an agent other than the state.[136]

Democratically elected actors are therefore incentivised to overreact in a period of emergency. This electoral incentive to effectuate an emergency response is also evident in crises triggered by natural disasters. In the United States, for example, Andrew Reeves argues that US presidential disaster declarations which then allow presidents to unilaterally authorise the release of federal funds to help states cope with natural disasters are twice as likely in states that are closely contested during election terms as those that are not. The release of such funds may result in a statistically significant increase of 1 per cent of the vote to the president or his

[129] See David Cole, 'Enemy Aliens' (2002) 54 *Stanford Law Review* 953; Christina E Wells, 'Questioning Deference' (2004) 69 *Missouri Law Review* 912–21.

[130] De Londras (n 20) 1–35.

[131] See David Garland, *The Culture of Control: Crime and Social Order in Contemporary Society* (Oxford University Press, 2001).

[132] ibid, 37–38.

[133] Jonathan Simon, *Governing Through Crime* (Oxford University Press, 2007) 259.

[134] Bruce Russett, *Controlling the Sword: The Democratic Governance of National Security* (Harvard University Press, 1990) 34.

[135] Young (n 20) 167.

[136] David Garland, 'The Common Place and the Catastrophic: Interpretations of Crime in Late Modernity' (1999) 3 *Theoretical Criminology* 353.

nominee in the affected state.[137] This incentivisation illustrates the powerful subjective forces at play when a state of emergency is declared.

The Broadening of Emergency Powers: Expanding the 'Penumbra'

As noted in Chapter 1, 'emergency' is an incredibly broad term enabling a degree of flexibility in accommodating unforeseen or unprecedented threats. Relatedly, if emergency situations could be defined in a concrete manner, norms could be created in advance to accommodate such instances, thus negating the necessity of having emergency powers in the first instance.[138] In other words, a state of emergency would not be necessary as a contingency plan would already be available to accommodate the crisis. Conversely, if conditions do not meet the parameters of the definition composed, a vital response may be denied the state when necessary. The flexibility inherent in definitions of emergency is therefore vulnerable to the powerful subjective forces noted above that are at play when a decision-maker declares a state of emergency. The result of this is that the emergency paradigm is being widened and applied to more quotidian phenomena that may not have triggered the declaration of a state of emergency in the past.

Terrorism as a Permanent Emergency

Subjective factors are particularly heightened in the context of terrorism. As noted above, 'individual separation'—the belief that we can separate friend from enemy—while challenged by the amorphous nature of terrorism, nevertheless results in counter-terrorist powers impacting most strongly on individuals from minority groups easily identifiable as different: 'the other'.[139] It was also noted that terrorism was not limited to attacks on military targets and 'battlefields' but could also involve the targeting of civilians in built-up urban areas. 'International terrorism' compounds this problem further by transcending state borders, posing a threat to multiple nations and, consequently, requiring a coordinated, multi-state response. Terrorism, therefore, is often conceptualised as a perfect storm for the emergency paradigm, challenging individual, geographical and temporal separations between normalcy and emergency.

To conclude that terrorism is permanent and omnipresent, however, assumes that a phenomenon such as terrorism exists. Terrorism is a term that notoriously defies attempts to define it. It has oscillated in meaning from referring to violence perpetrated by the state to violence exercised against the state, and back again.[140]

137 See Andrew Reeves, 'Political Disaster: Unilateral Powers, Electoral Incentives, and Presidential Disaster Declarations' (2011) 73 *Journal of Politics* 1142.

138 Gross and Ní Aoláin, (n 5) 171.

139 Cohen (n 20) 10–11; de Londras (n 20) 75–82.

140 Bruce Hoffmann, *Inside Terrorism: Revised and Expanded Edition* (Columbia University Press 2006) 5–17.

Its conceptual boundaries are particularly sensitive to the political climate in which it is being deployed or the discipline deploying it. The need for a definition of terrorism also varies according to the different fields undertaking the quest. Sociologists and criminologists require one in order to define the parameters of that which they study.[141] This mostly descriptive, as distinct from prescriptive, need, however, has not resulted in agreement, with a famous 1988 survey finding over 100 definitions used by terrorism researchers in the literature.[142] This has been described as 'a perverse situation where a great number of scholars are studying a phenomenon, the essence of which they have ... agreed to disagree upon'.[143] The prescriptive and, indeed, proscriptive factors that a legal definition must address means that the problem is even more acute for law.[144]

Conor Gearty thus argues that terrorism is 'an uncertain term with no shared meaning'.[145] Relatedly, Alex Schmid has described terrorism as a term used 'promiscuously for such a wide range of manifestations ... that one wonders whether it is a unitary concept'.[146] Ulman's discussion of Schmitt's theory of the partisan as including an implicit theory of the terrorist appears to suggest, for example, that freedom fighters should not be included within the definition of 'terrorist' due to their 'telluric' connection to the land they wish to liberate, resulting in them being more 'partisan' in nature than 'terrorist'. Yet it is this very issue that is subject to disagreement amongst states when attempting to define terrorism on an international scale. Jörg Friedrichs illustrates that the differences between states on whether or not freedom fighters are terrorists can be explained, not by legal but by political differences between states and their respective incentives or vested interests.[147] States dealing with attacks from such 'freedom fighters' sought their inclusion within the ambit of 'terrorism'. The UK, for example, under this alternative understanding sought to have the IRA designated as a terrorist organisation.[148] Conversely, many Arab states in the 1970s and 1980s argued that a freedom fighter is not a terrorist in order to avoid the label being applied to the Palestinian struggle.[149] A number of Arab states may, however, have changed their

[141] See Alex Schmid and Albert J Jongman, *Political Terrorism: A New Guide to Actors, Authors, Concepts, Data Bases, Theories and Literature* (Transaction Books, 1988) ch 1.

[142] ibid.

[143] D Brannan, P Esler and T Strindberg, 'Talking to "Terrorists" Towards an Independent Analytical Framework for the Study of Violent Substate Activism' (2001) 24 *Studies in Conflict and Terrorism* 3, 11; Lisa Stampnitzky, *Disciplining Terror: How Experts Invented "Terrorism"* (Cambridge University Press, 2013) 5.

[144] Jessie Blackbourn, Fergal Davis and Natasha C Taylor, 'Academic Consensus and Legislative Definitions of Terrorism: Applying Schmid and Jongman' (2013) 34 *Statute Law Review* 239, 255.

[145] Conor Gearty, 'Rethinking Civil Liberties in a Counter-Terrorist World' (2007) 2 *European Human Rights Law Review* 111, 111.

[146] Alex Schmid, 'Terrorism—The Definitional Problem' (2004) 36 *Case Western Reserve Journal of International Law* 375, 380.

[147] Jorg Friedrichs, 'Defining the International Public Enemy: The Political Struggle Behind the Legal Debate on International Terrorism' (2006) 19 *Leiden Journal of International Law* 69, 76.

[148] ibid, 80.

[149] ibid.

stance in the aftermath of the 'Arab Spring' and attempts—both successful and unsuccessful— by various opposition groups to usher in internal regime change.

Even states that legally make no distinction between 'terrorist' and 'freedom fighter' nevertheless act as if there is. The UK's definition of terrorism contained in section 1 of the Terrorism Act 2000 makes no such distinction; nevertheless, the breadth of this definition is such that it places enormous discretion on, for example, the Crown Prosecution Service, to decide what cases to actually prosecute. Moreover, this definition does not dictate government policy, resulting in the arbitrary application of the definition to the different opposition groups in the Syrian civil war. An absurd example of this clash between the legal and political understanding of terrorism is the case of Bherlin Gildo, a Swedish national who was being prosecuted in the UK for terrorist activities in Syria. The case against Gildo collapsed, however, when it became clear that British security and intelligence agencies were supporting the group with which he was affiliated.[150]

The term 'terrorist', much like the term 'state of emergency', is therefore applied to a vast array of phenomena, organisations and individuals. It is for this very reason that it is in the interest of the political branches or those empowered to label a phenomenon as 'terrorism' to keep it as such. The highly symbolic nature of the term immediately renders those labelled as terrorist illegitimate and conversely those fighting the terrorist virtuous.[151] In much the same way as declaring a state of emergency permits a response that ordinarily would not be possible, so too does terrorism warrant a response that is deviant from that which the ordinary criminal would be subject to. That stated, even certain criminal behaviour that does not ostensibly challenge the political legitimacy of the state as a primary goal, such as organised crime, can also be 'framed' to an extent that it constitutes a state of emergency.[152]

[150] Richard Norton-Taylor, 'Terror Trial Collapses after Fears of Deep Embarrassment to Security Services' *The Guardian* (1 June 2015) <www.theguardian.com/uk-news/2015/jun/01/trial-swedish-man-accused-terrorism-offences-collapse-bherlin-gildo> accessed 7 August 2017; Kevin Jon Heller, 'British Government Says "Oops, Our Bad" in Terrorism Case' *Opino Juris* (7 September 2015) <http://opiniojuris.org/2015/09/07/uk-government-says-oops-our-bad-in-terrorism-case/> accessed 7 August 2017.

[151] Young draws parallels between terrorism and counter-terrorism measures to suggest broad similarities between the two approaches, while both nevertheless appear to be the moral dichotomy of the other. Young (n 20) 149–50; Jeremy Waldron, *Torture, Terror and Trade-offs: Philosophy for the White House* (Oxford University Press, 2010) 77.

[152] See Alan Greene, 'Shielding the State of Emergency: Organised Crime in Ireland and the State's Response' (2011) 62 *Northern Ireland Legal Quarterly* 249. A particularly extreme example of this can be seen in Mexico where many individuals involved in organised crime may be trained militarily. Liz Campbell, 'Organised Crime and National Security: A Dubious Connection?' (2014) 17 *New Criminal Law Review* 220, 235. In the Philippines, President Rodrigo Duterte has taken this further, hyperbolising the threat of drugs into a severe national security question and using this to justify extra-judicial killings and other forms of extreme political violence against suspected drug dealers. See Danilo Andres Reyes, 'The Spectacle of Violence in Duterte's "War on Drugs"' (2016) 35 *Journal of Current South East Asian Affairs* 111; Sophie Cousins, 'Five Thousand Dead and Counting: The Phillipines' Bloody War on Drugs' *British Medical Journal* (26 November 2016) <https://doi.org/10.1136/bmj.i6177> accessed 8 August 2017.

To conclude, therefore, that terrorism poses a permanent threat is to ignore the immense political baggage that comes with this term. As terrorism is arguably a 'social construct',[153] 'an interpretation of events and their presumed causes',[154] it is fundamental to focus on who is interpreting and deciding that such events amount to 'terrorism' and why. The definition of terrorism may therefore tell us more about the categoriser than the categorised.[155] It follows that a permanent state of emergency justified by the threat of terrorism depends upon the subjective interpretation and labelling of an event as 'terrorist', as much as it does upon violent crimes actually occurring. Consequently, scrutiny of this decision to label an event or individual as 'terrorist' is of paramount importance when understanding why a permanent emergency may arise.

Economic Emergencies

The international state of emergency ushered in by the events of 9/11 and subsequent 'war on terror' was soon followed by another emergency in the form of a 'global economic crisis' or economic 'state of emergency'.[156] Conceptualising an economic crisis as tantamount to a state of emergency is not, however, a recent twenty-first century development. Indeed, to recall from Chapter 1, the Roman Republic often appointed a dictator in order to raise a levy on citizens and fund a military campaign.[157] Economic measures were thus of equal importance as specific military tactics. Since the early decades of the twentieth century, however, economic crises became to be more readily equated with military crises and therefore perceived, or represented as necessitating, an emergency response in and of themselves.[158] This increase in the scope of emergency powers correlated with a decrease in the use of martial law or state of siege as such mechanisms were not suitable for economic crises.[159] Yet the spirit and concepts that martial law and state of siege envisage can be seen from the responses taken to economic crises. Such was their success and malleability that these emergency powers came to surpass the need to declare martial law or state of siege. Thus the state of emergency became the predominant response mechanism for war, natural disaster or economic emergency.[160]

153 See Nachman Ben-Yehuda, *Political Assassinations by Jews: A Rhetorical Device for Justice* (State University of New York Press 1993) 51; Schmid (n 146) 384; Austin Turk, 'Sociology of Terrorism' (2004) 30 *Annual Review of Sociology* 271, 271–73.

154 Turk, ibid, 271.

155 David Anderson, 'Shielding the Compass' [2013] 3 *EHRLR* 233, 240.

156 See Alan Greene, 'Questioning Executive Supremacy in an Economic State of Emergency' (2015) 35 *Legal Studies* 594.

157 See text to n in ch 1.

158 William E Scheuerman, 'The Economic State of Emergency' (1999–2000) 21 *Cardozo Law Review* 1869, 1870–72, 1878–79. Economic crises have also been compared with natural disasters, with the US Supreme Court drawing this equivalence in *Home Building and Loan Association v Blaisdell* 290 US 423.

159 For a discussion on the evolution of the state of emergency and the corresponding reduction in the use of martial law, see Mark Neocleous, 'From Martial Law to the War on Terror' (2007) 10 *New Criminal Law Review* 489.

160 ibid.

Following World War I, however, states began in earnest to confront economic crises through emergency powers. France, for example, used a broad delegation of legislative power to the executive in order to tackle the conditions of 'severe economic distress' in 1924.[161] Similarly, Germany frequently resorted to the use of the infamous Article 48 of the Weimar Constitution to confer broad law-making powers on the executive, thus bypassing a legislature paralysed by diametrically opposing factions of communists and national socialists.[162] Article 48 and the vast discretion to rule by executive decree it enabled would ultimately play a key role in governing the Weimar Republic until Hitler's ascension to power.[163]

Roosevelt's New Deal programme in the United States represents an archetypal economic state of emergency.[164] In his inaugural speech Roosevelt drew equivalence between Abraham Lincoln's actions during the US Civil War and the Great Depression, making clear that he intended to 'ask the Congress for the one remaining instrument to meet the crisis: broad executive power to wage a war against the emergency, as great as the power that would be given me if we were in fact invaded by a foreign foe'.[165] Forty-eight hours after assuming office, Roosevelt utilised the Trading with the Enemy Act 1917, specifically designed to meet only wartime exigencies, to declare a bank holiday and force the closure of financial institutions.[166] Roosevelt then signed into law the Emergency Banking Act which restructured these financial institutions to ensure that viable institutions could then reopen once the bank holiday was lifted.[167] Roosevelt's actions subsequently paved the way for emergency powers in the form of executive action to be applied in the United States in instances beyond the original conception of emergency as a military phenomenon.[168] Moreover, many of these emergency measures undertaken by Roosevelt became entrenched, leading not to a restoration of the status quo ex ante, but to a fundamental reformation of the US economy and social order.

The post-2008 financial crisis had similar effects on the EU and its Member States, ushering in permanent change to the EU legal order and those of its

[161] Clinton Rossiter, *Constitutional Dictatorship Crisis Government in Modern the Democracies* (Transaction, 2002) 117–27.

[162] ibid, 41.

[163] Indeed, it was the primary catalyst for Hitler's ascension. See Rossiter (n 164) 33–60; Ellen Kennedy, *Constitutional Failure: Carl Schmitt in Weimar* (Duke University Press, 2004) ch 6; David Dyzenhaus, *Legality and Legitimacy: Carl Schmitt, Hans Kelsen and Hermann Heller in Weimar* (Oxford University Press, 1997) 32–37.

[164] BA Meyler, 'Economic Emergency and the Rule of Law', Cornell Law Faculty Publications, Paper 68 (2006) <http://scholarship.law.cornell.edu/lsrp_papers/68> 1, accessed 8 August 2017.

[165] Scheuerman (n 158) 1871. See also Roger I Roots, 'Government by Permanent Emergency: The Forgotten History of the New Deal Constitution' (1999–2000) 33 *Suffolk University Law Review* 259, 260–61. A transcript of Roosevelt's speech may be found at <www.bartleby.com/124/pres49.html> accessed 7 August 2017.

[166] Roots, ibid, 262. According to Belknap, the Trading with the Enemy Act was a World War I statute that had never been repealed. Michal R Belknap, 'The New Deal and the Emergency Powers Doctrine' (1983–4) 62 *Texas Law Review* 67, 73.

[167] US Senate Special Committee on the Termination of the National Emergency, 'Report of the Special Committee on the Termination of the National Emergency' (19 November 1973) 93-549, II, 4.

[168] ibid; Belknap (n 166) 68.

Member States. For example, the basis of the Fiscal Compact Treaty (FCT),[169] Europe's principal structural change in response to the economic crisis, is Article 122(2) of the Treaty on the Functioning of the European Union (TFEU):

> Where a Member State is in difficulties or is seriously threatened with severe difficulties caused by natural disasters or exceptional occurrences beyond its control, the Council, on a proposal from the Commission, may grant, under certain conditions, Union financial assistance to the Member State concerned. The President of the Council shall inform the European Parliament of the decision taken.[170]

In this regard, the EU legally, as well as rhetorically, equated the financial crisis to 'natural disasters or exceptional occurrences beyond [a Member State's] control'. The FCT effected a permanent change to the manner in which eurozone states set their macroeconomic budgets. The underlying rationale behind the FCT thus assumes that there were fundamental flaws in these budgetary processes prior to its enactment that needed to be addressed and prevented from reoccurring in future. Here, however, we see a dichotomy between the classical understanding of phenomena that trigger emergencies and economic crises. Whereas natural disasters may be 'exceptional circumstances beyond [a Member State's] control', economic crises are often seen as a result of the state's actions or its mismanagement of the economy. Responses are therefore not just firefighting but also preventative and future oriented in order to prevent such mismanagement from occurring again. A return to the status quo or 'normalcy' that existed prior to the crisis is therefore not desirable as this 'normalcy' is itself represented as being part of the problem. This is also true of the manner in which states respond to terrorist threats, no longer merely reacting but also seeking to prevent future attacks from happening by 'defending further up the field'.[171] Thus 'normalcy' in the sense of the status quo that existed before the crisis—be it economic or terroristic in nature—will not be restored, nor, as this rhetoric represents, should it. Former US Vice-President Dick Cheney succinctly describes this post-9/11 world of perpetual terrorist and perpetual counter-terrorist prevention measures as the 'new normalcy' and the same is applicable for the post euro-crisis EU.[172] The financial crisis therefore has not been so much an emergency for the EU warranting temporary firefighting responses. Instead it was more akin to a 'constitutional moment' or, at the very least, a constitutional challenge requiring fundamental institutional reforms.[173] It is, in essence, a catalyst for a 'new normalcy' in the eurozone area.

[169] Treaty on Stability, Coordination and Governance in the Economic and Monetary Union (Fiscal Compact Treaty; FCT), entered into force, 1 January 2013.

[170] Art 122(2) TFEU.

[171] D Anderson, 'Shielding the Compass' (2013) 3 *EHRLR* 233, 243.

[172] 'Richard B Cheney Delivers Remarks to Republican Governors Association', *FDCH Political Transcripts*, 25 October 2001.

[173] Bruce Ackerman, for example, describes Roosevelt's New Deal as a constitutional moment in the US. See B Ackerman, *We the People*, vol 1: *Foundations* (Harvard University Press, 1993) 289.

Relatedly, in contrast to natural disasters, the moment at which the economic state of emergency crystallises is not necessarily an unforeseen eruptive event outside of a decision-maker's control. Certainly, a collapse in financial markets may look like a natural, uncontrollable phenomenon; however, many of the measures taken by the EU post-2008 were not in the immediate aftermath of a market crash. Instead, their fruition is often used as part of the bargaining process by one side. This can be seen from the Cyprus negotiations in March 2013, for example. Cyprus's emergency did not crystallise until the European Central Bank (ECB) declared that it would no longer provide emergency liquidity to Cypriot banks, resulting in Cyprus having to introduce strict credit controls on banks and limiting withdrawals.[174] The Cypriot economic emergency in 2013 thus was not an external phenomenon wholly outside the control of the respective parties. Rather, the crystallisation of the emergency became a bargaining tool in the negotiations between the various stakeholders. Similar tactics were also evident during the 2015 bailout negotiations with Greece.[175]

The application of the emergency paradigm to 'economic crises' illustrates the increasing diversification of phenomena labelled as 'emergency'. These phenomena are notably less serious, or pose a uniquely different threat to that envisaged by traditional states of emergency, ie war, armed conflict or extreme natural disasters. While not wishing to downplay the severity of the effects that economic crises have on states and individuals, these impacts are of a wholly separate nature to that caused by violent or tumultuous phenomena such as war or natural disasters. Economic states of emergency, therefore, illustrate the decreasing 'shielding effect' of states of emergency. The threat-severity threshold that a crisis should reach before it warrants a declaration of a state of emergency is lowered. Economic states of emergency also blur the lines of separation between normalcy and emergency in another way as the cessation of an economic crisis is not easily identifiable. Thus, although the start of a crisis may be sudden—falling share prices and confidence, spikes in unemployment levels, falling gross domestic and national product (GDP and GNP), and collapse of government tax intake—the actual restoration of 'normal' economic conditions may be difficult, if not impossible, to ascertain.[176] The return to economic growth, full employment and a balanced state budget may be a gradual trend that is achieved over a prolonged period of time, rather than a sudden economic 'boom'. Therefore, when the economy has returned to an acceptable 'level' of normalcy, and correspondingly when such extraordinary powers are no longer needed, will be an issue of contestation. Indeed, it is rare, if ever, that

[174] Paul Carrel and Eva Kuehnen, 'ECB Sets Monday Deadline for Cyprus Bailout Deal' *Reuters* (21 March 2013) <www.reuters.com/article/us-ecb-cyprus-funding-idUSBRE92K09Z20130321> accessed 24 July 2017.

[175] 'Greece Debt Crisis: ECB "To End" Bank Emergency Lending' *BBC News* (28 June 2015) <www.bbc.co.uk/news/world-europe-33303105> accessed 24 July 2017.

[176] Eric Posner and Adrian Vermeule, 'Crisis Government in the Administrative State: 9/11 and the Financial Meltdown of 2008' (2009) 76 *University of Chicago Law Review* 1613, 1619–23.

economic states of emergency are purely defensive in nature. Often, the emergency measures introduced are not done purely to restore the status quo as it is the status quo that existed prior to the emergency that contributed to the problem in the first instance. Economic states of emergency therefore are invariably transformative, ushering in permanent changes.

De Facto Emergencies

While economic crises and terrorism can trigger official declarations of emergency,[177] it is very often the case that they are dealt with by stressing the abnormality of the crisis facing the state and employing measures such as those that would be employed during a state of emergency; however, no official state of emergency is actually declared. In other words, de jure a state of normalcy exists but de facto the state responds as if it is in a state of emergency.[178] This damages the emergency paradigm by completely abandoning the 'threat-severity threshold' that ought to quarantine these exceptional powers to exceptional situations. The 'shielding effect' of the emergency paradigm is thus destroyed leaving it only as an enabler of exceptional state power.

The Questiaux Report, commissioned by the UN Economic and Social Council in 1982, highlighted a number of states such as Suriname, Uganda and South Africa that it considered to be in periods of de facto emergency. Suriname was flagged for not declaring a state of emergency or state of siege, notwithstanding the fact that a 'de facto state of emergency' had existed following a coup d'état in 1980.[179] Uganda had lifted its official state of emergency within two months of when the then Chief of State had taken power; however, many legal instruments were subsequently enacted that were akin to emergency powers, eg the granting of immunity to military forces and restrictions on the exercise of public freedoms.[180] Apartheid South Africa was highlighted on account of legislation used that was akin to legislation passed as if a state of emergency existed.[181] As discussed previously, Israel during the Second Intifada stands as a more recent example of de facto states of emergency. Relatedly, the termination of Syria's official period of emergency in 2011 and subsequent descent into civil war cannot be considered to be a restoration of normalcy.[182]

De facto emergencies damage the emergency paradigm as de jure a state of normalcy exists; however, de facto conditions are more akin to a state of emergency. No clear dichotomy therefore exists between the two states.[183] The shielding effect

[177] See text to n 116 in ch 1.

[178] 'Study of the Implications for Human Rights of Recent Developments Concerning Situations Known as States of Siege or Emergency', UNESC E/CN4/Sub2/1982/15 (27 July 1982) 26.

[179] ibid, 27.

[180] ibid.

[181] ibid.

[182] See text to n 91 above.

[183] ibid.

of the state of emergency is thus completely negated. This damage to the emergency paradigm is again not necessarily caused by the phenomenon that triggers the de facto emergency response, but due to the failure (bona fides or mala fides) to declare a state of emergency.

De facto emergencies therefore place pressure on the emergency paradigm by incorporating emergency powers into a state of normalcy. This can be compared to the labelling of ever-more banal phenomena such as organised crime, economic states of emergency and indeed terrorism as equating to an emergency situation. These forces combine to blur the distinction between normalcy and emergency by 'inflating' normalcy to emergency, and by 'deflating' emergency down to normalcy. The key factor, however, in this inflation and deflation is the role of the decision-maker as it is their assessment of the situation that triggers the application of the emergency paradigm.

Conclusion

States of emergency, whether de facto or de jure, have serious consequences for democracy, human rights and the rule of law. Utilised effectively, a temporary aberration from these obligations can ultimately preserve the state and the liberal-democratic order. In addition, insistence on a de jure state of emergency can protect these rights further. If these restrictions become permanent, however, they fundamentally threaten the liberal-democratic nature of the state. It is only by containing the state of emergency and ensuring the above implications are temporary aberrations from the norm that they are justified. Accordingly, if this cannot be ensured, the state of emergency is an obsolete tool, inadequate for the modern state.

Arguments that suggest it is impossible today to separate normalcy from emergency, due to the more dangerous, factual conditions of modernity, do not adequately explain why the 'state of emergency' is now the norm. Rather, utilising emergency responses for low-level threats, stretches the malleable contours of 'emergency' to a point where it snaps, negating the distinction between normalcy and emergency. In addition, de facto states of emergency blur this distinction further by de jure preserving normalcy while altering it to such an extent that it correlates more consistently with the emergency paradigm.

Permanent emergencies are therefore not a result of empiricism, but of subjective political decisions. The emergency–normalcy dichotomy, and as a consequence, the shielding effect of the state of emergency, may therefore be preserved by more stringent controls on when an emergency is declared and a more careful analysis of when it ceases to exist. In the following chapter I will therefore seek to establish an argument in favour judicial review of this decision to declare a state of emergency.

While the above discussion is directed at the initial decision-maker regarding the existence of a state of emergency, there is no reason to assume that subsequent reviewers of this decision, ie the judiciary or the legislature, are immune to the influence of heuristics. Indeed, the dearth of democratic legitimacy surrounding the proper scope of judicial review and the lack of expertise of the judiciary on issues of national security act as additional factors in encouraging a deferential approach of the judiciary towards the executive or other decision-makers regarding the exercise of emergency powers. Consequently, I will not argue in the following chapter that the judiciary ought to review the decision to declare a state of emergency because of heuristics and the power of rhetoric at the hands of the political branches in shaping debate to corroborate their assessment as to the existence of an emergency. Rather, these theories corroborate the assertion that the propensity of emergencies to become perpetual is largely influenced by the subjective assessment of decision-makers. It is therefore rash to assert that the emergency paradigm is obsolete; rather, more effective controls on the decision to declare an emergency ought to be in place, in particular judicial review, notwithstanding the possibility that they may also be subject to heuristics, influenced by rhetoric, or exercise review in an exceptionally deferential manner. Instead, the argument for judicial review, which will be delineated in the following chapter, is based upon the theoretical implications on the rule of law of not having such review available: the prospect of proxy-constitutional amendments which potentially infringe upon the constituent power of a state.

3

Permanent States of Emergency and Constituent Power

Introduction

In chapter two, I argued that the emergency paradigm was not obsolete; rather, permanent states of emergency are largely caused by the subjective assessment of the decision-maker empowered to declare and perpetuate the emergency. In light of this, in this chapter I aim to establish what controls are necessary in order to ground this declaration of emergency within the legal order. In this regard, arguments pertaining to human rights or substantive conceptions of the rule of law which dominate the current literature on emergency powers will be avoided. The goal here instead is to move the debate away from these factors towards a more fundamental, theoretical understanding of the location of emergency powers within the constitutional structure. This will be done by invoking the concept of 'constituent power' against which the power to declare a state of emergency will be evaluated. In so doing, the aforementioned normative factors such as human rights or substantive conceptions of the rule of law may potentially be vindicated by stressing the importance of conceptualising the power to declare a state of emergency as a constituted power of the legal order—an argument that will be returned to in chapter five.[1]

The key to ensuring the juridical status of the state of emergency lies in Hans Kelsen's Identity Thesis and the idea that the state is identical to the legal order.[2] This will be compared and contrasted with the challenge posed by Carl Schmitt: that the state cannot be identical to the legal order as the state must exist prior to the legal order in order to create the stable conditions necessary for the founding of a constitution.[3] Schmitt thus preserves the potential for state power to

[1] See text to nn 127–44 in ch 5 of this book.

[2] See generally, Hans Kelsen, *Pure Theory of Law* (University of California Press, 1967), hereinafter *PTL*, and Hans Kelsen, *General Theory of Law and State* (Harvard University Press, 1949), hereinafter *GTLS*.

[3] The primary sources of Schmitt's work from which I shall draw are: Carl Schmitt, *Constitutional Theory*, trans J Seitzer (Duke University Press, 2008); Carl Schmitt, *The Concept of the Political*, trans G Schwab (University of Chicago Press, 2007); and Carl Schmitt, *Political Theology: Four Chapters on the Concept of Sovereignty*, trans G Schwab (University of Chicago Press, 2005).

be exercised that is not dependent upon legal validation. Schmitt's challenge to Kelsen's Identity Thesis will then be explored through the lens of emergency powers, and the consequences of stretching the concept of legality to rebut Schmitt by 'purifying' law from all other factors and creating a purely formal concept of legitimacy that is synonymous with legality. I will then outline an argument in favour of a robust enforceable constitution requiring a commensurably robust judiciary as a necessity in order to confront the 'Schmittian challenge' and affirm Kelsen's Identity Thesis. This will be established by elaborating on the relation between validity and effectiveness of constitutional norms, the hierarchy of norms within a constitution, and the possibility of unconstitutional norms or unconstitutional amendments. It will be shown that a permanent emergency has the potential to render constitutional norms invalid by making them permanently ineffective. Consequently, I argue that a permanent emergency has the potential to amount to a 'proxy-constitutional amendment' which can act as a claim for the constituent power. Such a claim must, however, be rejected.

Power beyond Law? The State of Emergency and the Legal Order

The juridical status of the state of emergency exposes the mechanics at the heart of the state and the legal order. As it appears that the law or the legal order is being departed from, states of emergency raise the question of whether this power is located within, or outside the law—whether it is a legal or political decision.[4] A superficial answer to this would be to argue that as the power to declare a state of emergency is enumerated in a legal norm, then it follows that it is legal in nature. This answer, however, while prima facie appearing uncomplicated, begs the question somewhat. Moreover, it reveals an understanding of the relation between law and state power that Carl Schmitt's critique focuses on.

Subsuming all state power within the law was the primary objective of Hans Kelsen's 'Pure Theory' of law.[5] According to Joseph Raz, the Identity Thesis—a fundamental component of the Pure Theory—attempts to solve three separate problems: the existence of law and its efficacy; the difference between making a new law and applying an existing one; and, finally, the relation between law and the state.[6] Kelsen's Identity Thesis considers the state to be identical to the legal

[4] Oren Gross, 'The Normless and Exceptionless Exception: Carl Schmitt's Theory of Emergency Powers and the "Norm—Exception" Dichotomy' (1999–2000) 21 *Cardozo Law Review* 1825, 1833; David Dyzenhaus, 'Schmitt v Dicey: Are States of Emergency Inside or Outside the Legal Order?' (2006) 27 *Cardozo Law Review* 2005, 2006–07.

[5] See generally Kelsen (n 2) *PTL* and *GTLS*.

[6] Joseph Raz, 'The Identity of Legal Systems' (1971) 59 *California Law Review* 795, 801.

order. No action can be attributed to the state that does not derive its validity from this legal order and no state power can exist outside of this legal order. Kelsen contended that there is a principle of legality which is the central feature of any legal system and which requires that all official action be in accordance with law.[7] For Kelsen, therefore, the law is supreme, autonomous and supersedes politics.

The legal order envisaged by Kelsen's Pure Theory is one of a unified hierarchy of norms. Like Immanuel Kant, Kelsen distinguishes a norm—an 'ought' statement—from an 'is' statement.[8] Unlike scientific theories, which are either true or false as based upon observation and causation, a norm, instead, is either valid or invalid by a process of imputation.[9] Thus when A occurs, the legal scientist is not concerned with what actually occurs subsequently, but rather with what *ought* to occur in a 'factually predictive' sense (as distinct from what ought *morally* to occur).[10] What renders a norm valid is its conformity with a higher norm: only norms may validate another norm.[11] It is this clear separation of the 'is' from the 'ought' that gives Kelsen's theory its 'pure' nature. For Kelsen 'is' and 'ought' (*sein* and *sollen*) 'denote different, illogically reconcilable structures of thought'.[12] The Pure Theory is thus 'pure' in the sense that it is purged of all other values or sociological insights that attempt to explain or legitimise legal norms. Law may be referred only back onto itself. It is therefore a pure and closed normative order.[13]

Kelsen's hierarchical normative order cannot and does not continue ad infinitum. One eventually reaches a norm that does not need a higher norm to validate it—the 'basic norm' or *Grundnorm* or *Ursprungsnorm* (origin norm).[14] Thus, if the statement 'a person who steals ought to be punished' is contained in a statute, then it would follow through a process of regression that 'one ought to obey the legislature'. In turn, if this norm of obeying the legislature is contained in the constitution, one would impute that 'one ought to obey the constitution'. If this process of regression is continued, 'Ultimately, we reach some constitution that is the first historically and that was laid down by an individual usurper or by some kind of assembly.'[15] On the validity of the basic norm, Kelsen argues that it is simply 'presupposed'. The validity of this first constitution is that presupposition, 'the final postulate, upon which the validity of all the norms of our legal

[7] David Dyzenhaus, *Legality and Legitimacy: Carl Schmitt, Hans Kelsen and Hermann Heller in Weimar* (Oxford University Press, 1997) 116.

[8] Ronald Moore, *Legal Norms and Legal Science: A Critical Study of Kelsen's Pure Theory of Law* (University of Hawaii Press, 1978) 7–12.

[9] *PTL*, 76–83.

[10] ibid.

[11] ibid, 193.

[12] Sylvie Delacroix, 'Schmitt's Critique of Kelsenian Normativism' (2005) 18 *Ratio Juris* 30, 31.

[13] This position has been subjected to substantial criticism from both positivist and anti-positivist schools. See text to n 114 in ch 4 for further discussion of this separation from the perspective of Ronald Dworkin. It is submitted, however, that these critiques are not fatal to my argument regarding the justiciability of the decision to declare a state of emergency.

[14] *PTL*, 193–211; *GTLS*, 115–18.

[15] ibid.

order depends'.[16] This is the basic norm: coercive acts ought to be carried out only under the conditions and in the way determined by the 'fathers' of the constitution or the organs delegated by them.[17] The basic norm is not, however, the constitution itself. The constitution is merely a collection of various norms that facilitate and guide the creation of further norms. The collection of norms that composes the historically first constitution is itself validated by the basic norm: one ought to obey the historically first constitution.

The State of Emergency and the Pure Theory of Law

Suggesting that the decision to declare a state of emergency is contained within a legal order permits one to assert that every action of the state may be validated by a legal norm, and, consequently, that the state is identical to the legal order. However, this syllogism also raises the peculiar instance of law being used to suspend itself. Law is a unique discipline in that it regulates its own creation, and in certain instances, law may be used to invalidate law.[18] However, a state of emergency is notably different in that it is not necessarily new law replacing old law; rather, law is being used to say that particular elements of law are no longer applicable. As noted in chapter one, these 'particular elements of law' may be the very fundamental norms that give the legal order its constitutional identity. Thus, for the Roman Republic, the dictator harkened back to the very elements of monarchical tyranny that the Republic was founded to protect against, breaking free from the inter-consular veto and the right of the Roman citizen to appeal through *provocatio*.[19] In modern constitutions, it may be core values such as human rights, democracy and the rule of law that are vulnerable.

Law's unique capacity to regulate its own creation is understood by the Pure Theory through what Kelsen terms the two aspects of legal normative orders: the static and the dynamic aspect. A static normative order is one in which the content of the lower-order norms may be derived from a higher norm.[20] In essence, the lower norm is merely a manifestation of an aspect of the higher norm. Thus, for example, the norm that 'one ought to have access to proper healthcare' may be derived from the higher-order norm that 'one has a right to life'. In contrast, a dynamic normative order is one in which the higher-order norm gives no guidance as to the substantive content of lower-order norms but instead confers power onto certain institutions to create the lower-order norms.[21] Thus, a constitution

16 ibid.
17 *GTLS*, 116.
18 *PTL*, 209; *GTLS*, 122–23.
19 See text to n 172 in ch 1.
20 *PTL*, ch IV.
21 *PTL*, ch V; Moore (n 8) 87–88.

may confer law-making power on a legislature. Most constitutions, therefore, are a collection of both dynamic and static aspects.[22] They are dynamic in that they specify specific institutions and confer norm-creating powers upon them and they may also be static in that they may prescribe what the contents of such norms ought to be and proscribe what they should not be. This is the primary role of rights provisions in constitutions, as any lower-order norms ought to conform with and respect the rights contained in the higher-order constitutional norms.

The dynamic aspect of the constitution may potentially explain the juridical status of the state of emergency. A state of emergency contained in constitutional provisions may be construed as a norm-creating power conferred on the body in question to act as it sees fit in an emergency. For example, if an emergency executive order is pronounced that empowers the police to 'in their absolute discretion, search the property of any individual without a warrant', then the syllogistic logic employed by the individual subject to such a search order would be:

> The order issued by the police to me is validated by the executive order. This executive order is validated by the declaration of a state of emergency, which is itself contained in the constitution. As one ought to obey the constitution, it follows that I ought to obey the directions of the police and consent to my property being searched.

Such syllogism would present no conflict to the basic norm and the validity of a state of emergency would flow from the existing, presupposed basic norm.

Power beyond the Law: Rejecting the Identity Thesis?

This syllogism is, however, based primarily upon the dynamic aspect of the constitution and would completely ignore any static norms of such a constitution. This would theoretically validate in law any emergency law, no matter how abhorrent or repugnant to the constitutional norms enshrined and effective under the constitution when in a state of normalcy. Even in a constitutional order that does not contain substantive human rights provisions, conceptualising a state of emergency as a dynamic norm-creating device is, nevertheless, problematic as the new method of producing legal norms—for example, through executive decree or truncated legislative procedure—invariably stands in conflict with the normal method prescribed by the constitution.[23] There must, by definition, be a conflict between the state of emergency and the prior existing legal order as it is the very constraints on power that exist in normalcy that necessitate the declaration of a state of emergency. Thus, prolonged emergency rule through the use of executive decree may call into question the legislature's role as the principal law-maker in a state. This apparent conflict may be countered and resolved by stating that the

[22] *GTLS*, 125–26.

[23] See text to n 158 in ch 5 regarding the challenges posed to the substantive limits to emergency powers supposedly explicit in Art 48 of the Weimar constitution.

emergency provision 'trumps' the ordinary mechanism of norm creation and so this is not a problem for the Identity Thesis; as long, however, as the emergency remains exceptional, ie temporary.

Kelsen is committed to subsuming all state power within the legal order and his basic norm is an attempt to do this by capping and enclosing the legal order with a metaphysical norm. For Kelsen, the sovereignty of a legal order is not an attribute of the one who possesses supreme power, but simply the expression of the autonomy of that legal order from all other normative orders; an autonomy which is assured by the basic norm.[24] The insistence on a separation between 'is' and 'ought' that lies at the heart of Kelsen's conception of law collapses the question of legitimacy into the question of legality. For Kelsen, therefore, every state is a *Rechtstaat*. This focus on form and ignoring the substantive content of law that lies at the basis of positivist constitutionalism led Carl Schmitt to argue that in such a system, 'a purely formal concept of law, independent of all content, is conceivable and tolerable'.[25] According to David Dyzenhaus, Schmitt

> thus alleged that the liberal equation of constitution with written constitution would turn an entire constitution into something provisional, a 'blank cheque statute'. A genuine constitution should not contain the discretionary power to grant another, radically different constitution.[26]

The above answer that the state of emergency can be constrained by the dynamic nature of the legal order therefore conceptualises the state as identical to the legal order but at the cost of reducing the constitution to 'a blank cheque statute'. Other theorists attempt to reject viewing all state power as legal. John Locke's theory of the prerogative—the power to do good without a rule and sometimes even against this—attempts to circumscribe the state within the rule of law, but still leave a zone beyond law in which the sovereign could act.[27] Locke, therefore, does not create a model of the state as identical to the legal order but leaves a zone beyond it. Again, however, this raises problem of the legitimacy of this power and its accountability as if the sovereign is above, or beyond the law, how can it be accountable to it? On this issue, Locke said that this could only take the form of public acquiescence. If the public did disagree with the approach taken by the holder of the prerogative, they had no recourse except to throw their arms to heaven.[28] Similarly, Clinton Rossiter, despite laying down eleven criteria for assessing whether an emergency is

[24] Dyzenhaus (n 7) 103.

[25] Carl Schmitt, *Legality and Legitimacy* (Duke University Press 2004) 20; Gary Jeffery Jacobson, 'An Unconstitutional Constitution? A Comparative Perspective' (2006) 4 *International Journal of Constitutional Law* 460, 466.

[26] Dyzenhaus (n 7) 52–53.

[27] John Locke, *Second Treatise of Government*, ed CB McPherson (Hackett Publishing, 1980) 84–88. See text to nn 174–84 in ch 6 for a more detailed discussion of Locke's theory of the prerogative and what Oren Gross terms 'extra-legal measures' to confront crises.

[28] ibid.

constitutional or not, admitted that 'whatever the theory, in moments of extreme national emergency the facts have always been with ... John Locke'.[29]

Carl Schmitt and the State of Exception

Theories such as Locke's therefore envisage state power existing beyond the law. This difficulty that a liberal-democratic constitutional order has in dealing with the state of emergency by either recognising a power beyond the law, or by attempting to circumscribe the exception within the law, forms the lynchpin of Schmitt's critique of liberalism and its political realisation by way of parliamentary democracy.

The Concept of the Political: The Friend–Enemy Distinction

Schmitt's challenge to conceptualising the state as identical to the legal order is that this deduction starts by assuming that stability and order within the state already exist, completely ignoring the fundamental importance of how this order was established in the first instance: by an irrational decision taken by the sovereign when it distinguished friend from enemy.[30] Ernst-Wolfgang Böckenförde argues that there are two common misconceptions about Schmitt's friend–enemy distinction.[31] Firstly, that the friend–enemy distinction turns political debate within the state to a friend–enemy distinction, ie opposing political parties or ideologies conceptualise themselves as friends and enemies; and secondly, that the friend–enemy distinction constitutes a normative theory of politics and the political order. Addressing the first misconception, the friend–enemy distinction refers not to politics within the state but instead constitutes the distinction that identifies the state as separate from other nations and groupings. Schmitt conceptualised a state as presupposing a relatively ethnically homogeneous populace or *Volk*.[32] However, identification of what exactly unites this population is not traceable back to a rational or objectively derivable constituent. Rather, what unites the *Volk* or nation is an irrational decision. Schmitt saw all ideologies and doctrines as metaphysical and claimed that conflicts between such ideologies

[29] Dyzenhaus (n 4) 2014, quoting Clinton Rossiter, *Constitutional Dictatorship: Crisis Government in the Modern Democracies* (Transaction Publishers, 2002) 219.

[30] Schmitt, *The Concept of the Political* (n 3) 38–39.

[31] Ernst-Wolfgang Bökenförde, 'The Concept of the Political: A Key to Understanding Carl Schmitt's Constitutional Theory' (1997) 10 *Canadian Journal of Law and Jurisprudence* 5, 5–6.

[32] WE Scheuerman, 'Revolutions and Constitutions: Hannah Arendt's Challenge to Carl Schmitt' (1997) 10 *Canadian Journal of Law and Jurisprudence* 141, 143; Dyzenhaus (n 7) 57; Aoife O'Donoghue, *Constitutionalism in Global Constitutionalisation* (Cambridge University Press, 2014) 56.

cannot be resolved through rational thought. Instead, such can only be resolved by an arbitrary or irrational decision.[33] When distinguishing between friend and enemy, this decision, therefore, is also lacking rationality.[34] As this decision is both constitutive and expressive of the state, it follows that the state is founded on this arbitrary decision of the sovereign. Relatedly, the nature of this decision as lacking rationality means that its legitimacy stems from its authority, not from its truth.[35] The decision made by the sovereign in distinguishing between those who are within the state (friend), and those who are outside of it (enemy) permits the founding of a state.[36] Only states, therefore, and not just any domestic or international association, are the bearers of politics.[37] To address the second misconception of the friend–enemy distinction: Schmitt did not posit the friend–enemy distinction as a normative theory, but as descriptive of how the political actually operates.[38]

Schmitt thus contends that Kelsen's Identity Thesis starts at the point at which the distinction between friend and enemy has already been made and the state is stable enough for Kelsen to postulate that the state is identical to the legal order. Schmitt considered the friend–enemy distinction to be vital, and argued that its intensity must be so extreme as to make war a possibility. Schmitt thus describes war as the 'existential negation of the enemy'.[39] It is only by defeating the enemy that the friend can be secure, and it is only by war that the enemy can be negated.[40] It follows from this that:

> Constitutional law then appears as the binding normative order and form determining the existence, maintenance, and capability for action of a political unity in the above sense. It is and must be the specific telos of constitutional law to facilitate, preserve and support the state as a political order and unity.[41]

[33] David Dyzenhaus, '"Now the Machine Runs Itself": Carl Schmitt on Hobbes and Kelsen' (1994–95) 16 *Cardozo Law Review* 1, 3.

[34] Nevertheless, the distinction must also have some grounding in fact in order for it to be effective and produce the requisite stability necessary to establish the legal order. See Hans Lindahl, 'Constituent Power and Reflexive Identity: Towards and Ontology of Collective Selfhood' in Martin Loughlin and Neil Walker (eds), *The Paradox of Constitutionalism: Constituent Power and Constituitonal Form* (Oxford University Press, 2007) 10.

[35] Or *autoritas non veritas facit legem*. See Schmitt, *Political Theology* (n 3) 52; Dyzenhaus (n 7) 58.

[36] Bökenförde (n 31) 10–12; Schmitt, *The Concept of the Political* (n 3) 44–45.

[37] George Schwab, 'Introduction' in Schmitt, *The Concept of the Political* (n 3) 6. The development of branches of law such as global constitutionalism and international political organisations such as the European Union has led to inquiries into constituent power at a level beyond the state. For example, see O'Donoghue (n 32); Neil Walker, 'Post-Constituent Constitutionalism? The Case of the European Union' in Loughlin and Walker (n 34) 247; and Bardo Fassbender, '"We the People of the United Nations": Constituent Power and Constitutional Form in International Law' in Loughlin and Walker (n 34) 269.

[38] Bökenförde (n 31) 10. That stated, Schmitt's utilisation of the friend–enemy distinction as a sledgehammer against liberalism is certainly making a normative argument. See text to n 46 below.

[39] Schmitt, *The Concept of the Political* (n 3) 33.

[40] ibid.

[41] Bökenförde (n 31) 8.

Schmitt's decisionism reveals itself by this founding of the state upon this presupposition of the political. Once the distinction between friend and enemy is made, the 'relative ethnic homogeneity' of the people is established and the order necessary to found a legal order is created.[42]

Schmitt's Critique of Liberalism: The State of Exception

While Böckenförde is keen to stress that Schmitt's friend–enemy distinction does not turn debate within a state into this distinction, as, in general, these contestations are not of the requisite intensity, he does argue that domestic groups which form and oppose each other within the state can potentially escalate in intensity to become equivalent to this friend–enemy distinction. It therefore becomes necessary to stabilise the domestic order to pre-empt looming tensions and prevent contestations from spiralling out of control and crossing the threshold of intensity necessary to satisfy the friend–enemy distinction being met.[43] In this regard, Schmitt argues that a liberal legal order is incapable of intervening to stabilise such tensions. Instead, liberalism perpetually postpones the decision necessary to distinguish friend from enemy and bring the order required to permit the establishment of a legal order.[44] Liberalism is the 'enemy of enemies' and Kelsen's Pure Theory was the embodiment of this liberal order.[45] Dyzenhaus argues that Carl Schmitt's critique of liberalism does not claim that liberalism is committed to

> a global neutrality between ideologies or to a position that attempts to find some substantive basis for contesting ideologies that assert a global superiority for themselves. He does not claim that liberalism is more naturally aligned with a positivist view about the nature of law or with a view that claims there is a higher law beyond the positive law to which the positive law is somehow subject. He does not claim that liberalism either presupposes its own truth or makes no claim to truth. And he does not claim that liberalism is either political or anti-or apolitical. Rather, what is distinctive about his position is its thesis that liberalism is doomed to shuttle back and forth between these various alternatives.[46]

Schmitt's position that the political supersedes the legal thus axiomatically stands as the antithesis of Kelsen's Identity Thesis. Kelsen's basic norm—that 'coercive acts ought to be carried out only under the conditions and in the way determined by the "fathers" of the constitution or the organs delegated by them'[47]—marks the point at which the legal scientist stops her inquiry and presupposes the validity

[42] Dyzenhaus (n 7) 57. Again, however, note the paradox that this entails as there must be a degree of relative homogeneity of the people already in factual existence prior to this decision being made. See Lindahl (n 34).
[43] Bökenförde (n 31) 8.
[44] ibid.
[45] Dyzenhaus (n 7) 41.
[46] ibid, 38–39.
[47] *GTLS*, 116.

of this basic norm. It is at this point, however, that Schmitt's critique of Kelsenian normativism begins. Kelsen and other liberal theorists presuppose the political and social stability that makes their subsequent presupposition possible, failing to inquire into what caused or permitted this stability to exist in the first instance.[48] For theorists such as Kelsen, 'the machine runs itself'.[49] However, Schmitt argues that it is disingenuous and incorrect to stop inquiry at this point. It is only by taking this 'order' as already established that they have the confidence to presuppose the validity of the basic norm.[50] For Schmitt, however, it is an existential decision, not some ultimate norm, that is the basis of a constitution.[51] It is the decision of the sovereign to distinguish between friend and enemy that delineates the parameters of the state, creating the relative cultural homogeneity within the state and the stability and order that flows from this. By ignoring the decision upon which the state is founded, this fiction allows liberal legal theorists such as Kelsen to believe that the state *is* the legal order and that no state action can be attributed to that which is not done through law.

Carl Schmitt and the State of Exception

This liberal fiction is fundamentally exposed, however, by the inevitable appearance of a 'state of exception'. Schmitt's famous declaration that '[s]overeign is he who decides on [*über*] the exception'[52] refers both to whether an exception exists or not and what ought to be done in such an exception. Despite the forcefulness and confidence of this declaration, Schmitt's conflation of these two separate questions is not prima facie clear. John P McCormick argues that this stems from Schmitt's deliberately ambiguous use of the word 'on' (*über*). This blurs the distinction between the two separate questions and belies his endorsement of such a separation a year earlier in *The Dictatorship* when discussing the institutional separation of these two questions in the Roman Republic.[53] This marks the evolution in Schmitt's thought from commissarial to sovereign dictatorship. In turn, these two separate questions are what Dyzenhaus identifies as the 'Schmittian Challenge'.

[48] Dyzenhaus (n 7) 68–70.

[49] See Dyzenhaus (n 33).

[50] Sylvie Delacroix, 'Schmitt's Critique of Kelsenian Normativism' (2005) 18 *Ratio Juris* 30, 33; Scheuerman (n 32) 143.

[51] Dysenhaus (n 7) 52.

[52] Schmitt, *Political Theology* (n 3) 1.

[53] John P McCormick, 'The Dilemmas of Dictatorship: Carl Schmitt and Constitutional Emergency Powers' (1997) 10 *Canadian Journal of Law and Jurisprudence* 163, 169. McCormick argues that this conflation is subsequently made deliberate when Schmitt states later in *Political Theology* that: '[H]e decides whether there is an extreme emergency as well as what must be done to eliminate it'. See Schmitt (n 3) 7. See also Dyzenhaus (n 7) 41 where he argues that Schmitt's critique of liberalism is 'dangerously unsystematic' because he had 'a genuine obsession with the arcane and the aphoristic and because he did not want to reveal his hand too clearly'.

In *The Dictatorship*, published in 1921, Schmitt follows the archetypal normalcy—emergency dichotomy and endorses a commissarial constitutional dictatorship to accommodate emergencies.[54] This commissarial dictatorship would follow closely the Roman dictatorship and the key elements of the emergency paradigm identified in chapter one, ie a crisis identified and labelled by a state to be of such magnitude that it is deemed to cross a threat-severity threshold, necessitating urgent, exceptional and consequently temporary actions by the state not permissible when normal conditions exist. However, only a year later, in 1922, Schmitt abandons this constitutional dictatorship in *Political Theology*, endorsing a potentially all-powerful sovereign that must not only operate in a period of emergency but would be a permanent feature of the state's legal and political landscape.[55]

For Schmitt, it is the essence of sovereignty both to decide what an exceptional situation is, and to make the decisions appropriate to that exception.[56] Schmitt draws an analogy between the sovereign's ability to intervene and act without legal authority and sometimes even against it, to the theological idea of a miracle by divine intervention which cannot be explained by the scientific laws of the universe.[57] Thus, what characterises the exception is unlimited authority; the suspension of the legal order.[58] With this decision, the exception, according to Schmitt, reveals the true nature of the state's authority.[59] In a manner similar to how the political necessarily existed prior to the establishment of the legal order, so too can it intervene in this legal order when it is necessary and it is for the sovereign, not the legal order, to decide when that is and what that intervention should entail. Schmitt argues, therefore, that the spectre of the initial decision made by the sovereign continues to haunt the legal order that is subsequently established thereunder.

Gross describes Schmitt's theory of the exception as his 'main weapon in his attack on liberalism'.[60] According to Schmitt, the decision as to the existence of the exception is a decision in the truest sense of the word:

> Because a general norm as represented by an ordinary legal prescription can never encompass a total exception, the decision that a real exception exists cannot be entirely derived from this norm.[61]

[54] See Carl Schmitt, *Dictatorship*, trans Michael Hoelzl and Graham Ward (Polity Press, 2014); Gross (n 4) 1834.

[55] McCormick (n 53) 163.

[56] Schwab, 'Introduction' in Schmitt (n 37) xii.

[57] Schmitt, *Political Theology* (n 3) 36 where Schmitt expressly states that: '[T]he exception in jurisprudence is analogous to the miracle in theology'; Noa Ben-Asher, 'Legal Holes' (2009) 5 *Unbound* 1, 3–6.

[58] Schmitt, *Political Theology* (n 3) 12.

[59] ibid, 13.

[60] Gross (n 4) 1827.

[61] Schmitt, *Political Theology* (n 3) 6.

As a legal norm requires a level of certainty and clarity to be effective, Schmitt argues that the exception cannot be circumscribed by law as there can be no norm applicable to chaos.[62] In so doing, Schmitt also reveals that he considers 'clarity and effectiveness' to be fundamental aspects of law and, in turn, the rule of law. While the paradigmatic example of a state of exception is war, the Schmittian exception relates to a much broader array of political phenomena that cannot be considered to be circumscribed by legal rules.[63] At best it can be 'characterised as a case of extreme peril, a danger to the existence of the state, or the like'.[64] Schmitt considers the exception therefore to be the 'purest expression and reflection of the political'.[65] This decisionist nature of Schmitt's theory is, according to Gross, normatively indefensible as it can lead to the justification of authoritarian dictatorship.[66]

Schmitt justifies dictatorial action on the basis of the pre-constitutional sovereign will of the people and not the principles embodied within the constitution itself.[67] Thus Aoife O'Donoghue argues that Schmitt's idea of the nation is associated with the commonality of the community.[68] In this regard, some may claim that Schmitt 'aims to rescue the primacy of democracy over the rule of law', given the prominence he appears to accord to the 'pre-constitutional sovereign will of the people'.[69] Schmitt, however, can only be considered 'democratic' in the extremely thin sense that he considers the legitimacy of the state to derive from the people or *Volk* as distinct from God.[70] Among the political regimes and constitutional orders that Schmitt was perfectly content to consider democratic was no less than the Third Reich. Thus, Christoph Möllers, suggests that the 'construction of the *Führer* permitted the establishment of a permanent revolutionary subject which, right to the very end of the Nazi era, referred to the German people as the source of its own legitimacy'.[71] The people therefore are a convenient substitute for God, albeit they are given a voice through an all-powerful sovereign speaking on their behalf.[72] In this regard, it is important to note the innate religious dimension that is latent in Schmitt's work and that is fundamentally

[62] ibid, 13.
[63] Gross (n 4) 1832.
[64] Schmitt, *Political Theology* (n 3) 6.
[65] Gross (n 4) 1831; Schmitt, *Political Theology* (n 3) 6.
[66] Gross (n 4) 1828.
[67] McCormick (n 53) 177.
[68] O'Donoghue (n 32) 56.
[69] Lindahl (n 34) 21.
[70] Ellen Kennedy, *Constitutional Failure: Carl Schmitt in Weimar* (Duke University Press, 2004) 176–78.
[71] Christoph Möllers, '"We Are (Afraid of) the People": Constituent Power in German Constitutionalism' in Loughlin and Walker (n 34) 87, 98.
[72] Thus, Ulrich K Preuss describes Schmitt's conception of the constituent power as the secularised version of the divine power to create the world ex nihilo: Ulrich K Preuss, 'Constitutional Powermaking for the New Polity: Some Deliberations on the Relations Between Constituent Power and the Constitution' (1992) 14 *Cardozo Law Review* 639, 640.

influenced by his strong Catholic faith.[73] Thus, Schmitt's fidelity to 'the people' is questionable at best. Rather, what is key is that, for Schmitt, constitutionalism can only be realised and made possible by a wilful exercise of political power.[74] Constitutionalism is therefore dependent on an underlying positive decision and not a norm of presupposed validity.[75] Consequently, Schmitt considers that the state cannot be equated to the legal order as there will always be actions of the state beyond law. From this, Schmitt deduces that: 'Sovereign is he who decides the exception.'[76]

Confronting the State of Exception: Preserving the Identity Thesis

Kelsen was aware that Schmitt believed his legal science was simply a neutral mask for liberalism's particular metaphysics.[77] NE Simmonds, evaluating Dyzenhaus' work on Schmitt, Kelsen and Heller, states that: 'Kelsen's relentless pursuit of a value-free legal science has the paradoxical effect of exposing the liberal legal order's rootedness in existential choice, so that the Pure Theory tends to confirm Schmitt's decisionism as the truth of liberal jurisprudence.'[78] To resist Carl Schmitt's challenge, Dyzenhaus argues that we must refuse to accept the two limbs of the Schmittian challenge—that the Sovereign can both decide on the existence of a state of exception and what must be done in lieu of this declaration. To do this, Dyzenhaus argues for maintenance of the rule of law during a state of emergency and that such a conception of the rule of law must be substantive or 'thick'.[79] One must imbue the legal order with some sense of value and avoid the positivist disposition of collapsing the issue of legitimacy into a thin form of legality. Consequently, Dyzenhaus rejects the contention that the state of emergency can satisfy rule-of-law constraints simply because it conforms with Kelsen's 'dynamic aspect' of a legal order.[80] This syllogism would, however, also be rejected by Schmitt: such an empty-formalistic conception of the rule of law is in fact a recognition of the failure of the liberal-democratic order, a cloaking device hiding the true nature of

[73] Kennedy (n 70).
[74] Scheuerman (n 32) 143.
[75] ibid.
[76] Schmitt, *Political Theology* (n 3) 1.
[77] Dyzenhaus (n 7) 120.
[78] NE Simmonds, '"Legality and Legitimacy: Carl Schmitt, Hans Kelsen and Hermann Heller in Weimar" by David Dyzenhaus [Oxford: Clarendon Press 1997]' (1998) 57 *Cambridge Law Journal* 195, 199.
[79] See D Dyzenhaus, *The Constitution of Law: Legality in a Time of Emergency* (Cambridge University Press, 2006).
[80] See text to n 22 above.

the state, namely that: 'Sovereign is he who decides the exception.'[81] In this regard, Schmitt himself clings to a concept of the formalist conception of the rule of law thicker than mere 'rule by law'[82] to argue that the state of exception cannot be prescribed by law. Given that the exception cannot be constrained by law as it is too vague a concept and so lacking clarity and certainty, Schmitt reveals himself as believing that clarity and certainty are necessary prerequisites for a norm to satisfy in order for it to be considered to be part of a legal order.[83]

In turn, I also reject arguments that a state of emergency contained within a constitutional provision can be described wholly by the dynamic aspect of law as such a power cannot be explained by reference to the hierarchy of norms alone. Instead, such a syllogism must reach for a more embryonic power, ie constituent power; a power beyond law which establishes the constitution and legal order in the first instance.[84] While this may suggest that I agree with Schmitt, I, however, take the opposite conclusion and contend that this claim for the constituent power through the state of exception must be rejected. Thus, the power to declare a state of emergency, while exceptional in the sense that it should be exercised rarely, must nevertheless be located within the legal order. The body exercising emergency powers must respect the constitutional constraints on the exercise of that power and, logically, there must also be constraints on this power for it to be legal.[85] These constraints must, I contend, be judicial in nature.

Conflicts between Norms: The Hierarchy of Norms

From a 'legal constitutionalist' perspective, the status of a constitution as a collection of the highest legal norms in a state is inextricably linked to the possibility of lower-order norms such as legislation being invalidated on the grounds that they are incompatible with constitutional norms.[86] This superiority of a constitution is necessarily and indelibly linked to whether judicial review of legislative action is available.[87] Alexander Hamilton in the *Federalist Papers* stated that:

> There is no position which depends on clearer principles than that every act of a delegated authority, contrary to the tenor of the commission, under which it is exercised, is void. No legislative act, therefore, contrary to the Constitution, can be valid. To deny this would be to affirm that the deputy is greater than his principal; that the servant is above

[81] Schmitt, *Political Theology* (n 3) 1.

[82] Brian Tamanaha, *On the Rule of Law: History, Politics, Theory* (Cambridge University Press, 2007) 92–93.

[83] Schmitt, *Political Theology* (n 3) 13.

[84] See text to n 147–68 below.

[85] Dyzenhaus (n 4) 2007.

[86] See text from nn 98–119 in ch 4 for a critique of judicial review from a political constitutionalist perspective.

[87] Carl Joachim Friedrich, 'The Issue of Judicial Review in Germany' (1928) 43 *Political Science Quarterly* 188, 195.

> his master; that the representatives of the people are superior to the people themselves; that men acting by virtue of powers may do not only what their powers do not authorize, but what they forbid.[88]

The procedural peculiarity surrounding the amendment of a constitution when compared against other norm-creating procedures (eg the ordinary legislative process) may also indicate a constitution's legal superiority. Thus, while law may be dynamic in the sense that it regulates its own creation, constitutional norms must possess a certain degree of resistance to change or repeal that distinguishes them from other legal norms such as legislation. In certain instances, this resistance to law's dynamic nature may be entwined with the issue of the availability of judicial review of legislative acts, as evidenced by debates in Weimar Germany.[89] Like the US Constitution, the matter as to whether judicial scrutiny of legislative acts for conformity with the constitution was possible was not expressly enumerated in the Weimar Constitution.[90] Gerhard Amschütz argued that no such power was available to the judiciary under the Weimar Constitution as this constitution could be amended by ordinary legislation.[91] Amschütz concluded that 'the Constitution and the statute are manifestations of the will of the very same power, the legislative power'.[92] Consequently, he argued that there was no distinction between ordinary legislative power and constitution-making power—the constituent power or *pouvoir constituent*. The constitution, therefore, under this argument, was not above the legislature but rather 'at its disposal' and the fact that qualifying majorities were required to amend the constitution did not alter this conclusion.[93] Carl Joachim Friedrich therefore argued that 'those in favour of judicial review must concentrate upon this central question: "is the Constitution a superior legal rule and a fundamental law or not?"'[94] Kelsen echoes this position, arguing that if a constitution lays down certain prescriptions and these are not followed, it must foresee this possibility and account for it:

> The constitution may then designate the organ that has to decide whether or not the prescriptions regulating the legislative function were observed. If this organ is different from the legislative organ, it forms an authority above the legislator. ... If no organ different from the legislative is called upon to inquire into the constitutionality of statutes, the

[88] Alexander Hamilton, 'Federalist No 78' in Clinton Rossiter (ed), *The Federalist Papers* (Signet Classics, 2003) 465–66.

[89] See Friedrich (n 87); Bernd J Hartmann, 'The Arrival of Judicial Review in Germany under the Weimar Constitution of 1919' (2003–04) 18 *BYU Journal of Public Law* 107.

[90] Hartmann, ibid, 1; in *Marbury v Madison* (1803) 5 US 137, the US Supreme Court held it had such a power to review the constitutionality of legislation. See text to nn 74–81 in ch 4 for further discussion of *Marbury v Madison.*

[91] Gottfried Dietze, 'Unconstitutional Constitutional Norms? Constitutional Development in Postwar Germany' (1956) 42 *Virginia Law Review* 1, 7–8.

[92] Friedrich (n 87) 192.

[93] ibid, 193.

[94] ibid.

> question whether or not a statute is constitutional has to be decided ... by the legislative organ itself. Then, everything that is passed by the legislative organ as a statute has to be accepted as a statute in the sense of the constitution. In this case, no statute enacted by the legislative organ can be considered to be unconstitutional.[95]

It was also suggested in Weimar Germany that not expressly prohibiting judicial review of the constitutionality of legislation would, like in the United States, eventually lead to the *Reichsgericht* (Weimar Germany Federal Supreme Court) declaring that it had such a power to do so.[96] This proved to be prophetic with the *Reichsgericht* eventually holding on 4 November 1925 that it had the power to review the constitutionality of statutes:

> Since the national Constitution itself contains no provisions according to which the decision of constitutionality of national statutes has been taken away from the courts, and has been transferred to another determinate authority, the right and the obligation of the judge to examine the constitutionality of statutes must be recognised.[97]

Amschütz's argument, therefore, was rejected by the *Reichsgericht* and consequently, in Weimar Germany, there was a fundamental difference between legislative power and 'constitution-making power'. This distinction is of fundamental importance for a state seeking to establish a constitutionalist framework for the control and exercise of state power. This is corroborated to an extent by Schmitt who argued that a genuine constitution would never permit its alteration into a fundamentally different document.[98] A constitution of a republic, for example, should not allow its alteration into an absolute monarchy. Thus, Schmitt also draws a distinction between the constitutional amendment power and the constituent power which can radically alter and transform the constitution.[99] That stated, the rejection of Amschütz's argument did not save the Weimar Constitution as it was through the use of the emergency clause in Article 48 that the constitution was reduced to a 'blank cheque statute' and this radical transformation of the constitutional order could take place.[100]

Conflicts between Constitutional Norms

The Pure Theory of law's concept of the unity of a legal order allows for no conflict between norms. Where there is conflict, Kelsen suggests that the Pure Theory can

[95] *GTLS*, 156.

[96] Friedrich (n 87) 190.

[97] (1920) 111 RGZ 320; per Friedrich's translation, Friedrich (n 87) 197; Hartmann (n 89) 124; Schmitt, *Constitutional Theory* (n 3) 230.

[98] Dyzenhaus (n 7) 52–53.

[99] See also Joel I Colón-Rios who draws a distinction between constitutional amendments and constitutional amendments to the 'fundamental core' of the constitution, the latter of which amounts to an expression of the constituent power. See Joel I. Colón-Ríos, *Weak Constitutionalism: Democratic Legitimacy and the Question of Constituent Power* (Routledge, 2012) ch 7.

[100] See text to nn 159–69 in ch 5.

rectify it. Conflict between two norms of different hierarchal status are resolved by the higher-order norm superseding the lower-order norm so that in effect there is no conflict.[101] If there is a conflict between norms of hierarchal parity, Kelsen argues that this can be resolved by either of two ways. Firstly, the most recently created norm must be considered as having priority over the older norm and the older norm must be considered to have been repealed by the newer norm in accordance with the principle *lex posterior derogate priori*.[102] Secondly, if both norms are created simultaneously, such as norms contained within the same piece of legislation constitution, such conflicts ought to be resolved through a process of holistic interpretation. A holistic or harmonious approach to constitutional interpretation views the constitutional norm in question to be part of a collection of norms, a broader tapestry revealing its true intention and meaning when viewed as a whole.[103] The constitutional norm in question is but one part of the jigsaw that is the constitution. This approach seeks to avoid conflicting constitutional norms that may arise when interpreting a norm solely in isolation. Instead, if there are two apparently conflicting constitutional norms, a harmonious interpretation seeks to resolve this conflict by reaching an understanding of the constitution that mediates between the conflicting norms.

Conflicts between constitutional norms may also be resolved by identifying a hierarchy of norms within the constitution itself.[104] This approach does not consider every norm contained within a constitution to be of equal importance, but instead identifies those norms which are most important, accords them the requisite position of hierarchy, and resolves conflicts between norms in favour of the higher norm. Constitutional norms may be identified as higher than others by an explicit indication in the text that accords them this superiority, or through a process of interpretation by the judiciary.[105] A hierarchy of constitutional norms may be invoked to resolve conflicts between different constitutional rights with some rights identified as more important and, consequently, 'trumping' others in certain situations.[106] Thus, bearing this in mind, how does one resolve a conflict between norms when one norm explicitly states that it must be interpreted in isolation, thereby excluding the possibility of harmonious interpretation? Is this requirement of interpretive isolation also a claim to hierarchal superiority? This question is particularly relevant when it involves constitutional emergency powers that permit the suspension of other constitutional norms.

[101] *GTLS*, 153–55.

[102] *GTLS*, 402.

[103] Gerard Hogan and Gerry Whyte, *JM Kelly: The Irish Constitution*, 3rd edn (Lexis Nexis, 1994) ci–civ.

[104] ibid, civ–cv.

[105] ibid, cvi–cvii.

[106] See, for example, *The People v Shaw* [1982] IR 1 where the Irish Supreme Court held that the right to life of a victim trumped the right to liberty of an individual who was suspected to have kidnapped her and was detained by the police longer than lawfully permitted in order to extract a confession as to her whereabouts. An express hierarchy of constitutional rights was acknowledged by Kenny J in this case. See also Hogan and Whyte, ibid.

When dealing with a constitutional norm that enables a state of emergency, one could potentially resolve any possible conflict of norms by arguing that the other norms are rendered conditional by the constitutional norm that enables a state of emergency. In other words, one ought to interpret every right or constitutional conferral of power as applicable only when a state of normalcy exists. If this is the case, then there is no conflict as the other norms are not applicable in a period of emergency. In effect, the constitutional norm that enables a state of emergency supersedes all other constitutional norms. However, according emergency powers a position of constitutional hierarchy vindicates Carl Schmitt, or at the very least, makes the legal order vulnerable to the Schmittian Challenge by reducing the constitution to a 'blank-cheque statute' in order to cling on to this thread of legality. Conversely, recognising a hierarchy of norms within a constitution is to argue instead that it gives rise to the potential for 'unconstitutional constitutional norms' or an interpretation of constitutional norms that is unconstitutional. This idea can assist in removing the state of emergency from its apparent constitutional apex and establishing the primacy of judicial review as a necessary control on the decision to declare a state of emergency in order to conceptualise it as validated by the legal order and successfully confront the Schmittian Challenge.

Unconstitutional Constitutional Norms: The Case for Judicial Review

The idea of unconstitutional constitutional norms appears, at first instance, to be oxymoronic. If a norm is enumerated in a constitution, then it is, axiomatically, a constitutional norm and therefore constitutional. Notwithstanding this, the concept of an unconstitutional norm has been approached by supreme and constitutional courts in a number of jurisdictions.[107] In order to identify whether unconstitutional constitutional norms or amendments may be possible, Rory O'Connell identifies four factors that need to be considered: (i) What is the amending procedure provided in the constitution? (ii) Does the constitution explicitly state that some provisions cannot be amended? (iii) Is there an express provision that amendments may be subject to judicial review? (iv) Does the constitution explicitly state that some provisions are hierarchically superior to others?[108]

[107] For an analysis of unconstitutional constitutional norms, see Yaniv Roznai, *Unconstitutional Constitutional Amendments: The Limits of Amendment Powers* (Oxford University Press, 2017); Rory O'Connell, 'Guardians of the Constitution: Unconstitutional Constitutional Norms' (1999) 4 *Journal of Civil Liberties* 48; Jacobson (n 25); Aileen Kavanagh, 'Unconstitutional Constitutional Amendments from Irish Free State to Irish Republic' in Eoin Carolan (ed), *The Constitution of Ireland: Perspectives and Prospects* (Bloomsbury Professional, 2012); Richard Stith, 'Unconstitutional Constitutional Amendments: The Extraordinary Power of Nepal's Supreme Court' (1996) 11 *American University International Law Review* 47.

[108] O'Connell, ibid, 52.

In the German and Indian constitutions, for example, there exists a clear hierarchy of norms within the constitution itself.[109] Other constitutions contain what are termed 'eternity clauses'—provisions that are stated to be unamendable and therefore 'eternal'.[110] If another constitutional norm conflicts with this higher constitutional norm, the conflict ought to be resolved in favour of the higher norm. This may take the form of interpreting the subservient constitutional norm in a manner so that it does not conflict with the higher constitutional norm, or in the most extreme cases, it will involve a declaration of invalidity of the offending constitutional norm. Such a declaration generally comes to light in instances involving constitutional amendments, as opposed to norms that have existed in a constitution since its inception; however, there is no conceptual reason why it should only be limited to amendments. Instead, such constitutional norms may remain unapplied by the courts, or may be cited as inapplicable and in this manner the superior constitutional norm is able to prevail. In this manner, such norms may lose their validity through a process of constitutional desuetude.[111]

The existence of unconstitutional constitutional norms requires that a state's constitutional or supreme court be empowered to invalidate constitutional amendments or provisions.[112] Judicial supremacy is mandated by these higher norms, but also must be constrained by them. Therefore, the exercise of judicial power in contravention of these norms would also be invalid and illegitimate. The issue of unconstitutional constitutional amendments came to the fore in India following Indira Gandhi's victory in the 1971 election and her party securing two-thirds of the seats in parliament. Parliament enacted the 24th, 25th, 26th and 29th Amendments to restrict judges' power, and property rights. However, in *Kesavananda v Kerala*[113] the Supreme Court again reviewed the constitutionality of constitutional amendments. Firstly, the court overruled the majority in *Golak Nath* which held that the human rights provisions of the Indian Constitution could not be amended,[114] arguing that Article 368 of the Indian Constitution (the amendment

[109] O'Connell, ibid; Dietze (n 91) 13–16.

[110] Colón-Ríos (n 99) 127.

[111] See text from nn 126–39 below.

[112] In *Golak Nath v Punjab*, AIR [1967] SC 1643, six of the eleven judges of the Indian Supreme Court held that the Indian Constitution does not permit the abridgment of rights, even by a constitutional amendment. The Constitution gives such rights a place of prominence within the constitution itself, ie that a hierarchy of norms could be identified within the constitution. Germany's constitution or Basic Law (*Grundgesetz*) was initially passed as a transitory document in 1949; however, withstanding the test of time, the Basic Law has remained in force and taken on the characteristics of a fully-fledged constitution. Art 1 of the Basic Law accords dignity a special place in the constitutional order, requiring all state authority to respect. Art 20 further declares the state as founded on popular sovereignty, the rule of law and separation of powers. Art 79 precludes the amendment of Arts 1 and 20, and also prohibits amendment of the federal nature of the German state. To date, the German Constitutional Court has not yet invalidated an amendment to the Constitution, or declared a constitutional norm invalid, yet the prospect remains that it does have the power to do so. See Donald P Konners, 'German Constitutionalism: A Prolegomenon' (1991) 40 *Emory Law Journal* 837, 837.

[113] AIR [1973] SC 1461.

[114] See n 112 above.

article) permitted the amendment of any part of the Constitution. However, the Court instead homed in on the concept of 'amendment', declaring that Parliament could only amend the Constitution and not abolish its essential features.[115] Some judges identified these essential features based on the fundamental values identified in the Indian Constitution. The six dissenting judges, however, argued that all parts of the Constitution were of the same hierarchy and therefore none could be given priority over others.[116]

The clash between Gandhi and the Supreme Court came to a head in 1975. In June 1975 the High Court declared Gandhi's victory in the 1971 election invalid due to the corrupt practices she and her party were found to have engaged in. Following this, Gandhi's Parliament passed the 38th Amendment, which provided that any decision to declare an emergency under India's constitution was unreviewable by the courts, and the 39th Amendment, which retrospectively altered the laws under which Gandhi was convicted of committing election offences.[117] Yet again, however, the Supreme Court struck down a constitutional amendment, this time the 39th Amendment on the grounds that precluding judicial review of electoral matters would render the concept of free and fair elections a myth.[118]

Once again, Gandhi responded with another constitutional amendment—the 42nd Amendment—which O'Connell describes as 'a war against the judiciary'.[119] This Amendment declared Parliament's constituent power to be absolute, asserted the superiority of legislation implementing directive policies over fundamental rights, and restricted the Court's range of remedies and actions. In response to this, the Supreme Court held in *Minerva Mills* that:

> Since the Constitution had conferred a limited amending power on Parliament, the Parliament cannot under the exercise of that limited power enlarge that very power into an absolute power. Indeed, a limited amending power is one of the basic features of our Constitution and therefore, the limitations on that power cannot be destroyed.[120]

The Indian experience of unconstitutional constitutional amendments illustrates how the amendment power has a close relation to the constituent power—the power that posits or founds the constitution in the first instance—yet the amendment power must still be conceptualised as a constituted power. The Indian approach is thus to state that an unlimited amendment power amounts to a claim for the constituent power and, consequently, such an interpretation would reduce the constitution to what Schmitt would term a 'blank cheque statute'. Consequently, the Indian Supreme Court found that the Indian Constitution did not prescribe an unlimited amending power. Indeed, it is debatable whether such power can actually be prescribed by law as such a power would, in reality, be the

[115] O'Connell (n 107) 69.
[116] ibid, 70.
[117] ibid, 70–71.
[118] ibid.
[119] ibid, 71.
[120] *Minerva Mills* AIR [1980] SC 1789.

constituent power—the powers constituted by the Constitution cannot reach or claim for a power that is beyond them. Therefore, the power to amend the Indian Constitution through the process prescribed by it is a constituted power. In this manner, the Indian Supreme Court essentially recognised the argument made by Schmitt that a true constitution cannot enumerate a power for it to be radically altered into a fundamentally different constitutional order.[121]

The Permanent State of Emergency as an Unconstitutional Constitutional Amendment

As established in chapter one, a state of emergency should, ideally, be a reactive or defensive mechanism. Its justification rests in the fact that it is temporary; required to restore normalcy and therefore negating its own necessity. A state of emergency should therefore be temporary and non-transformative.[122] Carl Schmitt's concept of sovereign dictatorship is not justified on the grounds of restoring normalcy, however; it is permanent. It is seen as always being needed and, as such, is not defensive but transformative. Even if the constitutional order established creates, for example, a parliamentary democracy based on a separation of powers, the constituent power possessed by the sovereign stands in the shadows, waiting to be revealed in the moment of exception. Relatedly, the communist dictatorship of the proletariat is, like commissarial dictatorship, envisaged to be temporary, but rather than restoring the prior status quo, its goal is to usher in a new communist utopian conception of society.[123] It is temporary, but transformative. The question this raises is the nature of the dictatorial power created by the state of exception and its relation to the intention of the dictator. If the form of the dictatorial regime and power invested in this office are identical, does the raison d'être of the dictatorship make a difference to its relationship with the pre-existing legal order? Is that pre-existing legal order or the norms contained therein still valid? Must we look to the intention of those deciding that an emergency exists and still exists in order to assess whether a declared state of emergency is defensive or revolutionary? Is the only answer to this question that one ought to look at the intention of whoever has declared a state of emergency?

As stated previously, Kelsen's Pure Theory of law views the legal order as a system of norms validated by higher norms, all made valid by presupposing

[121] See text to n 101 above.

[122] Thus, McCormick argues that the change in Schmitt's thoughts between writing *The Dictator* and writing *Political Theology* was a change from commissarial to sovereign dictatorship. McCormick (n 53) 163; Rossiter also insists that the temporariness of a state of emergency is necessary, stating that: 'It is the crisis alone which makes the dictatorship constitutional; the end of the crisis makes its continued existence unconstitutional': Rossiter (n 29) 306.

[123] McCormick (n 53) 165–67.

the validity of the basic norm. To state that a norm's validity is imputed from a higher norm is not the entire picture, however. Kelsen asserts that the relationship between the validity and effectiveness—whether a norm is actually followed or not—of a legal norm is one of the most difficult problems in positivist legal theory.[124] Two diametrically opposed streams of thought on this issue can be identified: first, that which asserts a norm is valid, regardless of its efficacy; and second, that which holds that a norm is not valid unless it is effective.[125] Kelsen rejects the first argument—that a norm is valid regardless of its efficacy—as this ignores the observed reality that a legal norm, and, indeed, a legal order as a whole, ceases to be effective to such an extent that they no longer actually exist.[126] In such instances it is wrong to say that such norms are still valid. The second position—that validity and effectiveness are identical—is also problematic as it falls into the trap of confusing the 'is' with the 'ought'[127] and conceptualises norms as true or false, rather than valid or invalid.[128] As a result, Kelsen settles upon a medium between these two conflicting positions, arguing that effectiveness is a necessary condition of validity, but it is not identical to validity.[129] Deriving from this, Kelsen recognises the concept of desuetude or *desuetudo*: that a norm can become invalidated if it falls into disuse and is ineffective for a substantial period of time.[130]

Constitutional Desuetude

Kelsen describes desuetude as a 'negative custom' surrounding a norm. While the norm in question exists in the sense that it is enumerated in the manner in which the legal order stipulates that a valid norm has been created, it has not been exercised for an extended period of time. In this regard, the norm in question is lacking the modicum of effectiveness necessary to ensure its validity. Desuetude is generally concerned with norms contained in statutes, particularly in civil legal systems; however, constitutional theorists have begun to explore the concept of desuetude in the context of constitutional norms. Richard Albert, for example, argues that desuetude requires three elements: (1) sustained (2) conscious non-use, and (3) political repudiation are necessary in order to render a rule desuetudinal.[131] Albert then applies this theory to the British

[124] *PTL*, 211.
[125] Raz (n 6) 801.
[126] *PTL*, 211.
[127] ibid, 212.
[128] ibid.
[129] ibid, 211–14; *GTLS*, 122.
[130] *GTLS*, 119–20.
[131] Richard Albert, 'Constitutional Amendment by Constitutional Desuetude' (2014) 62 *American Journal of Comparative Law* 641, 651.

powers of disallowance and reservation which are entrenched in the Canadian Constitution to argue that they evince evidence of desuetude.[132]

Non-use of a constitutional power is also a key indicator of what Adrian Vermeule describes as 'constitutional atrophy'.[133] Vermeule argues that certain constitutional provisions may, due to their disuse over time, lose their political legitimacy such that a future attempt to revive the power amounts to 'an illegitimate attempt to change the rules of the political game'.[134] Albert argues that the vehicle for constitutional amendment by desuetude is custom. Custom or 'convention' is also a key factor in Vermeule's argument regarding the atrophy of constitutional powers. A political actor may fail to exercise a power out of fear that they will face a political backlash. Vermeule gives the example of the Crown veto over legislation in the UK as an illustration of this point with the last veto over legislation exercised by Queen Anne in 1708.[135] Today, it is unimaginable that the Crown would now veto a piece of legislation. The distinction between atrophy and desuetude appears to be this relation between validity and effectiveness, with Vermeule stating that constitutional powers that have atrophied lose their legitimacy; he does not, however, go so far as to say they lose their legal validity. This may be due to the fact that desuetude is not recognised in many common law legal systems, owing to the fact that ineffective legal norms can often be repealed or amended by a simple act of parliament.[136] Albert, in contrast, argues that constitutions may be amended through desuetude, which would suggest that the prior existing constitutional norms that have been amended have lost their validity. However, he uses the term 'political validity' as distinct from legal validity, which again may be symptomatic of the contested status of desuetude in the legal orders from which his examples are drawn.[137] In this regard, I argue that such norms do not merely lose their political validity but, in line with Kelsen's theory on the relation between the validity and effectiveness of legal norms, their legal validity too. Albert further contends that constitutional desuetude is only possible in jurisdictions covered by

[132] ibid, 656–69.

[133] Adrian Vermeule, 'The Atrophy of Constitutional Powers' (2012) 32 *OJLS* 421.

[134] ibid, 423.

[135] ibid, 432.

[136] Moreover, the fact that a statute can be simply repealed means that British constitutional law is reluctant to label many constitutional changes as permanent. Thus, for example, where statute supersedes prerogative powers, these powers are considered to go into 'abeyance' and thus the possibility of their restoration remains. See *De Keyser's Royal Hotel* [1920] AC 508, 539–40; Robert Craig, 'Casting Aside Clanking Medieval Chains: Prerogative, Statute and Article 50 after the EU Referendum' (2016) 79 *MLR* 1019; Gavin Phillipson, 'A Dive into Constitutional Waters: Article 50, the Prerogative and Parliament' (2016) 79 *MLR* 1064. While a detailed analysis of the abeyance of prerogative powers is beyond the scope of this book, the relationship between the validity and effectiveness of legal norms would, I suggest, cast doubt over whether or not the prerogative power in question is actually in abeyance or whether it is actually invalid. Rather, much would depend upon the circumstances surrounding repeal of the legislation in question that has forced the prerogative into abeyance which would raise questions as to the validity of the aforementioned prerogative power and whether it has been repudiated.

[137] Albert (n 131) 654.

a written constitution.[138] Moreover, while Albert and Vermeule focus mostly on the constitutional powers of specific actors—ie dynamic constitutional norms—there is no reason why the idea of constitutional desuetude or atrophy cannot apply to other static constitutional norms, eg constitutional rights.[139] In addition, Vermeule's theory of constitutional atrophy applies to both written and unwritten constitutions. I will return to this issue in chapter six when discussing how unwritten constitutional orders such as that of the UK which proclaim the sovereignty of Parliament confront the Schmittian challenge and whether norms in the British Constitution can be identified as falling into desuetude.[140]

The Permanent State of Emergency and the Validity and Effectiveness of Constitutional Norms

This potential for norms to lose their validity through desuetude establishes the primacy of 'temporariness' in order to ensure a state of emergency is contained within the legal order and Kelsen's Identity Thesis is maintained. A declaration of a state of emergency as prescribed by the constitution has the potential to suspend certain constitutional provisions by rendering them temporarily ineffective. Thus, if the state of emergency has suspended the writ of habeas corpus, one cannot petition the court for relief using this writ. A situation may arise, however, where such norms have been suspended perpetually and have not been applicable for years or even decades. If a norm or norms within a constitution are by and large ineffective, and have been so for a prolonged period of time, it would be disingenuous to describe them as norms as the 'ought' that they prescribe is not being obeyed. According to Raz:

> Laws guide human behaviour. … A law, the existence of which is unknown, or that is never acted on by the police nor enforced by judges or juries does not guide the behaviour of most people, not even that of law-abiding people. There seems, therefore, to be no reason to regard it as part of the legal system, since its complete inefficacy has deprived it of the main characteristic of law, that of guiding behaviour.[141]

The constitutional norms perpetually suspended by the permanent emergency lack the necessary element of efficacy required for a norm to be valid. This has stemmed from the factual reality that the emergency has not fulfilled its raison

[138] ibid, 650.

[139] The ineffectiveness of such norms may be more difficult, however, due to their status as 'principles' rather than hard-and-fast rules. See text to nn 126–30 in ch 6 regarding Dworkin's distinction between rules and principles and the impact that the Schmittian Challenge has on conceptualising rights as principles.

[140] See text to nn 83–172 in ch 6.

[141] Raz (n 6) 802.

d'être; that it is a temporary aberration from the status quo. A declaration of a state of emergency that has the potential to render certain constitutional norms ineffective and create a permanent state of emergency can render constitutional norms permanently ineffective and therefore invalid. The constitution, therefore, has been changed in a manner inconsistent with the ordinary amendment procedure. If there is no possibility for judicial review of the decision to declare a state of emergency, then there is no reason in law to assume that it will be temporary. It is only by the possibility of this decision being subject to scrutiny that one can consider it to be potentially temporary. To recap, the assessment of an issue that acts as a limit on the power of a decision-maker, if it truly is to be a limit on their power, cannot be exclusively assessed by the decision-maker and consequently is amenable to judicial review. Thus, if the existence of a state of emergency is wholly at the discretion of those who declared it, then the requirement that it be temporary is not a legal one.

The logical question that flows from this issue is assessing the permanence of a state of emergency. At what stage does the derogation or suspension of a legal norm impact upon its efficacy to such an extent that it loses its validity? Like the concept of emergency itself, 'temporariness' is a term that eludes precise definition. When an emergency is declared, and constitutional norms are suspended or derogated from, they arguably become immediately ineffective but one cannot say that these norms have immediately lost their validity. This ineffectiveness can, however, be explained initially by a harmonious interpretation between the emergency power and the suspended constitutional norm by interpreting the suspended norms as 'one ought to obey, but not during a period of emergency'. This harmonious interpretation only works, however, upon the assumption of a separation between normalcy and emergency, with restoration of normalcy being the raison d'être of the emergency. Without this assumption, harmonious interpretation fails and a conflict between the two constitutional norms remains. It would be disingenuous to resolve the conflict in favour of the perpetually suspended norm as it is a norm that is clearly not being obeyed. If one resolves it in favour of the emergency constitutional norm, then one is back to the position of the emergency constitutional power being used to invalidate another constitutional norm. The issue this points to therefore is not when an emergency becomes permanent, but whether there is a *possibility* of a permanent emergency coming into existence under the constitutional structure. It is a thought experiment designed to highlight the difficulties and consequences of perpetuating an emergency at the discretion of a political actor. This thought experiment shows that the decision to declare and perpetuate a state of emergency must be subject to the rule of law and judicial review in order to permit a harmonious interpretation of the constitution. An interpretation of a constitutional provision that precludes judicial review of the existence of a state of emergency has the potential to permit a permanent state of emergency as the reasons pertaining to the existence of a state of emergency do not have to be substantially justified in law.

The problem of the perpetuation of a state of emergency even when judicial review is available can be solved, I contend, by arguing that each time the emergency is reviewed by the judiciary, it is still done so on the grounds that it is temporary and with a view to bringing it to an end. The suspended norms still exert their existence in the assessment process, with the existence of the emergency being referred back to the necessity of such powers, and consequently the necessity of derogation from the suspended norms.[142] In contrast, when the existence and perpetuation of an emergency is at the sole discretion of a body, the decision is justified on the grounds of authority, not on a reasonable calculation of the costs and opportunity costs of declaring an emergency, ie one cannot say that it was done in accordance with the rule of law by reference back to the suspended norms and their influence.

Permanent States of Emergency and the Repudiation of Constitutional Norms

Albert argues that constitutional desuetude can be distinguished by dormancy. A dormant constitutional provision is one that has not been used in some time; however, it has not been subjected to the public repudiation that the norm subject to constitutional desuetude has been.[143] A dormant constitutional norm, therefore, does not suffer from the same illegitimacy that the desuetudinal one does and so its revival is perfectly legitimate. With regards to constitutional norms indefinitely suspended as a result of a permanent state of emergency, it may be argued that these norms are not potentially desuetudinal but merely dormant, waiting for the right conditions to arise whereby they can be revived. The difficulty, however, with this is that it may fall prey to the Schmittian challenge by once again stretching the concept of legality so broadly as to legitimise any action of the state from a legal perspective. One making such an argument would do well to heed Ellen Kennedy's assertion that to state that an individual has rights even though they cannot enforce them is to fall into the sinister trap laid by Schmitt.[144]

In the context of emergency powers, it is highly unlikely that suspended constitutional norms will be expressly repudiated in the sense that, for example, political actors or the courts state that these norms no longer have a value. This argument, however, ignores the fact that a declaration of a state of emergency *is* an express assertion that the impugned constitutional norms in question should not be followed; that they are, at best inappropriate for the exceptional conditions facing the state, or, at worst, that they counterproductive and jeopardising the security

[142] See, however, ch 5 for a discussion regarding the contention that such review may, however, be carried out in such a deferential fashion that it acts as a mere cloak of legality, thus doing more harm than good to the rule of law.

[143] Albert (n 131) 675–77.

[144] Kennedy (n 70) 176–178.

of the state. A declaration of a state of emergency therefore *is* a repudiation of the suspended constitutional norms and repeated assertions that the emergency cannot be ended amount to a repeated repudiation of the suspended constitutional norms. In essence, a state of emergency is a declaration that the rules of the game have changed and a renewal of the declaration is a restatement of the fact that the rules of the game have still changed. However, it should also be a declaration that they have only *temporarily* changed. Consequently, temporariness is of paramount importance when assessing whether a permanent state of emergency has caused certain constitutional norms to fall into desuetude.

The Permanent State of Emergency as a Claim for the Constituent Power

In a legal system where the legislature lacks the power to amend the constitution, a statute that attempts to do so will be invalid. It is invalid, not because it is in conflict with a higher normative value such as dignity, but because it lacks the power to act in the way it has attempted to act, ie it is ultra vires the powers given to the legislature by the constitution. It is attempting to do something that the constitution has not empowered it to do.[145] While this statement is incredibly rudimentary, it is of vital importance as it applies in instances where the legislature in a state may not necessarily intend to amend the constitution explicitly but the statute they pass in actuality has this effect; or, in instances where an interpretation of the constitution or a constitutional norm proffered would have the effect of transferring the power to amend the constitution from one branch to another. In other words, it would be an attempt by the legislature to claim the amendment power that may not be prescribed to it under the constitution.

As noted above, Schmitt's theory of sovereignty and the decision to declare a state of exception can be viewed as an expression of, or a claim for, the constituent power that founds the constitution. Andreas Kalyvas discusses the merging of these conceptions of sovereignty and constituent power, arguing that sovereignty's traditional understanding as command-based authority has had a negative effect on the normative value of sovereignty in political and legal science. Instead,

[145] Thus, if the Irish Oireachtas attempted to amend the Constitution without a referendum, such a statute would be invalid on the grounds that it encroaches on the power of the people to amend the Constitution under Art 46 of the Irish Constitution. Indeed, in his dissenting judgment in *State (Ryan) v Lennon* [1935] 1 IR 170, Kennedy CJ argued that even though Art 50 of the Constitution of Saorstát Éireann gave the power to amend the Constitution via ordinary legislation to the Oireachtas within the first eight years of the Constitution's operation, it was not an unlimited power. Rather, it was subject to the 'ultimate authority of the people'. This was evidenced by that fact that Art 50 contained the words 'subject to the provisions of Article 47' which contained the ordinary amendment procedure by referendum. [1935] 1 IR 170, 213 fn 26. See also Kavanagh (n 107).

Kalyvas suggests that a better understanding of sovereignty is to consider it in terms of constituent power, an understanding he attributes to (amongst others) Carl Schmitt.[146] For Schmitt, sovereignty is not the ultimate 'coercive power of command' but is instead the power to found, to posit or constitute, ie a constitutive power.[147] Emmanuel Joseph Sieyès recognised this formulation of the constituent power as 'the moment of a constitution's founding and an expression of the essential relation between the people and the state'.[148] Under this understanding, the constituent power determines the constitutional structure. Hence, the constituent power creates the 'constituted powers' that derive their validity from the constitution and are exercised through institutions created by the constitution. The constitution thus presupposes the constituent power and Illan Rua Wall argues that Sieyès makes constituent power into the very constitution itself.[149] The constitution, therefore, is an expression of the constituent power.[150]

Martin Loughlin argues that Hans Kelsen and others who try to conceptualise a legal order as a closed system of norms ignore this constructive concept of the constituent power.[151] According to this 'normative' account, what authorises the 'original constitution', ie what is the constituent power, cannot be answered through law but can only be presupposed. Again, this is the critique of the Pure Theory of law as only being pure because it ignores the foundational moment, permitting the assumption of a closed system of norms, thus collapsing the concept of legitimacy into the concept of legality.[152] While Schmitt's conception of the constituent power can be understood as constructive, there is also a tense and ambivalent relation towards the constitutional order by the constituent power that has founded it.[153] Constituent power therefore is both constructive and destructive.[154] It is constructive in the sense that it posits or creates the new constitutional order; however, it is also potentially destructive too, as it negates

[146] Andreas Kalyvas, 'Popular Sovereignty, Democracy and the Constituent Power' (2005) 12 *Constellations* 223, 225.

[147] ibid.

[148] Emmanuel-Joseph Sieyès, *What Is the Third Estate?* [1789] <http://pages.uoregon.edu/dluebke/301ModernEurope/Sieyes3dEstate.pdf> accessed 11 August 2017; Illan rua Wall, 'Notes on an "Open" Constituent Power' (1 May 2013) available at SSRN: <http://ssrn.com/abstract=2259008 or http://dx.doi.org/10.2139/ssrn.2259008> accessed 7 August 2013, 1.

[149] Illan rua Wall, 'A Different Constituent Power: Agamben & Tunisia' (25 November 2011) in *New Critical Legal Thinking: Law and the Political* (Birkbeck Law Press/Routledge, 2012) available at SSRN: http://ssrn.com/abstract=2090896 (accessed 7 August 2017) 15.

[150] ibid.

[151] Martin Loughlin, 'The Concept of Constituent Power' (2014) 13 *European Journal of Political Theory* 218, 221–23.

[152] Kelsen rejects the notion of a people or *Volk* existing prior to the legal order and possessing the constituent power as it is only by the ratification of the constitution and presupposition of the *Grundnorm* that can one recognise the *Volk*. This is the so-called 'paradoxical self-creation' at the heart of the constituted order. See generally Loughlin and Walker (n 34); Illan rua Wall, *Human Rights and Constituent Power* (Routledge, 2012) 79.

[153] Kalyvas (n 146) 227.

[154] Wall (n 148) 2.

or destroys the established interests of the prior order.[155] For some theorists of constituent power, this potential for destruction remains, even when the new order is established. The constituent power is a 'moment without end'[156] and thus constituent power has 'an open sense of temporality'.[157]

In other words, the constituent power under Schmitt's 'open' formulation is not subservient to the constitutional order it has founded. It existed prior to, or outside of, any legal norm and cannot therefore be subsumed within one. The spectre of the initial decision haunts the order it has established and as '[s]overeign is he who decides upon the exception', Schmitt intimates a clear link between constituent power and the state of emergency. Schmitt appears to suggest that deciding when an exception exists indicates where sovereignty and therefore the constituent power lies. The two distinct decisions to declare and act in a state of exception are therefore conflated by Schmitt, which he considers to amount to an expression of the constituent power. Under this understanding, there is no possibility that law can control the decision as to the existence of a state of emergency as it is the exercise of the constituent power which lies beyond the law.

The 'tense and ambivalent' relation between constituent power and the constitution has been termed 'the paradox of constitutionalism': 'that government power is generated from the people while at the same time must be divided and constrained through institutional forms'.[158] Conceptualisations of constituent power often stress a fundamental link between constituent power and the people, with constituent power being invoked as a legitimating principle of authority emerging from the people from the 'bottom up' in contrast to the 'divine right of kings' which legitimated monarchies.[159] Thus, Sieyès' conception of constituent power is aimed at liberating the potential of the Third Estate in France, arming it with the political philosophy necessary to engage in nation building.[160] For some, constituent power therefore has become bound to the idea of democracy, with Antonio Negri boldly proclaiming that: 'When we talk about constituent power we are talking about democracy.'[161] As noted above, Schmitt's invocation of the *Volk* has been seen by some to be him preferring democracy over the rule of law. However, I also argued that Schmitt can only be considered democratic in the sense that he considers the legitimacy of the state to derive from the people or *Volk* as distinct from God. Consequently, I contended that what is key is that, for

[155] ibid.

[156] ibid.

[157] ibid; Loughlin (n 151) 227–31. Wall also attributes 'open' constituent power to Giorgio Agamben and Antonio Negri. See Antonio Negri, *Insurgencies: Constituent Power and the Modern State*, trans Maurizia Boscagli (University of Minnesota Press, 1999); Kevin Attell, 'Potentiality, Actuality, Constituent Power' (2009) 39 *Contemporary Italian Thought* 35. See text to nn 153–72 in ch 6 for a discussion of 'open' 'relational' constituent power in the context of the UK.

[158] Martin Loughlin and Neil Walker, 'Introduction' in Loughlin and Walker (n 34) 1.

[159] Martin Loughlin, *Foundations of Public Law* (Oxford University Press, 2010) 223–24.

[160] Sieyès (n 148).

[161] Negri (n 157).

Schmitt, constitutionalism can only be realised and made possible by a wilful exercise of political power.[162]

While Kelsen's theory has been criticised for beginning only at the point at which the legal order has already been established, the idea of constituent power can, I contend, nevertheless help the Identity Thesis confront the Schmittian challenge to which Kelsen's theory is potentially vulnerable. Constituent power is a necessary concept in order to demonstrate the limits of the constituted order and, by extension, the emergency powers contained therein. Thus, O'Donoghue argues that the 'pivot of constituent and constituted powers underpins constitutional orders'.[163] In this regard, formal constitutional amendment powers must be considered to be constituted powers. This is clear from the intricate procedures enumerated by constitutions that regulate the amendment procedure. Even in constitutions that can be amended by plebiscite of the people, 'the people' in such form are not exercising constituent power. Rather, both the people and the manner in which they speak are defined or constituted by the constitution. However, when changes are wrought to the constitutional order beyond that envisaged by the constitution, or the constitutional order altered so radically that it no longer resembles the initial order envisaged by the constitution, these changes cannot be explained through Kelsen's Identity Thesis without resorting to simply the dynamic understanding of the constitution outlined above; an argument that, I contend, is vulnerable to the Schmittian Challenge. Rather, this must be explained instead as amounting to a *claim* for the constituent power—a power beyond the law. It is only by recognising this possibility that the Identity Thesis can be saved from the Schmittian Challenge. However, by recognising this as a 'claim', the Identity Thesis mandates that it must also be rejected as it is not for a constitutional court, or, indeed, any constituted organ, to declare whether or not a claim for the constituent power has been successful. In this regard, the idea of 'constituent power' guides and shapes the evolution of the constitution in stipulating what must be considered 'constituted powers'. Consequently, it must be considered as revealing the limits of these powers so as to avoid vindicating the Schmittian Challenge.

As stated previously, Schmitt's infamous statement that '[s]overeign is he who decides upon the exception' is actually a conflation of two separate decisions: sovereign is he who both decides as to whether an exception exists and what ought to be done in order to confront the exception.[164] Consequently, I contend that Schmitt's merging of the constituent power with the exception is therefore dependent upon these two questions being decided by the same party. If the constitutional emergency provisions apply the principle of heteroinvestiture[165] as applied by the Roman dictatorship and separate these two questions, then the emergency

162 Scheuerman (n 32) 143.
163 O'Donoghue (n 32) 56.
164 See McCormick (n 54).
165 See text to n 48 in ch 1.

provisions do not equate to Schmitt's 'sovereign', ie they are not a manifestation of the constituent power. Schmitt may have argued on this point that even if an emergency provision were to apply the principle of heteroinvestiture, nevertheless in a period of true existential crisis where there is no possibility of following the legal protocols enumerated in the constitution, then the sovereign would reveal itself and decide accordingly. However, such a criticism would not only be valid against a constitution that recognises a separation of normalcy and emergency, but also one that also professes that 'the same law in war applies in peace'.

To reiterate, a permanent state of emergency can amount to an amendment of the constitution by rendering the impinged norms in question invalid by permanently removing their effectiveness. As effectiveness is a necessary condition of validity, one cannot say that the impinged norms are still valid. An argument, therefore, that permanent emergencies are possible under constitutional emergency provisions must also contend with the concept of a declaration of a state of emergency acting as a proxy-constitutional amendment. It is not a power, however, that is a limited amendment power such as that envisaged by the Indian Supreme Court.[166] Nor is it an amendment power envisaged by the constituent power as it is one that conflicts with the express constitutional amendment protocol enumerated in the constitution, ie it is not a constituted power. A claim grounded in law that the constitution permits one body the exclusive right to assess the existence of a state of emergency must fail, precisely because it requires one to reach for the constituent power to legitimate it, ie it requires one to argue a Schmittian understanding of the state of exception in a court. It requires that emergencies be potentially permanent and that such emergencies therefore are not reactive/defensive mechanisms; that is to say, they are not commissarial dictatorships, but amount to sovereign dictatorships. Such a claim, by excluding judicial review and reaching for the constituent power, claims a power that lies beyond the law and therefore such an argument cannot be grounded in law. Such an argument therefore must be rejected.

Constituent Power and the State of Emergency: The Case of Ireland

A concrete example of this possibility can be seen from the provision of emergency powers in the Irish Constitution. Enacted in 1937, Ireland's Constitution provides for emergency powers as follows:

> Nothing in this Constitution other than Article 15.5.2° shall be invoked to invalidate any law enacted by the Oireachtas which is expressed to be for the purpose of securing the

[166] See *Minerva Mills* (n 120); O'Connell (n 107) 71.

public safety and the preservation of the State in time of war or armed rebellion, or to nullify any act done or purporting to be done in time of war or armed rebellion in pursuance of any such law.[167]

With the words 'Nothing in this Constitution', the Oireachtas—the Irish legislature—is almost given carte blanche not only to suspend basic fundamental rights but theoretically also to revise the operation of the separation of powers in Ireland, and in essence rewrite the Constitution, eg by enlarging the government and decreasing the powers of the president.[168] Since the Twenty-First Amendment of the Constitution Act 2001, however, the Oireachtas may not introduce the death penalty even during a state of emergency. To date, an emergency has been declared in Ireland twice. The first was declared on 2 September 1939 following the outbreak of World War II. This lasted until September 1976 with the government on numerous occasions refusing to lift the declaration for precautionary reasons.[169] On the day the emergency was lifted in September 1976, another emergency was immediately declared arising out of the escalation of hostilities in Northern Ireland. This was to last until February 1995, bringing the 56-year long emergency to an end. As the Irish Constitution entered into force in 1937, the state has therefore been in a de jure state of emergency for longer than it has been in a state of normalcy.

Despite a state of emergency existing in Ireland from 1939 to 1995, the impact of this entrenched emergency on the legal order was minimal. Once the Emergency Powers Act 1939—the principal legislation enacted in lieu of this declaration of emergency—was allowed to lapse on 2 September 1946, no legislation derived its validity from a declaration of a state of emergency, notwithstanding the repeated refusal by successive governments to repeal the state of emergency in subsequent decades.[170] The result was that even though the Oireachtas had the capacity to pass legislation that would be incompatible with the ordinary provisions of the Constitution, it did not do so. The resultant legal order during the state of emergency from 1946 to September 1976 was therefore identical to how the legal order would have existed were the state in a period of normalcy. The Constitution and

[167] Art 28.3.3° continues: 'In this sub-section "time of war" includes a time when there is taking place an armed conflict in which the State is not a participant but in respect of which each of the Houses of the Oireachtas shall have resolved that, arising out of such armed conflict, a national emergency exists affecting the vital interests of the State and "time of war or armed rebellion" includes such time after the termination of any war, or of any such armed conflict as aforesaid, or of an armed rebellion, as may elapse until each of the Houses of the Oireachtas shall have resolved that the national emergency occasioned by such war, armed conflict, or armed rebellion has ceased to exist.' For analysis of the drafting and amendment of Art 28.3.3°, see Alan Greene, 'The Historical Evolution of Article 28.3.3° of the Irish Constitution' (2012) 47 *Irish Jurist* 117.

[168] James Casey, *Constitutional Law in Ireland*, 3rd edn (Roundhall Sweet & Maxwell, 2000) 181; Alan Greene, 'Declaring a State of Emergency under Article 28.3.3° of the Irish Constitution: A Purely Political Question?' in Eoin Carolan (ed), *The Constitution of Ireland: Perspectives and Prospects* (Bloomsbury, 2012).

[169] Greene (n 167) 139–40.

[170] Greene (n 167) 140.

all the norms contained therein, therefore, were 'by and large effective' with every provision enforceable at all times. One could not say, therefore, during Ireland's perpetual emergency that certain constitutional norms were invalidated as they were rendered ineffective by the emergency. This is not to say, however, that the theoretical state of emergency posed no threat at all to the Irish constitutional order. Rather, the perpetuation of the state of emergency indicates the weakness of the quarantining effect of Article 28.3.3°, notwithstanding the comparatively narrow conditions of war, armed conflict or armed rebellion which the Irish Constitution states should exist for an emergency to be declared. There is no mention of natural disaster or other 'public emergencies threatening the life of the nation'. In the Irish context, scrutiny of the existence of a state of emergency by the political branches alone is a weak control on such emergency powers, potentially setting a precedent for a more malevolent government to take advantage of.

If Article 28.3.3° is interpreted so as to permit suspension of constitutional norms and to preclude judicial review of the decision to declare an emergency, then such an interpretation cannot be grounded in law to legitimise it. While initially this interpretation could be explained by the dynamic nature of legal systems—by conceptualising Article 28.3.3° as a norm-creating power conferred on the Oireachtas—if such emergency norms were created that rendered other constitutional norms ineffective for the duration of the emergency, this argument would lose its legitimacy if the emergency became permanent. This would result in the perpetual suspension of constitutional norms, rendering them perpetually ineffective and depriving them of their validity, amounting to a proxy-constitutional amendment. This is irreconcilable with a conception of the state as identical with the legal order. Such an interpretation, by attempting to argue that it was in conformance with the Constitution, would reduce the Irish Constitution to 'a blank cheque statute'. This is not just repugnant to even a formalist conception of the rule of law, it is antithetical to it. It is a claim, not for a power that is conferred on the Oireachtas by the Constitution but a claim for the power that conceived the Oireachtas in the first instance. It would permit the invalidation of constitutional norms by proxy and in a manner not foreseen by the constitutional drafters.

Consequently, this interpretation of Article 28.3.3° would, in actuality, be an affirmation of Carl Schmitt's concept of sovereignty, or a claim to the constituent power that founded the Constitution; a claim for a power that lies beyond the legal order exists beyond the state that has a 'tense and ambivalent relation' with the order that it founded.[171] It would therefore mean that the state is not identical to the legal order. This power, like Schmitt's sovereign, would then reveal itself in a time of emergency. Legality could only be clung on to by harkening back to the dynamic nature of Article 28.3.3°, emptying the discrete enumerated conditions of war, armed rebellion or armed conflict threatening the vital interests of the state of any real meaning. Consequently, conceptualising the powers conferred under

[171] Kalyvas (n 146) 227.

Article 28.3.3° as 'temporary' would be incorrect. Article 28.3.3°, therefore, can be conceptualised as a legal norm-creating power only if judicial review of the decision to declare a state of emergency is available. Only in this way can the requirement that an emergency be temporary be a legal one, and only if this raison d'être of Article 28.3.3° is put on a legal foothold can it prevent a commissarial dictatorship transforming in to a revolutionary, transformative sovereign dictatorship.

Conclusion

If an emergency is intended to restore normalcy once a particular severity threshold has been reached, as argued in chapter one, then emergency provisions only make sense in law if they are interpreted as permitting temporary derogations from constitutional norms. There must therefore be some mechanism of reviewing the decision to declare a state of emergency in order to ensure it fulfils its raison d'être. A legalistic argument attempting to preclude judicial review of the state of emergency must fail as it removes the requirement that a state of emergency be a temporary departure from the status quo. With this temporariness not grounded in law, constitutional emergency powers have the capacity to become permanent, thus rendering other constitutional norms ineffective and depriving them of their validity. This argument is, in essence, a claim for the constituent power that has constituted the constitutional order in the first instance. It is a reformulation of the 'Schmittian Challenge' to the idea that all state power can be circumscribed by law. For this reason, it must be rejected.

4

Permanent States of Emergency and Legal Black Holes

Introduction

Chapter three grappled with the 'Schmittian Challenge'—attempting to subsume all state power within a legal order without weakening the legal order to such an extent that it is incapable of controlling this state power as a result. This challenge is particularly acute during a state of emergency, or what Schmitt terms a 'state of exception'. To answer this, I argued that a permanent state of emergency has the potential to invalidate constitutional norms by depriving them of the necessary degree of efficacy required for validity. This potential means that an unfettered power to declare a state of emergency and assess its continued existence amounts to a claim for the constituent power that founds the constitution. To counter this, I argued that this decision must be a legal one and that Kelsen's Identity Thesis—that the state is identical to the legal order—is maintained. The only way this can be done is if this decision is amenable to judicial review.

This answer, however, raises further questions regarding the proper role and function of judicial review. Arguing for judicial review in the area of national security is to push the judicial branch into reviewing decisions where its legitimacy is at its weakest. Moreover, doing so by way of Kelsen's formalist account of the rule of law raises concerns as to the quality of such review, which can, in turn, have damaging consequences for a more substantive conception of the rule of law or other values such as human rights. The following two chapters will address these critiques. Firstly, in this chapter, I shall confront arguments that courts should play a minimal role in issues of contentious public policy and, particularly, regarding questions of national security. This will be done using an account of the rule of law that is broader than simple 'rule by law' but narrower than that used by many in the literature who seek to defend judicial review by fortifying the rule of law with substantive content such as human rights. This narrower conception is thus insulated from the critiques levied at these more substantive conceptions, for example, arguments that claim that human rights are merely political disputes, and consequently placing their resolution in the hands of the judiciary is anti-democratic or anti-republican. It will be demonstrated using this narrower conception of the rule of law that a permanent state of emergency does not merely give rise to the creation of a legal black hole; rather, it reveals a zone beyond law and, consequently, this scenario must be rejected by insisting that the question as to the existence of a state of emergency exist be a legal issue. I shall then address concerns in chapter five from the substantive rule of law perspective that overly deferential judicial review can add a veil of legitimacy to measures that damage human rights, thus doing more harm than had the judiciary admitted it cannot review the measure in the first instance. In so doing, the relation between judicial review and the rule of law will be examined and whether maintaining Kelsen's Identity Thesis can truly resist the Schmittian Challenge.

Legal Black Holes

Kelsen's Identity Thesis, explored in chapter three, is arguably the 'purest' manifestation of legal formalism and the attempt to constrain all state power within law. However, the extent to which Kelsen goes to in order to purify his theory of other sociological, political and moral factors raises fundamental questions as to what value, if any, there is to this formalist conception of the rule of law. As we saw in chapter three, one could contend that Kelsen's Identity Thesis could be viewed as conceptualising the rule of law as merely a mechanism through which all state power flows—essentially, rule *by* law.[1] Kelsen's idea of 'dynamic norms'—legal norms that stipulate how other legal norms are created—could potentially reduce the rule of law to simply that a statement by a body authorised to make law is law.[2] As Schmitt contended in his critique of Kelsen's legal positivism, in order to conceptualise the state as synonymous with the legal order and ensure all state power is exercised through law, Kelsen's theory is purified of normative values. It therefore says nothing about the substantive content of such norms and a morally repugnant legal norm would not be invalid if it can derive its validity from a higher norm, eg a dynamic norm permitting a decision-maker to create such a morally repugnant norm. As noted in chapter three, this makes Kelsen's theory vulnerable to validating and legitimising serious rights abuses.[3] To say therefore that such abuses are in conformity with the rule of law due to the dynamic nature of legal norms is a pyrrhic victory for the rule of law. This is the Schmittian challenge and one which he contends that Kelsen's pure theory of law is incapable of answering.

This pyrrhic victory, brought about by conceptualising the rule of law solely on the basis of legal authority to make a decision, can legitimise the creation of what are labelled legal black holes: zones formally created by law within which,

[1] See text to n 25 in ch 3 of this book.
[2] Hans Kelsen, *Pure Theory of Law* (University of California Press, 1967) ch 5, hereinafter *PTL*.
[3] See text to n 25 in ch 3.

no recourse to the law can be made.[4] A black hole is created when there is no legal control on the body exercising the conferred power in question, leaving the decision-maker free to exercise her absolute discretion. At best, under this conception of the rule of law, the only question the judiciary can ask is whether or not the legal black hole was correctly formed.[5] Legal black holes thus correlate closely with the classic ultra vires theory of judicial review: as long as the legal black hole was validly created, eg by the legislature, and the decision-maker stays within the limits of their discretion, there can be no review of the decision they reached.[6] When assessing whether a state of emergency was properly created, this narrow, 'rule by law' approach would suggest that one should only look at whether the decision-maker who made the declaration was the one formally identified as being empowered to do so rather than assessing or reviewing the conditions being used to justify the declaration of a state of emergency. Focus is thus on the assessor rather than on what they have assessed.

The term 'legal black hole' was first used by British Court of Appeal Judge Lord Phillips MR in *Abassi v Secretary of State for Foreign Affairs* to describe the legal situation of the appellant, a detainee in Guantanamo Bay.[7] Elaborating upon the use of this term, Judge Johan Steyn, writing extra-judicially on Guantanamo Bay, argued that the decision by the United States to detain individuals captured on the battlefield in Afghanistan in an offshore prison and strip them of their rights of due process amounted to placing these individuals in a legal black hole where they could not challenge the legality of their detention.[8] Key to this idea of a legal black hole therefore is the ousting of the federal courts' jurisdiction to review their detention. Instead, a military commission, lacking all the procedural safeguards of a habeas corpus petition, was initially proposed to review the detention of these so-called 'enemy combatants'. 'Enemy combatant' was itself a term formulated in an attempt to oust the applicability of the Geneva Conventions and international humanitarian law regarding the detention of prisoners of war. It had no basis in international law or domestic law, save as a brief descriptive term in the US Supreme Court judgment of *Ex parte Quirin*.[9] The US government thus sought to place the so-called enemy combatants in a legal limbo where neither international humanitarian law nor US domestic law—habeas corpus in particular—applied.

Much like the Roman dictator was appointed in order to circumvent the ancient right to appeal (*provocatio*) that demarcated the Roman citizen from other non-rights bearers, so too was the use of Guantanamo Bay an attempt to circumvent the

[4] Noa Ben-Asher, 'Legal Holes' (2009) 5 *Unbound* 1, 3–6.

[5] David Dyzenhaus, *The Constitution of Law: Legality in a Time of Emergency* (Cambridge University Press, 2006) 41–43.

[6] Mark Elliott, *Beatson, Matthews and Elliott's Administrative Law: Text and Materials*, 4th edn (Oxford University Press, 2011) 11–14.

[7] *Abassi v Secretary of State for Foreign Affairs* [2002] EWCA Civ 1598 [64] (Phillips MR).

[8] See Johan Steyn, 'Guantanamo Bay: The Legal Black Hole' (2004) 53 *ICLQ* 1.

[9] *Ex parte Quirin* (1942) 317 US 1, 31; David Luban, 'The War on Terrorism and the End of Human Rights' (2002) 22 *Philosophy and Public Policy Quarterly* 1, 11.

right to habeas corpus that individuals in the United States, regardless of citizenship, benefit from.[10] However, while the appointment of the dictator turned all of Rome into what Giorgio Agamben terms 'the camp', the legal black hole of Guantanamo Bay sought to draw clear geographical contours between the norm and the exception, exploiting the territorial reach of the US Constitution.[11] This was based on a 1959 US Supreme Court judgment in *Johnson v Eisentrager* in which Court held that non-US citizens held outside the United States had no constitutional or statutory habeas corpus entitlements.[12] By placing the individual beyond the geographical bounds of the US Constitution in Guantanamo Bay prison, they are stripped of their legal rights and reduced to *Homo sacer*—bare life.[13] Furthermore, the US also developed a complex network of state and non-state actors, and the express collaboration or acquiescence of other states in order to create a massive covert apparatus for the transfer of suspected enemy combatants to Guantanamo Bay and other so-called 'black sites'.[14]

Legal black holes are thus inherently linked to so-called ouster clauses—statutory provisions that expressly attempt to exclude judicial review of executive or administrative decisions. Legal black holes may also be created impliedly, with Adrian Vermeule arguing that administrative law in the United States is, in fact, replete with legal black holes that are the product of judicial interpretation.[15] Writing extra-judicially in 1985, US Supreme Court Judge Sandra Day O'Connor reasoned that US judges were more willing to accept ouster clauses than their British colleagues, suggesting that the presence of a constitutional clause protecting the courts' jurisdiction meant that the US Bench needed to be less wary of attempts to oust judicial review than the British judiciary which, prima facie at least, is at the mercy of parliamentary sovereignty.[16] Thus in the seminal case of *Anisminic Ltd v Foreign Compensation Commission*, the UK House of Lords found that despite the apparently clear wording of the statute indicating otherwise, judicial review had not been ousted from the decision of the Foreign Compensation Commission (FCC) regarding compensation for British property seized by the Egyptian government during the Suez crisis.[17] Section 4(4) of the Foreign Compensation Act 1950 stated that: 'The determination by the commission of any

[10] See text to n 38 in ch 1.

[11] Giorgio Agamben, *Homo Sacer: Sovereign Power and Bare Life* (Stanford University Press, 1998) 96.

[12] *Johnson v Eisentrager* (1950) 339 US 763.

[13] See text to n 56 in ch 5 regarding how the US Supreme Court confronted this issue with a view to closing the legal black hole.

[14] See 'Study of the CIA's Detention and Interrogation Program—Foreword, Findings, and Conclusions, and Executive Summary', S Rpt 113–288 (9 December 2014) < www.intelligence.senate.gov/publications/committee-study-central-intelligence-agencys-detention-and-interrogation-program> accessed 9 August 2017; Open Society Justice Initiative, *Globalizing Torture: CIA Detention and Extraordinary Rendition* (Open Society Foundations, 2013).

[15] See Adrian Vermeule, 'Our Schmittian Administrative Law' (2009) 122 *Harvard Law Review* 1095.

[16] Sandra Day O'Connor, 'Reflections on Preclusion of Judicial Review in England and the United States' (1985–86) 27 *William and Mary Law Review* 643, 645.

[17] *Anisminic Ltd v Foreign Compensation Commission* [1969] 2 AC 147.

application made to them under this Act shall not be called into question in any court of law.' This raised the question of whether the FCC was effectively empowered to err in law if it misinterpreted the eligibility of a claimant for compensation.

Notwithstanding the classic justification of judicial review in common law jurisdictions as merely ensuring decision-makers stay within the bounds of their discretion as laid down by the will of Parliament, the House of Lords nevertheless found that that the prima facie clear wording of section 4(4) did not preclude judicial review:

> If the draftsman or Parliament had intended to introduce a new kind of ouster clause so as to prevent any inquiry … I would have expected to find something much more specific than the bald statement that a determination shall' not be called in question in any court of law.[18]

Anisiminic therefore cannot be simply explained as the courts giving effect to parliamentary intention. Rather, the courts are giving effect to other constitutional principles when conducting judicial review. While not expressly stated in *Anismninic*, subsequent cases and the academic literature analysing *Anisminic* view the case as an example of the courts vindicating the constitutional principle of the rule of law. In so doing, a close nexus is revealed between the rule of law and the judicial function.[19]

Much like 'emergency', however, the rule of law is itself a contested concept that notoriously evades definition.[20] At its narrowest conception, a formalistic understanding of the rule of law states that so long as correct procedures are followed in making law, then this is good law, regardless of the substantive content of the law in question. Hence, Joseph Raz's influential account of the rule of law starts with FA Hayek's explanation as:

> Stripped of all technicalities [the rule of law] means that government in all its actions is bound by rules fixed and announced beforehand—rules which make it possible to foresee with fair certainty how the authority will use its coercive powers in given circumstances and to plan one's individual affairs on the basis of this knowledge.[21]

From this, Hayek declares that the rule of law embraces concepts of equality, certainty and generality. Raz's conception of the rule of law derives from this core requirement that law must be capable of guiding the behaviour of its subjects.[22] In order to enable law to fulfil this function, Raz's formalist account of the rule of law protects the role of courts in interpreting and applying rules. Furthermore, the judicial branch should be independent and hold open hearings free of bias in

[18] ibid.

[19] See *Evans v Attorney General* [2015] UKSC 21 [54] (Neuberger L).

[20] Jeremy Waldron, 'Is the Rule of Law an Essentially Contested Concept (in Florida)' (2002) 21 *Law and Philosophy* 138, 138–140.

[21] Friedrich August Hayek, *The Road To Serfdom* (Routledge, 1944) 75–76; Joseph Raz, *The Authority of Law*, 2nd edn (Oxford University Press, 2009) 210.

[22] Raz, ibid, 214; Brian Tamanaha, *On the Rule of Law: History, Politics, Theory* (Cambridge University Press, 2007) 93.

order to maximise its rule-applying function and mitigate alternative motives for deciding a case in a particular way. Raz also contends that the discretion of law enforcement agencies possess should not undermine the purposes of the relevant legal rules that confer this discretion in the first instance.[23]

At a minimum, therefore, the rule of law requires the principle of legality: that law should be ex ante promulgated in a clear manner, so that individuals may be certain that their conduct is in conformity with it.[24] Clarity and certainty also appear in Lon Fuller's and AV Dicey's formulation of the rule of law,[25] and indeed in Carl Schmitt's conception of law.[26] As noted in Chapter 3, Schmitt's argument that states of exception cannot be circumscribed by law due to the inability of law to prescribe ex ante the possible conditions that may warrant the ushering in of a state of exception is a testament to this.[27] Clarity and certainty also have a degree of normative value to them, even if the law that they refer to is one that would be abhorrent to most standards of morality or judicial cultures today.[28] Raz thus views the value of the rule of law like the quality of a knife:

> A good knife is, among other things, a sharp knife. Similarly, conformity to the rule of law is an inherent value of laws, indeed it is their most important inherent value. … A knife is not a knife unless it has some ability to cut. The law to be law must be capable of guiding behaviour, however inefficiently.[29]

Under this formalist conception, the rule of law therefore possesses a negative value, acting to reduce the damage to clarity and certainty that can flow from unbridled discretion. Much like a knife, however, the means to which the rule of law can be deployed can vary from good to evil. Consequently, it is the other values found in the common law that ensure that Dicey's conception of the rule of law and that espoused by the House of Lords in *Anisminic* is one that is deployed for 'good' rather than 'evil'. *Anisminic* resulted in much soul-searching as to the constitutional justification of judicial review in the UK, a debate that continues to this day and one which Mark Elliott contends has never been sufficiently articulated.[30] This debate reveals insights into the separation of powers, constitutionalism, democracy and the rule of law that are relevant, not just to the British

[23] Raz (n 21) 218.

[24] Lon Fuller, *The Morality of Law* (Yale University Press, 1969) 74.

[25] AV Dicey, *Introduction to the Study of the Law of the Constitution*, 6th edn (Macmillan, 1902) 183–84.

[26] See Carl Schmitt, *Political Theology: Four Chapters on the Concept of Sovereignty*, trans George Schwab (University of Chicago Press, 2005); John P McCormick, 'The Dilemmas of Dictatorship: Carl Schmitt and Constitutional Emergency Powers' (1997) 10 *Canadian Journal of Law and Jurisprudence* 163, 169.

[27] See text to n 85 in ch 3.

[28] Thus the Code of Hammurabi reflected at a minimum level of a formal concept of the rule of law. By prescribing an 'eye for an eye' the punishment is known before an individual conducts their affairs. See R Pound, 'The End of Law as Developed in Legal Rules and Doctrines' (1914) 27 *Harvard Law Review* 195, 199.

[29] Raz (n 21) 226.

[30] See Mark Elliott, *The Constitutional Foundations of Judicial Review* (Hart Publishing, 2001).

constitutional order but to all constitutions seeking to strive for these values, and, particularly, in extreme conditions when these values are put under stress. In turn, this debate reveals the consequences of ousting judicial review and the creation of a legal black hole in the particular context of the suspension of constitutional norms.

National Security and Judicial Review

The classic justification of judicial review of executive power is that government must never act without legal authority.[31] This is perfectly in line with Kelsen's Identity Thesis. This core requirement of a formalist conception of the rule of law is manifested in the concept of jurisdiction: that a decision-maker only acts lawfully so long as he does not transgress the limits of his power. If the decision-maker steps beyond these limits he has acted ultra vires and his decision is void ab initio. Courts identify the limits of a decision-maker's power by interpreting the express and implied terms of the legislation and also principles such as natural justice and reasonableness.[32] Similar principles are also vindicated through judicial review in civil legal systems.[33] The assessment of an issue that acts as a limit on the power of a decision-maker, if it truly is to be a limit on their power, cannot be exclusively assessed by the decision-maker alone and, consequently, it is amenable to judicial review. The limits of these powers may be vague, however, and judicial interpretation is inevitable. Consequently, the legitimacy of the judiciary in determining these limits is further clarified and justified as merely the court's application of legislative intention and keeping the decision-maker empowered by the legislature within the parameters of their powers. The self-justification of the ultra vires doctrine therefore is that its application, and, in turn, judicial review, 'consists of nothing other than an application of the law itself and the law of Parliament to boot'.[34] For courts to allow decision-makers to act beyond these limits would be to circumvent the legislature's will. In this manner, the judiciary's democratic deficit is tempered by the contention that it is merely implementing the democratic will of the legislature.[35]

[31] ibid, ch 1.

[32] *Council of Civil Service Unions v Minister for the Civil Service* [1985] AC 374.

[33] Thus, US Supreme Court Justice Felix Frankfurter suggested that AV Dicey's later work admitted that an administrative state similar to the French *le droit administratif* was evolving in the UK. See Felix Frankfurter, 'The Task of Administrative Law' (1927) 75 *University of Pennsylvania Law Review and American Law Register* 614, 615.

[34] Lawrence Baxter, *Administrative Law* (Juta, 1984) 303.

[35] See Eric A Posner and Adrian Vermeule, *Terror in the Balance: Security, Liberty and the Courts* (Oxford University Press, 2007); Bruce Ackerman, 'The Emergency Constitution' (2004) 113 *Yale Law Journal* 1029; Fiona de Londras and Fergal Davis, 'Controlling the Executive in Times of Terrorism: Competing Perspectives on Effective Oversight Mechanisms' (2010) 30 *OJLS* 19, 24–33 (per Davis).

Somewhat paradoxically, however, the lack of democratic legitimacy of the judiciary is itself integral to its proper functioning in a constitutional order. The judiciary has famously been described as the 'least dangerous branch'.[36] As it holds neither purse nor sword, the propensity for the corruption of power should be much less in the judicial branch than in the legislature or executive.[37] Relatedly, it can be said that on the whole, the judiciary is the branch of government most removed from the others.[38] Its role—to interpret rather than make law, make findings of fact against individuals and ensure fair trials—requires a level of independence and isolation from political forces.[39] The judiciary, in comparison to the other branches of government, ought to be more resistant to politicisation and influence by measures such as remuneration protection, security of tenure and appointment rather than election.[40] The judiciary can also be described as a counter-majoritarian force, checking the power of the democratically elected branches of government.[41] Whilst this is axiomatically anti-democratic, it nevertheless forms an important part of an understanding of democracy conceptualised as not simply a process for making decisions, but a broader view of democracy founded on the principles of majority rule but with respect for human rights and the rule of law, ie a constitutionalist conception of democracy. It is for this reason that the judiciary is generally entrusted to enforce legal human rights obligations.[42] Moreover, it is for these reasons that the safeguards in place to ensure the independence of the judiciary often come under strain in a state of emergency that was declared under questionable circumstances. Relatedly, many serious abuses of human rights and emergency powers occur in constitutional jurisdictions where the independence of the judiciary is not wholly secure.[43]

However, these very institutional aspects of the judicial branch that situate it above the slings and arrows of politics also place it above mechanisms of

[36] See Alexander Bickel, *The Least Dangerous Branch: The Supreme Court at the Bar of Politics*, 2nd edn (Yale University Press, 1986).

[37] Alexander Hamilton, 'Federalist No 78' in Clinton Rossiter (ed), *The Federalist Papers* (New American Library, 1961) 463–71.

[38] ibid; Charles Montesquieu, *The Spirit of Laws*, trans Thomas Nugent (Continental Press, 1949) 173–75.

[39] See Paul J DeMuniz, 'Politicising State Judicial Elections: A Threat to Judicial Independence' (2002) 38 *Willamette Law Review* 367, 367–70.

[40] Raz thus stresses the importance of judicial independence for vindicating the rule of law. Raz (n 21) 216–17. Many US states do elect their judiciary; however, at the federal level they are appointed. An elected judiciary may, according to Jonathan Simon result in decisions taken by judges being skewed in favour of a populist outcome. This is especially pronounced in criminal justice matters. See Jonathan Simon, *Governing through Crime* (Oxford University Press, 2007) 130; DeMuniz, ibid.

[41] Bickel (n 36) ch 1.

[42] That stated, the judiciary does not have a monopoly on this role. See text to n 15 in ch 7 of this book for a discussion of what David Dyzenhaus terms a culture of control. Moreover, dialogic models of rights review seek a more collaborative relationship between the judiciary and other branches of government. See Stephen Gardbaum, *The New Commonwealth Model of Constitutionalism* (Cambridge University Press, 2012).

[43] See text from nn 56–59 in ch 7 for a discussion of how the independence of the judiciary in Turkey came under pressure following the declaration of a state of emergency in July 2016.

democratic accountability. In turn, many of the processes put in place to ensure that the judiciary makes *good* decisions are potentially counterproductive in a time of emergency. We saw in Chapter 1 that consolidation of powers in one branch of government in order to expedite decision-making was symptomatic of an emergency response.[44] While this consolidation occurred in the extraordinary constitutional officer of the dictator in the Roman Republic, today it is the executive, rather than the legislature or judiciary, that is considered best placed to act in a state of emergency. The executive is the branch of government most capable of acting quickly and decisively given the general consensus that exists in cabinet or the absence of formal procedures that may slow down such decision-making.[45] Relatedly, the executive is afforded a level of secrecy, making it a more suitable forum in which sensitive material pertaining to national security can be discussed.[46] In contrast, a slow legislative procedure is often seen as dangerous, hampering the swift and decisive response that is represented as necessary to dispose of the threat.[47] That stated, many constitutions do vest the power to declare a state of emergency in the legislature, although this is often accompanied by a clause allowing the executive to declare a state of emergency in the event that the legislature cannot meet sufficiently swiftly.[48] Moreover, in Westminster-style parliamentary democracies, the executive invariably dominates the legislature, thus making the separation between the two notional, particularly in a state of emergency.[49]

The branch of government considered to be least suited to determine issues of national security is the judiciary. In general, courts make decisions at a pedestrian pace, in an open public forum—institutional features that, while valuable in most contexts for securing justice and the rule of law, are inapposite for national security issues.[50] Judith N Shklar argues that Aristotle saw the rule of law as 'the law of reason': that judges must reason syllogistically in order to make fair decisions and to do so must avoid passion or emotion that may distort their logic.[51] The rule of law, therefore, for Aristotle was about mediation. It was a 'powerful psychology'; a way of life. Providing justifications for such decisions helps to show the syllogism that they used. Consequently, the method by which judges make decisions is necessarily dependent upon the existence of legal norms and the justification of their

[44] See text to n 163 in ch 1 of this book.

[45] Posner and Vermeule (n 35) 3; de Londras and Davis (n 35) 27.

[46] De Londras and Davis (n 35) 27.

[47] Commentators such as Ackerman do envisage a role for the legislature in determining the existence of an emergency; however, these models often leave it to the executive to make the initial declaration, which is subsequently scrutinised by the legislature. Bruce Ackerman, *Before the Next Attack: Preserving Civil Liberties in an Age of Terrorism* (Yale University Press, 2006) ch 4 See also text from nn 36–39 in ch 7 of this book for a further analysis of Ackerman's super-majoritarian escalator.

[48] See, for example, Art 77 Constitution of Italy.

[49] De Londras and Davis (n 35) 36 (per de Londras).

[50] ibid, 20–24; Posner and Vermeule (n 35) ch 5.

[51] Judith N Shklar, *Political Thought and Political Thinkers*, ed Stanley Hoffmann (University of Chicago Press, 1998) 23–24.

decisions. It also depends on the requirement that there is sufficient time in order to enable a court to reason syllogistically; time that is, axiomatically, unavailable at the onset of an emergency.

In contrast, there is no guarantee that political branches will reach their decisions syllogistically or enunciate reasons for their decisions. Aristotle stressed that judges be insulated from emotive or heated arguments in order to help them reason syllogistically.[52] In contrast, political branches are polemic and emotive. Decisions may be reached, not by analysing all facts and arguments and using reason, but for the advancement of vested interests and through the application of a parliamentary whipping system. Thus, we saw in chapter two that emergencies are not purely objective conditions but that subjective assessments come into play that the executive is capable of exploiting. To argue for judicial review of the decision to declare a state of emergency is to thrust the judiciary into the arena of national security where democratic accountability is considered paramount. In emergencies, therefore, 'the judiciary is at sea'.[53]

This unsuitability of the judiciary in matters of national security is illustrated in the jurisprudence of the upper echelons of the UK courts. In the infamous *Liversidge v Anderson* judgment, the majority of the UK House of Lords refused to review the power of the Home Secretary to intern individuals without trial if he had 'reasonable cause' to believe they had 'hostile associations'.[54] 'Reasonable cause', despite the ostensibly objective implication of the word 'reasonable', was interpreted as being a subjective test and therefore the courts could not review the Home Secretary's decision. Quoting with approval the judgment of Lord Parker in *The Zamora (1)* case,[55] Lord Macmillan held that:

> Those who are responsible for the national security must be the sole judges of what the national security requires. It would be obviously undesirable that such matters should be made the subject of evidence in a court of law or otherwise discussed in public.[56]

A similar conclusion was reached *CCSU v Minister for Civil Service* (the *GCHQ* case), where Lord Diplock stated that:

> National security is the responsibility of the executive government; what action is needed to protect its interests is, as the cases … establish and common sense itself dictates, a matter upon which those upon whom the responsibility rests, and not the courts of justice, must have the last word. It is par excellence a non-justiciable question. The judicial process is totally inept to deal with the sort of problems which it involves.[57]

These judgments encapsulate the familiar mantra that as the judiciary suffers from a democratic deficit, it should not be involved in issues pertaining to national

[52] ibid.

[53] Posner and Vermeule (n 35) 18.

[54] *Liversidge v Anderson* [1942] AC 206. As conferred by regulation 18B of Defence (General) Regulations 1939.

[55] *The Zamora (1)* [1916] 2 AC 77, 107.

[56] ibid, 253.

[57] *Council of Civil Service Unions v Minister for the Civil Service* (n 32) hereinafter the *GCHQ* case.

security. In light of this, Lord Justice Brown, commenting extra-judicially, noted that the very words 'national security' have acquired over the years an almost mystical significance.[58] The mere incantation of the phrase instantly discourages the court from satisfactorily fulfilling its normal role of deciding where the balance of public interest lies.[59] *Liversidge* therefore amounts to the creation of a legal black hole where no judicial review of the decision to detain an individual under section 18B of the Defence (General) Regulations 1939 was available. This creation, however, was not the express product of Parliament but rather the result of judicial interpretation.

The key distinction therefore between the judicial abdication seen in *Liversidge* and judicial fortitude in *Anisminic* is, undoubtedly, the subject matter in question: national security. This propensity of the judiciary to capitulate to claims of national security has led David Dyzenhaus to argue that in such instances it would be better for the judiciary to admit that they cannot hold the executive to account rather than engage in an incredibly deferential exercise that couches the executive's decision in the veil of the rule of law.[60] Thus, even when judges have the legal authority to review an exercise of executive power, they have done so in such a way as merely to 'rubber-stamp' the decision of the executive.

We have also seen that *Anisminc* further illustrates that reliance upon legislative intention can only take courts so far when justifying judicial review, even in common law systems where parliamentary sovereignty stands as the apex norm of the constitutional order. This is particularly the case in states of emergency where statutory provisions are drafted in broad terms permitting expansive discretion and facilitate flexible decision-making. In such cases, the resources that judges can draw upon to identify the limits of a decision-maker's powers are sparse. Giving effect to legislative intention also fails to justify judicial review of inherent executive power or prerogative powers that do not derive from legislation, as in such instances there is no legislative intention to be determined. Instead, subjecting prerogative powers or inherent executive power to judicial review is wholly seen as a fundamental component of the rule of law.[61] In turn, as courts become increasingly more willing to utilise concepts such as fair procedures and rationality to check decision-makers' powers, the link between these principles and legislative intention becomes increasingly more remote. The classic ultra vires justification of judicial review has therefore been modified to an extent to incorporate this reality. In the UK, Mark Elliott argues that courts, when interpreting statutes, are considered to be 'constitutionally entitled to assume that it was Parliament's intention to legislate in conformity with the rule of law'.[62] Moreover, the judiciary will

[58] Brown LJ 'Public Interest Immunity' [1994] Public Law 579, 589.

[59] ibid.

[60] Dyzenhaus (n 5) 49. See text from nn 1–17 in ch 5 of this book for a more thorough exploration of this argument.

[61] Thus, in the *Case of Proclamations* (1611) 2 Co Rep 74, 76, Edward Coke famously stated that: '[T]he King hath no prerogative, but that which the law of the land allows him.'

[62] Elliott (n 30) 109.

insist on a clear statement from Parliament that it intended to legislate contra the rule of law before it interprets a statutory provision giving effect to such a consequence.[63] Judicial review of statutorily conferred powers therefore acts not only as a checking power on the decision-maker to whom power has been conferred, upon but also upon Parliament's capacity to create and confer such powers in the first instance. It is this tension between the courts and the legislature, rather than between the courts and the executive, that is the most contentious in constitutional orders today.

From Administrative Review to Constitutional Review

The role of courts in reviewing administrative or governmental decisions is difficult to untangle from its role in reviewing legislation. Paul Daly attempts to maintain a distinction between administrative review and constitutional review by stressing that the latter focuses on decisions that affect fundamental rights.[64] Administrative review refers to a situation whereby the legislature has taken a decision to confer decision-making authority on a body other than a court; in contrast, in constitutional review, the protection of fundamental rights has been delegated to the courts themselves. As a result of this latter question, Daly argues that it does not matter how much power has been delegated to the initial decision-maker as the court must vindicate its constitutional duty to interpret and vindicate these fundamental constitutional rights.[65] Consequently, the standard of review exercised will be much more rigorous than in the context of administrative review where courts must respect the authority conferred on the initial decision-maker. Daly's primary motivation in maintaining the distinction between administrative and constitutional review, therefore, is due to his concern that abandoning the distinction would 'jeopardise the protection of fundamental rights'.[66] However, he does also caution about overstating this argument.[67] Ultimately, the distinction rests on the fact that one is the result of judicial interpretation of constitutional provisions; the other is the result of judicial interpretation of various statutory provisions. However, the interpretation of the latter invariably raises questions of the former, even in constitutional orders affirming parliamentary sovereignty as demonstrated by *Anisminic* and more recently in *Evans v AG*.[68] The distinction between administrative and constitutional review therefore becomes difficult to maintain, and consequently it has been argued by Dyzenhaus, Hunt and Taggart

[63] See *Evans v Attorney General* [2015] UKSC 21.

[64] Paul Daly, *A Theory of Deference in Administrative Law: Basis, Application and Scope* (Cambridge University Press, 2012) 187.

[65] ibid, 189.

[66] ibid, 194.

[67] ibid.

[68] *Evans* (n 63).

that it should be abandoned.[69] At the very least, however, the distinction between the two should not be overstated.[70]

The Constitutional Validity of Legislation

By interpreting a statute creatively, even in a manner contra the very will of the legislature, courts can still potentially claim that they are ensuring the decision-maker stays within the bounds of discretion that the statute permits. Thus, constitutional review can be presented as administrative review. Such creative and flexible interpretation can only be stretched so far until it snaps, however, and the issue may not merely require the reinterpretation of a statute, but rather a finding from a court that the statute is itself so flawed that it is rendered void. Most common law jurisdictions avoid this by affirming the sovereignty of parliament and denying the judiciary the capacity to strike down legislation. This is justified once again on the grounds of the superior democratic legitimacy of the legislature.[71] Despite these concerns, which are shared across many states, numerous constitutions have, nevertheless, taken the opposite approach, clearly enumerating the power of the judiciary to strike down legislation as unconstitutional.[72] However, simply to leave the constitutional justification for judicial review of legislation at whether or not the constitution stipulates it would necessarily imply that a constitution's express silence on this issue infers that the judiciary lacks such power. As well as being factually incorrect, this would also be to ignore the normative factors justifying judicial authority to strike down legislation.

The US Constitution, for example, is silent as to the capacity of judicial review of legislation; nevertheless, in the famous case of *Marbury v Madison*, the US Supreme Court found that it had such power:

> The powers of the Legislature are defined and limited; and that those limits may not be mistaken or forgotten, the Constitution is written. To what purpose are powers limited, and to what purpose is that limitation committed to writing, if these limits may at any time be passed by those intended to be restrained? The distinction between a government with limited and unlimited powers is abolished if those limits do not confine the persons on whom they are imposed, and if acts prohibited and acts allowed are of equal obligation. It is a proposition too plain to be contested that the Constitution controls any legislative act repugnant to it, or that the Legislature may alter the Constitution by an ordinary act.[73]

[69] See David Dyzenhaus, Murray Hunt and Michael Taggart, 'The Principle of Legality in Administrative Law: Internationalisation and Constitutionalisation' (2001) 1 *Oxford University Commonwealth Law Journal* 5.

[70] Daly (n 64) 194.

[71] Moreover, as we shall see in ch 6 when discussing alternatives to constitutional models of emergency accommodation, the evolution of common law constitutionalism may be heading in the direction of the judiciary having to such strike down powers. See text to n 107 in ch 6.

[72] See, for example, Art 34.3.2° Constitution of Ireland.

[73] *Marbury v Madison* (1803) 5 US 137, 176–77.

As a result, the Court found that an act of the legislature which is repugnant to the constitution is void and the courts must refuse to give it effect.[74] *Marbury* therefore scales up the ultra vires doctrine of judicial review from executive or administrative authority to legislative competence. Similar to the justification of judicial review of executive or administrative decisions, this judicial strike down of legislation is justified on the grounds of ensuring that the legislature's discretion conferred on it by the constitution does not exceed these constitutional bounds. The legislative power is conceptualised as a limited power whose contours are set down by the constitution and it can only be limited if its pronouncements in the form of legislation are reviewable. *Marbury* thus affirms the argument discussed in Chapter 3 that for a constitution to be superior to legislation, legislation incompatible with the constitution should be invalid.[75] The legislative power is therefore a limited, constituted power established as such by the exercise of constituent power in creating the constitutional order. The resultant shift towards 'constitutionalism' post-*Marbury v Madison* has been described by Mark Tushnet as requiring

> that a nation be committed to the proposition that a nation's people should determine the policies under which they will live, by some form of democratic governance. Yet constitutionalism also requires that there be some limits on the policy choices that people can make democratically.[76]

In the context of emergencies and national security, Davis and de Londras argue that this question is now one of whether 'constitutionalist limitations are desirable in a situation of exigency such as a terrorist threat and if so, who ought to determine where those limitations lie'.[77]

This question of 'who decides' is particularly contentious as the unconstitutionality of a piece of legislation is rarely straightforward or universally agreed upon. Raz's formalist account of the rule of law, discussed above, requires formal statements to be backed up by more general principles and it is in this more nebulous manner that constitutions are drafted.[78] Consequently, it is regarding the dispute over these more general principles on which much of the debate as to the legitimacy of judicial review of legislation centres. In *Marbury*, the reason given by Marshall CJ that it should be the judiciary to decide is that: 'It is emphatically the province and duty of the Judicial Department to say what the law is.'[79] Alexander Bickel argues, however, that *Marbury* side-steps the question of why it should be the judiciary, rather than another branch of government, that determines whether the legislature acted unconstitutionally.[80] According to this argument,

[74] ibid.

[75] See text to n 90 in chapter 3.

[76] Mark Tushnet, *Weak Courts, Strong Rights: Judicial Review and Social Welfare Rights in Comparative Constitutional Law* (Princeton University Press, 2008) 19.

[77] Fergal F Davis and Fiona de Londras, 'Introduction' in Fergal F Davis and Fiona de Londras (eds), 'Critical Debates on Counter-Terrorism Judicial Review (Cambridge University Press, 2014) 15.

[78] Raz (n 21).

[79] *Marbury* (n 73) 177.

[80] Bickel (n 36) 3–14.

the judiciary is not the only branch of government that must interpret the often inherently vague constitutional norms, raising the question of whether its interpretation should prevail. The legislature, too, for example, must also interpret the constitution when drafting legislation to determine what is or is not permissible. It follows that if the legislature has already carried out an interpretive exercise, why should the unelected judiciary trump the elected legislature?

Political Questions and Judicial Review

This difficulty is further compounded when the constitution itself expressly confers the decision-making power on a specific body other than on the judiciary. Reviewing such decisions which were expressly conferred on another branch of government by the constitution raises concerns as to whether the court has overstepped its own constitutional parameters. The 'political questions doctrine', as it is known in the US, or the concept of justiciability in the UK, is, according to BV Harris, recognition of the fact that the capabilities of the courts may be limited, and that there are certain questions upon which they cannot adjudicate.[81] While the usefulness of this doctrine has been questioned by commentators such as TRS Allan, who side-step this problem by arguing that the issue instead can be framed in terms of whether the petitioner has established enforceable rights,[82] or Chris Finn, who prefers that the test be one of whether the petitioner has established grounds for review,[83] the concept of justiciability provides a 'big picture' or hyperopic constitutional lens through which one can view whether a question is appropriate for the courts.[84]

In the UK, Harris identifies two different categories of decisions regarding justiciability: primary justiciability and secondary justiciability.[85] Harris considers primary justiciability to be those decisions that, of their nature, are not amenable to judicial review; or what Paul Daly labels as the category of decision.[86] Thus in *GCHQ*, Lord Roskill stated that:

> Prerogative powers such as those relating to the making of treaties, the defence of the realm, the prerogative of mercy, the grant of honours, the dissolution of Parliament and the appointment of ministers as well as others are not, I think susceptible to judicial review because their nature and subject matter are such as not to be amenable to the judicial process.[87]

[81] BV Harris, 'Judicial Review, Justiciability and the Prerogative of Mercy' (2003) 62 *CLJ* 631, 631.
[82] ibid 632; TRS Allan, *Law Liberty and Justice* (Oxford University Press, 1993) ch 9.
[83] Harris, ibid; Chris Finn, 'The Justiciability of Administrative Decisions: A Redundant Concept?' (2002) 30 *Federal Law Review* 239. 246.
[84] Harris, ibid, 633.
[85] ibid, 644–46.
[86] Daly (n 65) 269
[87] *GCHQ* (n 32) 418 (Roskill L).

In contrast, Harris labels as 'secondary justiciability' issues those decisions that prima facie may be subject to judicial review but that the decision taken may only be overturned if the body taking the decision acts in 'clear disregard' of the constitution. Secondary justiciability may therefore be seen in terms of judicial deference to the body making the decision and thus is still in line with the separation-of-powers doctrine, according respect to the decision of the legislature or executive, notwithstanding the court's assertion that it may review the decision in question.

The key precedent in identification of a 'political question' in the US is the judgment of Justice Brennan in *Baker v Carr*:

> Prominent on the surface of any case held to involve a political question is found a textually demonstrable constitutional commitment of the issue to a coordinate political department; or a lack of judicially discoverable and manageable standards for resolving it; or the impossibility of deciding without an initial policy determination of a kind clearly for non-judicial discretion; or the impossibility of a court's undertaking independent resolution without expressing lack of the respect due coordinate branches of government; or an unusual need for unquestioning adherence to a political decision already made; or the potentiality of embarrassment from multifarious pronouncements by various departments on one question.[88]

Originally, the political questions doctrine was based primarily on the first element of Justice Brennan's test—a textually demonstrable constitutional commitment of the issue to a coordinate political department.[89] Thus, the political questions doctrine dealt with the textual interpretation of the Constitution and an assessment of whom the US Constitution entrusted to make the decision in question. This could potentially remove the question from judicial scrutiny and, in essence, create a legal black hole within which the decision-maker was free to exercise their discretion. Over time, however, as evidenced by the remainder of Justice Brennan's test, the political questions doctrine was expanded to take more prudential matters into account, with the US Supreme Court focusing more on which body is 'best placed' to make such a decision.[90] Rachel Barkow argues that this new focus on prudential matters has ultimately led to the decline of the political questions doctrine.[91] As the political questions doctrine became less and less grounded in the technical language of the US Constitution and more distracted instead by efficacy issues, the Supreme Court was able to expand its jurisdiction to essentially cover almost any question that would arise before it. Rather than state that a certain subject matter was a priori beyond the jurisdiction of the Court, the Supreme Court would instead adopt the position that it does have the jurisdiction to review such a decision. However, in some cases it then defers to the political

[88] *Baker v Carr* (1962) 369 US 186, 217.

[89] ibid. See also Rachel Barkow, 'The Rise and Fall of the Political Question Doctrine' in Nada Mourtada-Sabbah and Bruce E Cain (eds), *The Political Question Doctrine and the Supreme Court of the United States* (Lexington Books 2007) 23, 23–33.

[90] Barkow, ibid, 34–35.

[91] ibid.

branches and their decision. The US Supreme Court has subsumed the political questions doctrine into the concept of judicial deference and thus it stands at the extreme point on this spectrum of deference, rather than as a separate and distinct sphere of political decisions over which the Court has no power to inquire into. It follows that secondary justiciability rather than primary justiciability is the dominant model in the US. Indeed, it has been argued that there is now no such thing as the political questions doctrine.[92] Notwithstanding these criticisms, arguments that certain decisions are 'political' in nature and hence non-justiciable, particularly where there is a 'textually demonstrable commitment' that it is so, are still made and so the concept cannot be wholly dismissed, particularly in areas such as national security where the judiciary's legitimacy is weak.[93]

A similar approach to political questions can be seen in Canada where in *Re: Secession of Quebec*[94] the Canadian Supreme Court identified three distinct grounds upon which a court may refuse to answer a question on the basis that it is non-justiciable. (i) If to do so would take the court beyond its own assessment of its proper role in the constitutional framework of the democratic form of government. (ii) If the court would be unable to give an answer which lies within its own area of expertise, namely the interpretation of law. (iii) If, notwithstanding that the issue does not come within grounds (i) or (ii), the court decides to exercise its discretion to refuse to answer the question on a pragmatic basis. Like in the US, ground (i) is based primarily on textual indications, with grounds (ii) and (iii) reflecting more prudential concerns.

In Ireland, Daly argues that primary justiciability or purely political questions do not exist, with the exception of very discrete areas, namely review of the text of a bill to amend the Constitution or the convening of the Houses of the Oireachtas (the Irish bicameral legislature).[95] Such decisions are firmly established by clear constitutional provisions and so echo the US notion of the importance of a 'textually demonstrable commitment' when establishing a purely political question. Daly instead argues that secondary justiciability is the dominant model in Ireland. While the nature of the subject matter may not give rise to an issue of primary justiciability, it is nevertheless relevant when assessing to what degree of scrutiny a decision should be subject. Thus, depending on the matter in hand, the Court may apply a test of 'correctness' or exercise a greater level of deference and apply the lower standard of 'clear disregard' when reviewing the decision in question.[96]

[92] See generally, Louis Henkin, 'Is there a "Political Question" Doctrine?' (1976) 85 *Yale Law Journal* 597.

[93] See text to n 35 above.

[94] (1998) 161 DLR (4th) 385, 401–02.

[95] P Daly, '"Political Questions" and Judicial Review in Ireland' [2008] 2 *Judicial Studies Institute Journal* 116. See also the judgment of Keane CJ in *Maguire v Ardagh* [2002] 1 IR 385, 537 where he lists specific activities of the Oireachtas that are non-justiciable.

[96] Daly notes, however, the discrepancies in the application of this doctrine when assessing whether a 'clear disregard' or 'correctness' standard should be followed. Daly, ibid, 124–27.

The question which follows from these examples is that if there is a textually demonstrable commitment that the decision to declare and review the existence of a state of emergency is vested in a branch other than the judiciary, does this make the issue a 'purely political question'? Can this oust judicial review? Can the constitution itself create a legal black hole? Conversely, if judges appear to go against the express wording of the constitution and, indeed, legislation where the power under review is contained in statute, can the judiciary still claim to be vindicating the rule of law?

Sceptical Views of Judicial Review and the Rule of Law

Creative judicial interpretation can pose a major challenge to the constitutional justification of judicial review and the contention that courts vindicate the rule of law; rather, it potentially provides ammunition for schools of jurisprudence which contend that the judicial function is actually an exercise in political subjectivity.[97] Such 'rule scepticism' rejects the idea of legal disputes being settled by predetermined norms. Instead, decisions made by the judiciary are no less shaped by political discourse and policy decisions than the other branches of government.[98] It follows that judicial decision-making is itself based on discretion and, consequently, contra to conceptions of the law as clear, certain and autonomous in itself. These ideas have been particularly powerful in the UK where political constitutionalists such as JAG Griffith instead argue that the British Constitution *is* politics and judges are making political decisions.[99] For Griffith, society is fundamentally about conflict.[100] There is, therefore, no such thing as what Ronald Dworkin would term a community morality as the community fundamentally disagrees and conflicts on these very important issues.[101] The codification of such conflicts within 'woolly principles and even woollier exceptions' does not resolve them, but shifts debate from political branches that are democratically accountable, such as parliament, to less-accountable branches, such as the courts.[102] Accountability, therefore, should be maximised in a political constitution, or a 'republican constitution' with decision-makers working in such conflict-ridden areas held responsible for their decisions.[103] Griffith's aphoristic[104]

[97] MDA Freeman, *Lloyd's Introduction to Jurisprudence*, 7th edn (Thomson Sweet & Maxwell, 2007) 803–06.

[98] ibid.

[99] See JAG Griffith, 'The Political Constitution (1979) 42(1) *MLR* 1.

[100] ibid, 2.

[101] ibid, 2–6.

[102] ibid 14, 16.

[103] Graham Gee and Grégoire CN Webber, 'What Is a Political Constitution?' (2010) 30 *OJLS* 273, 282.

[104] Graham Gee, 'The Political Constitutionalism of JAG Griffith' (2008) 28 *LS* 20, 23.

response to theorists such as Dworkin who argue that judges search for 'one right answer' and find this answer based in 'community morality' is that such 'community morality' is 'nonsense at the very top of a very high ladder'.[105] With politics and law essentially reduced down to conflicts and disputes, Griffith famously contended that 'law is politics carried on by other means'.[106] Although this statement has been softened to an extent by some later political constitutionalists, the arguments of Griffith and other political constitutionalists pose a robust challenge to judicial review, the rule of law and the conclusion that there is a positive relation between the two.[107]

The key challenge therefore that this raises is the fact that many of the norms that may be suspended during a state of emergency are inherently vague, even in times of normalcy. Thus, HLA Hart argues that in penumbra cases of judicial interpretation, there will often be no 'right answer' which the judge can find, and instead said judge must make a choice on how to interpret the rule in question.[108] Hart considers such a choice to be essentially political. The major challenge that Hart inadvertently poses to the rule of law is that such a choice of rules is then applied to the facts of a case in a retrospective manner. A case is therefore decided not by clearly prescribed rules beforehand, but by an ex post facto formulated rule. Consequently, Jeremy Waldron argues that when there is disagreement as to the scope of a norm, the resolution of this should be left to the branch of government whose entire raison d'être is to deal with disagreement: the legislature.[109]

Defences of judicial review must therefore confront this counter-majoritarian difficulty. This challenge is particularly acute in areas such as national security where democratic legitimacy and accountability for decisions is considered paramount. John Hart Ely, for example, attempted to resolve this tension between democracy and judicial review by advocating a justification of judicial review that enhanced democratic participation and accountability.[110] Ely's answer, however, was difficult to maintain as Ronald Dworkin demonstrated that his distinction between procedural and substantive norms collapsed under scrutiny.[111] Dworkin's own justification of judicial review draws a distinction between policy and principle, arguing for robust judicial scrutiny of questions of the latter, and embracing this counter-majoritarian dimension of the judiciary, lauding judicial review as a bulwark against the tyranny of the majority, protecting a vulnerable minority. Dworkin's—and, indeed, his ideal judge Hercules'—conception of democracy is thus much

[105] Griffith (n 99) 11.

[106] JAG Griffith, 'The Common Law and the Political Constitution' (2001) 117 *LQR* 42, 64.

[107] See, for example, Adam Tomkins, 'In Defence of the Political Constitution' (2002) 22 *OJLS* 157, 169.

[108] Hart describes the 'open texture of law as leaving 'a vast field for a creative activity which some call legislative': HLA Hart, *The Concept of Law*, 2nd edn (Oxford University Press, 1994) 204–05.

[109] Jeremy Waldron, *Law and Disagreement* (Oxford University Press, 1999) 23–24.

[110] See John Hart Ely, *Democracy and Distrust: A Theory of Judicial Review* (Harvard University Press, 1980).

[111] Ronald Dworkin, 'The Forum of Principle' (1981) 56 *New York University Law Review* 469, 516.

more substantive than simply majority rule.[112] This counter-majoritarian dimension is, nevertheless, particularly important in issues of national security when the vulnerability of minority groups may be heightened. Dworkin takes particular issue with HLA Hart's conception of a legal order as merely consisting of a hierarchy of rules.[113] Hart's conception of the penumbra surrounding a rule is tempered by the fact that he considers it only to be in exceptional cases and, by and large, the core of settled law is large enough that the legitimacy of the legal order is not challenged by the penumbra.[114] Dworkin, contests this, arguing that what is considered the 'core' is itself a product of interpretation. Every time a judge makes a decision in the penumbra, that particular instance becomes settled law in future, so that if another similar case were to arise, the case law would provide the answer. Judicial review therefore shrinks the penumbra; however, the resultant core is merely an area of provisional agreement as to interpretation.[115] As such, Hart's theory capitulates due to its misplaced faith in the narrowness of the penumbra. In contrast, Dworkin's solution is that that judicial review in penumbra cases does not amount to the application of retroactive rules.[116] Judges do not make decisions in a vacuum but instead are always constrained by law, even in hard cases.[117] There are controlling standards or principles that a judge must always follow. These principles, much like signposts, point the judge in the direction of what the correct interpretation is and, as a result, Dworkin argues that there is always only one right answer.[118] Consequently, Dworkin argues that in such instances a party is on notice that a case may go either way, and as such is not wholly taken aback when a finding goes against them.

This does not, however, solve the vagueness problem antithetical to the rule of law as the principles which Dworkin argues are embedded in the legal culture of a system are either unenumerated, or nebulous, or both. Disagreements as to the scope of constitutional norms therefore still, even under Dworkin's theory, pose profound challenges to the judicial review of legislation and the assertion that it vindicates the rule of law. In turn, the judiciary's integral role in maintaining Kelsen's Identity Thesis which I advocate for is also challenged. One can therefore side with Waldron and argue that in light of this disagreement, the legislature should decide as it is the best forum through which disagreement can resolve itself

[112] Ronald Dworkin, *Law's Empire* (Belknap Press, 1986) 397–99.

[113] See Ronald Dworkin, 'The Model of Rules' (1967) 35 *University of Chicago Law Review* 14.

[114] HLA Hart, 'Positivism and the Separation of Law and Morals' (1958) 71 *Harvard Law Review* 593, 607.

[115] See Dworkin (n 113); David Dyzenhaus, *Legality and Legitimacy: Carl Schmitt, Hans Kelsen and Hermann Heller in Weimar* (Oxford University Press, 1997) 7.

[116] Dworkin (n 114) 22–29.

[117] ibid; see also Ronald Dworkin, 'Hard Cases' (1975) 88 *Harvard Law Review* 1057.

[118] Dworkin (n 112) ch 7. Critics of Dworkin, however, argue that there cannot be 'one right answer' as objectively valid as judges with different political ideologies will come to different conclusions about the same problem. Dworkin responds to these 'external skeptics' by stating that what makes the decision 'right' is that the judge as a participant in legal practice experiences them as right. See Freeman (n 97) 1398–99.

as legislation is itself the very product of this disagreement. The opposite approach to take is the Dworkinian one where the judiciary should have the capacity to review legislation: in matters of interpretation, there is only one right answer, which judges are best placed to discover. Against this debate as to the role of courts in interpreting vague constitutional principles, a further challenge is mounted to judicial review when these general principles espoused by a constitution point away from the judiciary having a role in reviewing a decision. This can arise when the constitution implies that certain decisions are non-justiciable or 'political questions' beyond the reach of courts.

Legal Black Holes and Zones Beyond Law

We have seen that when there is disagreement as to the constitutionality of a norm, debate abounds as to which branch of government should ultimately decide. However, in a state of emergency, I contend that things are different. When a state of emergency is declared—either by the legislature or executive—and new norms are enacted, there is an express declaration made that these norms are unconstitutional. They are incompatible with the ordinary norms of the constitution which is why the state of emergency had to be declared. There is no disagreement therefore regarding the constitutionality of the enacted norms. It is this express unconstitutionality that negates the challenge to judicial review posed by Bickel's restatement of the question in *Marbury v Madison*.[119] When an emergency is declared by the legislature, it has carried out its interpretive duty under the constitution and decided that the measures enacted in lieu of this declaration are unconstitutional. It is an express admission that the ordinary bounds of the constitution no longer bind. It is an express admission that even if we consider that the constitutional norm is a legal norm in the sense that it has legal 'traction' when the legislature takes it into account when drafting legislation, a declaration of an emergency also states that the enacted response—be it by legislation or executive order—is not a manifestation and application of these legal norms; rather, it is a disapplication of these norms. Quite aside from the executive, to allow even the legislature unfettered discretion to decide that the ordinary bounds of the constitution are inapplicable is to allow the legislature to exceed the scope of its power as enumerated under the constitution. It is, in essence, a capitulation to the Schmittian Challenge discussed in Chapter 3, emptying the rule of law and legal order of any normative value. It would be to allow an ultra vires application of the legislature's emergency powers to go unchecked, negating the distinction between the legislature's constituted power and the constituent power that created and empowered the legislature in the first instance. What we have therefore is not a legal black hole created by law

[119] See text to n 81 above.

within which the decision-maker has unbound discretion; rather, what is revealed is a zone beyond law. The consequences of a non-justiciable declaration of a state of emergency is thus radically different from other non-justiciable questions.

Zones Beyond Law v Legal Black Holes: The Irish Example

This point is best illustrated by way of an example, with Ireland's experience of an entrenched state of emergency an excellent case study. As discussed in Chapter 3, Article 28.3.3° of the Irish Constitution contains a clear, textually demonstrable commitment that the decision to declare a state of emergency rests with the Oireachtas. Moreover, a literal reading of Article 28.3.3° allows for potential suspension of every article of the Irish Constitution.[120] Whether the Oireachtas' declaration of an emergency is amenable to judicial scrutiny has not yet been answered by the Irish courts although it was raised in *Re Emergency Powers Bill 1976*.[121] Following the declaration of a state of emergency in September 1976—one day after the cessation of the emergency declared in September 1939 upon the outbreak of World War II—the Oireachtas passed the Emergency Powers Bill 1976.[122] The justification given for this new declaration was 'the armed conflict now taking place in Northern Ireland'.[123] During the course of the parliamentary debate on the existence of the emergency, it was stated that the government's decision was motivated by explosions at the Special Criminal Court in Dublin on 15 July 1976, and the murder of the British Ambassador, Christopher Ewart-Biggs, on 21 July 1976.[124] These events were described as 'a direct challenge to the authority of the institutions of State and to their ability to discharge the functions entrusted to them under the Constitution'.[125] Before the Emergency Powers Bill could enter into force, however, the then Irish President Cearbhall Ó Dálaigh referred it to the Supreme Court to for a pre-emptive test of its constitutionality under Article 26 of the Irish Constitution.[126]

[120] This was the case until the 21st Amendment of the Constitution Act 2001 which amended, amongst other provisions, Art 28.3.3° to preclude the reintroduction of the death penalty. However, if Art 28.3.3° is interpreted literally, there is nothing preventing the Oireachtas using Art 28.3.3° to amend the Irish Constitution and delete this prohibition on the death penalty. Consequently, this is only a restraint if the amendment power vested in the people through a referendum by Art 46 of the Constitution is also inviolable in a state of emergency. Consequently, this further illustrates the importance of conceptualising the decision to declare a state of emergency as a constituted power.

[121] *In the Matter of Article 26 of the Constitution and in the matter of the Emergency Powers Bill 1976* [1977] IR 159, hereinafter *Re Emergency Powers Bill*. For a detailed analysis of all arguments made in this case, see David Gwynn Morgan, 'The Emergency Powers Bill Reference I' (1978) 13 *Irish Jurist* 67 and David Gwynn Morgan, 'The Emergency Powers Bill Reference II' (1979) 14 *Irish Jurist* 252.

[122] See text from nn 171–74 in ch 3.

[123] 292 *Dáil Debates* col 256 (1 September 1976).

[124] 292 *Dáil Debates* cols 4–5 (1 September 1976). See also Morgan, 'The Emergency Powers Bill Reference I' (n 121) 67–68.

[125] 292 *Dáil Debates* cols 4–5 (1 September 1976).

[126] Art 26 of the Constitution of Ireland permits the president, at his/her absolute discretion following consultation with the Council of State, to refer a Bill to the Supreme Court for a pre-emptive

As the substantive content of the Bill could not be challenged in lieu of a valid declaration of a state of emergency,[127] the two key questions to be answered by the Supreme Court were: firstly, whether the Supreme Court could review the resolution of the Oireachtas to declare a state of emergency; and, secondly, if it did have such competence, whether a state of emergency existed or not in this instance. Material from President Ó Dálaigh's personal papers, himself a former Chief Justice of the Irish Supreme Court, indicates that he was highly critical on the factual question of whether a state of emergency in accordance with the meaning envisaged in Article 28.3.3° existed.[128] It is clear, then, that there was a disagreement between the government and the Oireachtas on one side and the President on the other as to the existence of a state of emergency. The Irish experience surrounding *Re Emergency Powers Bill 1976* is therefore an excellent case study, demonstrating the difficulties of involving courts in decisions on the existence of an emergency. It also serves to illustrate the difficulties in engineering a constitution that strikes the correct balance between, on the one hand, effective scrutiny of the decision to declare a state of emergency; and on the other, a system that is flexible enough to enable a decisive response. This is particularly the case given that Ireland's emergency powers provisions are some of the most expansive in the world. In addition, Ireland's parliamentary democracy is one in which the executive dominates, meaning that the parliamentary approval of both houses of the decision to declare a state of emergency is largely an exercise in rubber-stamping.[129] The office of president is a largely ceremonial role of head of state and is officially part of the Irish legislature along with the two houses of Parliament with minimal powers, the most substantial being that exercised by Ó Dálaigh under Article 26 in referring a bill to the Supreme Court to test its constitutionality. Had a provision been included in Article 28.3.3° that considered the opinion of the president as to the existence of a state of emergency, as was suggested during the course of the debate on the First Amendment of the Irish Constitution,[130] the resolution to declare a state of emergency in September 1976 would have encountered a serious obstacle.

On the issue of whether the Supreme Court could review the decision of the Oireachtas to declare a state of emergency, the Attorney General initially argued

test as to its constitutionality before it becomes law. The Supreme Court must issue a single judgment only as to the Bill's constitutionality. If it is found to be constitutional, the president must sign it into law; if it is found to be repugnant to the Constitution, the president must refuse to sign it and the Bill does not become law.

[127] Art 34.3.3° Constitution of Ireland; Morgan, 'The Emergency Powers Bill Reference II' (n 121) 254; See also *State (Walsh) v Lennon* [1942] IR 112, 121, per Duffy J, who expressly stated in that case that upon a valid declaration of emergency under Art 28.3.3°, 'the applicants have come for relief to a Court which has no power to give them relief'.

[128] 'Council of State Schedule', IE UCDA P51/210; see also Alan Greene, 'Declaring a State of Emergency under Article 28.3.3° of the Irish Constitution: A Purely Political Question?' in Eoin Carolan, *The Constitution of Ireland: Perspectives and Prospects* (Bloomsbury Professional, 2012) ch 18.

[129] Greene, ibid.

[130] 77 *Dáil Debates* col16.

that only the Oireachtas could declare a state of emergency and hence it was beyond the scope of the courts to review such a declaration. Once the consequences of this position were made clear, however, the Attorney General revoked this submission on the grounds that 'it [the submission] did not arise in this case'.[131] These consequences are not listed in the report; however, the lack of any review by the legal sphere of the decision to declare a state of emergency would put this question firmly in the hands of the political and thus amount to a capitulation to the Schmittian Challenge.

The Attorney General then submitted that there exists a presumption that the facts stated in the resolutions declaring a state of emergency are correct and that this presumption should be acted upon unless and until it is displaced. This was accepted by the Supreme Court.[132] From this, O Dálaigh concluded that the Supreme Court had power to review the declaration of a state of emergency as this presumption could only be displaced if the courts had the competence to review such a declaration.[133] The reasoning employed by the Court is somewhat curious on this issue, however, as it went on to state explicitly that: 'The Court expressly reserves for future consideration the question whether the Courts have jurisdiction to review such resolutions.'[134]

In the Irish context, the presumption that a state of emergency existed was not overturned by the Supreme Court and the Bill was ultimately upheld. It was signed into law on 16 October 1976 by President Ó Dálaigh.[135] That same day an IRA attack killed a member of the Garda Síochána (the Irish police force) in Mountmellick, County Laois.[136] The following day, Defence Minister Paddy Donegan, addressing Irish troops at Columb Barracks, Mullingar, called President Ó Dálaigh a 'thundering disgrace' for referring the Bill to the Supreme Court.[137] Donegan then submitted his resignation to the Taoiseach Liam Cosgrave, but Cosgrave refused to accept it. Ó Dálaigh, considering his position to be untenable given the damaged relationship between the Defence Minister and the President in his symbolic role as Commander-in-Chief of the armed forces, resigned on 22 October 1976.[138]

[131] *Re Emergency Powers Bill* (n 121) 176.

[132] ibid, 175.

[133] In Ó Dálaigh's private papers, there is a copy of the judgment handed down by the Supreme Court. Ó Dálaigh has underlined the word 'presumption' in the phrase 'the Court accepts the existence of that presumption', and beside this he has written the word 'EXAMINABLE', IE UCDA P51/210, thus indicating that Ó Dálaigh considered this as confirming the jurisdiction of the courts to review the declaration of a state of emergency, notwithstanding the subsequent express statement of the Supreme Court that it was reserving judgment on this issue for a future case. See Greene (n 128).

[134] *Re Emergency Powers Bill* (n 121) 176; Gerard Hogan and Gerry Whyte, *JM Kelly: The Irish Constitution*, 4th edn (Bloomsbury Professional, 2003) 446–47.

[135] D Walsh, 'Emergency Bill Becomes Law after Court Verdict', *Irish Times*, 16 October 1976.

[136] J Corcoran, 'Memories of Darkest Day Haven't Gone Away', *Irish Independent*, 9 October 2011.

[137] D Walsh, 'FF Seeks Donegan's Dismissal for Remark about President', *Irish Times*, 19 October 1976.

[138] D Walsh, 'O Dálaigh Will not Stand Again', *Irish Times*, 23 October 1976.

The Non-Justiciability of Article 28.3.3° and Constituent Power

As noted above, the Supreme Court expressly refused to state whether or not it could review the decision to declare a state of emergency under Article 28.3.3°. Excluding judicial review may, however, give rise to theoretical problems regarding the constitutional order of the Irish state and other states that permit the suspension of constitutional norms in a period of emergency. As argued in Chapter 3, such issues of primary justiciability which a priori exclude judicial review go to the very root of the constitutional order. If the power to suspend constitutional norms—which is often what a declaration of a state of emergency entails—is not amenable to judicial review, then the impact of this 'political question' is unique from that of other non-justiciable questions. As argued in Chapter 3, a state of emergency renders the constitutional norms that it suspends inapplicable for the period of time that the emergency is in place. If the emergency lasts in perpetuity or becomes permanent, this ineffectiveness becomes similarly permanent. As effectiveness is a necessary condition of validity, although not equal to validity, it follows that a permanent emergency may have the capacity to render certain constitutional norms invalid. This invalidity has stemmed directly from the decision to declare a state of emergency and its perpetuation.

Such an interpretation of Article 28.3.3° would conceptualise a constituted power as unlimited. In essence, it would amount to an expression of state power that can only most accurately be described as 'constituent' in nature. It would potentially allow for the constitution to be amended and changed in a manner fundamentally different from that initially envisaged; something which Schmitt argues a true constitution cannot allow. Similarly, it would allow for the amendment of constitutional norms which make up what Joel Colón-Ríos terms the 'fundamental core' of a constitution.[139] Even if there are norms within the Irish Constitution that can be identified as amounting to a 'fundamental core' and these norms are not expressly suspended by a state of emergency, exclusion of judicial review of this decision to declare a state of emergency would still violate this 'fundamental core'.[140] This is because the *process* by which the amendment of the constitution has taken place—the perpetual suspension of constitutional norms by way of a state of emergency—has been in a manner not envisaged by the constitution.

[139] Joel I Colón-Ríos, *Weak Constitutionalism: Democratic Legitimacy and the Question of Constituent Power* (Routledge, 2012) ch7.

[140] In *In the Matter of the reference to the court of the Regulation of Information (Services Outside the State for Termination of Pregnancies Bill 1995* [1995] 2 ILRM 81, the Irish Supreme Court rejected the argument that there were limits to the people's amendment power under the Constitution. This would suggest that there is no 'fundamental core' of constitutional norms in the Irish Constitution. Aileen Kavanagh, however, suggests that this reluctance may be due to the people's superior democratic legitimacy and any proposed amendment that would impact on this democratic legitimacy could be found unconstitutional. Thus, Kavanagh suggests that there are actual limits to the people's amendment power under the Irish Constitution. Amendment of the Constitution by way of a permanent state of emergency would certainly satisfy this threshold. See Aleen Kavanagh, 'Unconstitutional Amendments from Irish Free State to Irish Republic' in Carolan (n 128) 331–54.

This violates the amendment process enumerated in the constitution which is itself a norm that makes up the fundamental core of the constitution.

The Irish example thus illustrates that we can differentiate emergency powers that result in the suspension of constitutional norms from other so-called legal black holes. In order to recognise a legal black hole, a background of law is needed upon which this legal black hole can be projected.[141] Noa Ben-Asher thus deploys the metaphor of a bagel to conceptualise the legal black hole. The hole in the centre of the bagel is 'shaped by the bagel'. It comes into existence through the bagel. 'Its "holeness" is directly attributed to the bagel.'[142] The legal black hole that was contended to have been created, for example, in *Anisminic*—when the legislature enacts a statute ousting judicial review from a tribunal's determination regarding whether an individual is entitled to compensation—is fundamentally different from that created by the declaration of a state of emergency and the suspension of constitutional norms until further notice. The latter, without judicial review, would amount to a claim for the constituent power that founds the legal order. It is a claim for a power beyond law that Schmitt is referring to. As such, it does not give rise to a legal black hole, but is instead recognition of a zone beyond law. This power does not need a background in law to be recognised, nor is it created by law; rather, Schmitt reverses the bagel metaphor, arguing that that law needs this background of state power in order for it to be law. This outcome is incompatible with a conception of the state as identical to the legal order. It is to argue for an interpretation that the constitutional provision has conferred the constituent power upon the decision-maker, a concept that is as worrying from a human rights and rule of law perspective as it is conceptually untenable. As a result, it illustrates the importance of judicial review of the decision to declare a state of emergency as one that cannot be displaced by concerns regarding the democratic legitimacy of judicial review or textually demonstrable commitments in the constitution vesting the ex ante decision to declare a state of emergency in a branch of government other than the judiciary.

In turn, this distinction between legal black holes and zones beyond law poses a challenge to theorists such as Adrian Vermeule who argues that the entire tapestry of US administrative law is Schmittian in nature. Vermeule argues that he needs 'only a modest version of Schmitt' in order to describe administrative law in the US as 'Schmittian';[143] however, in so doing, he blurs this above distinction between legal black holes and zones beyond law. The attempt to create a legal black hole in *Anisminic*, should it have been successful, would, nevertheless, still have been limited to the conferred power in question—namely the decision whether or not to award compensation to a British owner of an asset seized by Egypt.[144] Vermeule therefore underplays the distinction between commissarial and

141 Ben-Asher (n 4) 3–6.

142 ibid, 9.

143 Vermeule (n 15) 1100.

144 *Anisminic* (n 17).

sovereign dictatorship; between constituent and constituted power. It is this obviation of the distinction between the two that so fundamentally separates Schmitt's *Dictatorship* from *Political Theology* a year later. Moreover, it is this distinction that must be maintained in order to avoid fundamentally weakening the legal order and capitulating to the Schmittian Challenge.

Conclusions

Permanent states of emergency pose a profound challenge to the prior existing constitutional order. There are strong institutional and efficacy arguments against judicial review of emergency powers, and particularly, ex ante judicial input into the decision as to whether there exists a state of emergency. One must bear in mind, however, that relevance of the authority to assess the existence of a state of emergency in the first instance does not dissipate once an emergency is declared. It is also pertinent when deciding the question of whether an emergency still exists. Once a state of emergency is declared, the exception becomes the status quo and judicial review will not alter this status quo until after judgment is pronounced. These initial fears of slow decision-making dissipate in this instance and so too do the efficacious arguments against judicial review.

The implications of ousting judicial review over the decision to declare a state of emergency where such a decision leads to the potential for constitutional norms to be suspended cannot be ignored. Despite prudential concerns as to the efficacy of judicial review of emergency powers and unease as to the counter-majoritarian difficulty that affects the judiciary, I have argued that the fundamental questions raised as to the nature of the state and whether all state power can be circumscribed by law must not be discounted. This chapter has established this argument for judicial review by relying upon constituent power and a conception of the rule of law as viewing all state power as circumscribed by law and exercised through law. It has sought to do so in order to insulate this argument for judicial review from the critiques levied at the more substantive conceptions of the rule of law that seek to rely upon the normative basis of human rights to justify their claims. Nevertheless, these more substantive concerns also raise challenges for the justification for judicial review raised in this chapter. This chapter has focused on *why* courts should have the authority to review the decision to declare a state of emergency; however, it has not said anything about whether or not this will ensure that such review is rigorous. It is in the degree of scrutiny that this theory may encourage critiques of these more substantive conceptions of the rule of law, and therefore it is to these critiques that the following chapter will turn.

5

Permanent States of Emergency and Legal Grey Holes

Introduction

In chapter four, I argued that despite prudential and democratic concerns regarding the role of the judiciary on questions of national security, judicial review of the decision to declare a state of emergency cannot be ousted, even when there is a clear textually demonstrable commitment in a constitution vesting this power to declare an emergency in another branch of government. That the judiciary has the power to review the existence of a state of emergency—or any decision for that matter—does not mean, however, that such review will be robust. Overly deferential, weak review poses its own unique problems to the constitutional order as distinct from those posed by non-justiciable declarations of emergency. These critiques also pose profound challenges to the claim that judicial review of the decision to declare a state of emergency can answer the Schmittian Challenge. In this chapter, I shall contend that these arguments, which are often based on a substantive conception of the rule of law, are not necessarily inimical to the argument I laid out in chapter three. Rather, these 'thicker' conceptions of the rule of law may be corroborated and fortified by invoking the concept of constituent power to justify judicial review and giving the judiciary stronger grounds upon which to justify its constitutional role. Moreover, it is not clear as to whether or not a more substantive conception of the rule of law will actually give rise to more robust review. Indeed, it may lead to the opposite and to judges taking a more 'minimalist' approach to constitutional questions concerning the existence of a state of emergency. Finally, invoking the concept of constituent power to demonstrate the limitations of constituted powers may legitimise judicial review of emergency powers that impact on constitutional norms beyond human rights or other substantive values.

Legal Grey Holes

Chapter four discussed the problem of 'legal black holes'—zones of administrative discretion within which there are few, if any, legal controls on decision-makers so long as they stay within the bounds of their jurisdiction. This is often achieved by precluding judicial review through the use of ouster clauses.[1] We also saw, however, that the effective ousting of judicial review may be done by the judiciary itself rather than by the express terms of a statute or constitution. Thus, in *Liversidge v Anderson*, the majority of the British House of Lords found that 'reasonable cause' was a subjective test to be exercised by the minister in question when deciding whether to detain individuals without trial.[2] This effectively debarred the appellant from challenging his detention. This approach of the majority was subject to a scathing critique from the dissenting Lord Atkin:

> I know of only one authority which might justify the suggested method of construction: "'When I use a word,' Humpty Dumpty said in rather a scornful tone, 'it means just what I choose it to mean, neither more nor less.' 'The question is,' said Alice, 'whether you can make words mean so many different things.' 'The question is,' said Humpty Dumpty, 'which is to be master—that's all.'" ... After all this long discussion the question is whether the words "If a man has" can mean "If a man thinks he has." I am of opinion that they cannot, and that the case should be decided accordingly.[3]

Taking Lord Atkin's dissent as inspiration, David Dyzenhaus presents a particularly robust attack on such judicial capitulation with his concept of legal grey holes.[4] Dyzenhaus looks beyond the idea of legal black holes discussed in chapter four, arguing that while there may be ostensible attempts from the judiciary to impose a legal constraint on such powers and bring them within the rule of law, often these may be merely token gestures and wholly ineffective in constraining or reviewing the exercise of power. Instead, such a judicial approach provides a level of formal legitimacy, perpetuating rather than constraining the emergency power in question.[5] Grey holes, therefore, are legal spaces in which there are 'some legal constraints on executive action—it is not a lawless void—but the constraints are so minimal they pretty well permit government to do as it pleases'.[6] Consequently, Dyzenhaus argues that these 'grey holes' permit the government to 'have its cake and eat it too', by allowing the executive to appear to be governing, not only by law but in accordance with the rule of law.[7] As a result, legal grey holes might be even more dangerous from the perspective of a substantive conception of the rule of law than true black holes—decisions which the judiciary expressly admit they have no power to review or which review is ousted due to the wording of the statute.[8]

[1] See text to n 8 in ch 4.
[2] *Liversidge v Anderson* [1942] AC 206.
[3] ibid, 245.
[4] David Dyzenhaus, *The Constitution of Law: Legality in a Time of Emergency* (Cambridge University Press, 2006) 41–43.
[5] ibid, 42.
[6] ibid.
[7] David Dyzenhaus, '*Schmitt v Dicey:* Are States of Emergency Inside or Outside the Legal Order?' (2005–06) 27 *Cardozo Law Review* 2026.
[8] Dyzenhaus (n 4) 210.

Dyzenhaus does not therefore consider the availability of judicial review of emergency powers to be prima facie of benefit to the rule of law and human rights.[9] One must also look to the actual degree of review exercised. Judges may defer to such an extreme degree that mere lip-service is paid to judicial review and the rule of law. Such instances should be indistinguishable from the position where no capacity to review is declared in the first instance. Legal grey holes are therefore the product of undue judicial deference to the political branches on national security issues. As noted in chapter four, judicial deference is the manner by which courts accord respect to the initial decision-maker on the grounds of their superior expertise, competence or legitimacy.[10] Deference thus expands on the idea of judicial review as not just a checking mechanism in ensuring decision-makers act lawfully, but also viewing administrative law as facilitating legitimate government action in the public interest.[11] However, if judicial scrutiny is too light-touch, rather than facilitating good and legitimate government decisions, it legitimises bad ones. This is particularly acute in matters of national security whether the legitimacy of the judiciary is at its weakest and, as we saw in chapter two, the potential for governments to overreact is greatest.[12]

In this regard, Dyzenhaus considers Cass Sunstein's 'minimalist' approach to constitutional interpretation as one that is comfortable with legal grey holes.[13] Sunstein's theory of judicial interpretation argues that both in normalcy and emergency, courts should leave their constitutional interpretations under-theorised.[14] Sunstein rejects Ronald Dworkin's approach of courts becoming moral philosophers and formulating a grandiose theory of constitutional interpretation. Instead, by leaving their perspective of the constitution under-theorised and deciding cases on as narrow a ground as possible, this leaves room for popular and democratic debate to be had on areas of constitutional disagreement. By favouring 'shallowness and narrowness' over 'breadth and depth', the minimalist judge thus seeks to strike a balance between judicial review and democracy.[15] However, in so doing, Dyzenhaus argues that minimalism paves the way for overly deferential

[9] That stated, Paul Daly is sceptical of some of the more extreme interpretations of Dyzenhaus's argument, stating that: 'It would be strange to suggest (and in my view Dyzenhaus does not) that Canada was in violation of the rule of law when patent unreasonableness was a standard of review or that the rule of law is violated by the use by English courts of the super-*Wednesbury* standard of review.' Paul Daly, *A Theory of Deference in Administrative Law* (Cambridge University Press, 2012) 284.

[10] See text from nn 88–96 in ch 4; see also Aileen Kavanagh, 'Defending Deference in Public Law and Constitutional Theory' (2010) 126 *LQR* 222, 223.

[11] Murray Hunt, 'Sovereignty's Blight: Why Contemporary Public Law Needs the Concept of Due Deference' in Nicholas Bamforth and Peter Leyland (eds), *Public Law in a Multi-Layered Constitution* (Hart Publishing, 2003) 337, 349–54. Andew Bickel refers to this legitimating function of judicial review as 'the mystic function'. Andrew Bickel, *The Least Dangerous Branch: The Supreme Court at the Bar of Politics*, 2nd edn (Yale University Press, 1962) 29–33.

[12] See text to n 116 in ch 2.

[13] Dyzenhaus (n 4) 42–50; Cass Sunstein, 'Minimalism at War' [2004] *Supreme Court Review* 47.

[14] Sunstein, ibid, 48.

[15] ibid.

judicial review that legitimises draconian measures taken in the name of national security.[16] Dyzenhaus thus takes issue with Sunstein's attempt to rehabilitate the majority judgment in the infamous *Korematsu* whereby the US Supreme Court validated the detention of US citizens of Japanese descent during World War II as constitutionally permissible.[17]

Emergency Powers and Legal Grey Holes in Practice

While Dyzenhaus is primarily concerned with common law constitutional models where the legitimacy of judicial review must be squared with the sovereignty of Parliament,[18] US Supreme Court judgments on the constitution in times of war such as *Korematsu* illustrate that deference on issues of national security is also manifest in other constitutional traditions. While it is not possible here to provide a comprehensive comparative analysis of how numerous jurisdictions approach the issue of judicial review and national security, the disparate constitutional traditions noted here should suffice to convey concerns as to the performance of respective courts in reviewing issues of national security. Moreover, the relative stability of these constitutional orders illustrates how even established constitutional orders that claim a high regard for the rule of law can, nevertheless, struggle under claims of national security superiority.

Ireland

To recall from chapter four, in 1976 the Irish Supreme Court refused to decide whether or not it had the capacity to review the declaration of a state of emergency under the Irish Constitution following an increased intensity of the conflict in Northern Ireland.[19] This avoidance of a question of fundamental constitutional importance can itself be equated to Sunstein's idea of minimalism.[20] Moreover, judicial review in other related areas of national security in Ireland further exhibits an overly deferential tendency—for example, the judicial approach taken to reviewing the Irish government's decision to establish special courts. The Irish Constitution permits the establishment of non-jury special courts when 'the ordinary courts are inadequate to secure the effective administration of justice, and the preservation of public peace and order'.[21] This constitutional provision is closely tied to the more expansive emergency powers enabled by Article 28.3.3° with the rationale behind the provision being to provide for limited emergency powers

16 Dyzenhaus (n 4) 47.
17 ibid; *Re Korematsu* (1944) 323 US 214. See also text to n 17 in ch 6 for a critique of *Korematsu* in the context of 'business as usual' approaches to emergencies.
18 See text to nn 83–172 in ch 6 for a further discussion of common law constitutionalism.
19 See text to n 123 in chapter 4.
20 Sunstein (n 13).
21 Art 38.3.1° Constitution of Ireland.

for when conditions are less serious than those envisaged by Article 28.3.3°.[22] The power to give effect to this constitutional provision was enabled by Part V of the Offences against the State Act 1939 (OASA 1939), which was enacted less than two years after the entry into force of the Irish Constitution. The OASA 1939 is a piece of permanent legislation; however, the exceptional nature of the special courts is affirmed by virtue of the fact that Part V 'shall not come into or be in force save as and when and for so long as is provided by the subsequent sub-sections of this section'. Section 35(2) of Part V empowers the government to assess whenever 'the ordinary courts were inadequate to secure the effective administration of justice'. In *Re MacCurtain*, both the High and Supreme Courts rejected an argument that section 35(2) was an unconstitutional delegation of legislative authority to the executive.[23] In the High Court, Duffy J stated that:

> The Oireachtas clearly considered the Government to be the authority best situated, from its position and the information at its disposal, to determine whether or not Special Tribunals were necessary in the circumstances set out in the section. In my opinion, the provision that the Government may make such a proclamation when satisfied that the ordinary Courts are inadequate is clearly meant to be an essentially executive decision of the highest executive authority in the State.[24]

Duffy J continued by holding that the government had no obligation to disclose the reasons as to why it reached such a decision.[25] *MacCurtain* is thus a classic restatement of the grounds for executive supremacy on issues of national security. The Supreme Court further elaborated upon the unsuitability of courts to asses this question in *Kavanagh v Ireland*:

> The question of whether the ordinary courts are or are not adequate to secure the effective administration of justice and the preservation of public peace and order is primarily a political question, and for that reason, is left to the legislature and the executive.[26]

Only if mala fides on the part of the executive can be shown will the decision to establish Special Criminal Courts be voided.[27] However, the lack of a requirement to adduce reasons justifying this finding makes any scrutiny of this decision by the judiciary or legislature impossible, notwithstanding the provision in section 35(5) that the Dáil Éireann can at any time pass a resolution annulling the government's decision to establish such courts.[28] Thus although it would appear that

[22] Alan Greene, 'The Historical Evolution of Article 28.3.3° of the Irish Constitution' (2012) 47 *Irish Jurist* 117, 119; Alan Greene, 'Declaring a State of Emergency under Article 28.3.3° of the Irish Constitution: A Purely Political Question?' in Eoin Carolan, *The Constitution of Ireland: Perspectives and Prospects* (Bloomsbury Professional, 2012) 373; See Fergal F Davis, *The History and Development of the Special Criminal Court 1922–2005* (Four Courts Press, 2007).

[23] *Re MacCurtain* [1941] IR 83.

[24] ibid, 86.

[25] ibid.

[26] *Kavanagh v Ireland* [1996] 1 IR 321, 354.

[27] ibid 361.

[28] Greene, 'Declaring a State of Emergency' (n 22) 391–92.

the decision to establish special courts is justiciable, the reasoning followed by the Irish courts negates such review of any meaningful check on executive power while simultaneously legitimising the executive's decision. The result is that the decision to establish special courts is rubber-stamped by the judiciary, giving it the constitutional seal of approval and creating a legal grey hole in the Irish constitutional order.

Article 15 ECHR and the Meaning of 'Public Emergency Threatening the Life of the Nation'

A similarly overly deferential judicial approach can also be seen in international human rights courts such as the ECtHR, particularly on the issue of whether an emergency exists under Article 15 ECHR. To recall from chapter one, Article 15 ECHR states that:

> In time of war or other public emergency threatening the life of the nation, any High Contracting Party may take measures derogating from its obligations under this convention to the extent strictly required by the exigencies of the situation.[29]

Like many definitions of emergency, Article 15's articulation of a 'time of war or other public emergency threatening the life of the nation' is broad, leaving space for considerable flexibility as to its scope. This form of words has been mirrored in the constitutional provisions of a number of states; indeed, the ECHR system is an excellent illustrative example of how courts review emergency powers, not just because of the commonality of the wording of Article 15 but also due to the numerous different constitutional traditions covered by the Convention system and its compulsory jurisdiction.[30] Moreover, the Convention's exhibition of certain constitutionalist traits means that it manifests many of the aspects of apex constitutional courts in domestic legal systems.[31]

That stated, the ECtHR's vulnerable legitimacy in its infancy was arguably key to its early case law on states of emergency.[32] *Lawless v Ireland* was the first case to assess the existence of a state of emergency under Article 15, and the first to be heard before the ECtHR.[33] Lawless was a member of the Irish Republican Army (IRA) who was interned in Ireland under the Offences against the State (Amendment) Act 1940, the provisions of which were subject to a derogation

[29] Convention for the Protection of Human Rights and Fundamental Freedoms (European Convention on Human Rights), as amended by Protocols 11 and 14 (hereinafter ECHR).

[30] See text to n 93 in ch 1.

[31] Fiona de Londras, 'Dual Functionality and the Persistent Frailty of the European Court of Human Rights [2013] *EHRLR* 38,40; Kanstantsin Dzehtsiarou and Alan Greene, 'Restructuring the European Court of Human Rights: Preserving the Right of Individual Petition and Promoting Constitutionalism' [2013] *Public Law* 710, 713.

[32] *Lawless v Ireland*, Judgment of 1 July 1961, 3 EurCtHR (ser A, 1961); Brice Dickson, *The European Convention on Human Rights and the Conflict in Northern Ireland* (Oxford University Press, 2010) 37.

[33] Dickson, ibid.

notice lodged with the ECHR. On the question as to the existence of an emergency, the ECtHR was unanimous in upholding Ireland's derogation, finding that the phrase 'public emergency threatening the life of the nation', when given its natural and customary meaning, referred to 'an exceptional situation of crisis or emergency which affects the whole population and constitutes a threat to the organized life of the community of which the state is composed'.[34]

These conditions were found to exist in Ireland for three reasons: first, that there was a secret army operating within the state engaged in unconstitutional activities; second, that this same army was also operating beyond the state in Northern Ireland, jeopardising the relations between Ireland and its neighbour; and finally, that there was a marked increase in terroristic activities from autumn 1956 to July 1957.[35]

The factual conditions in *Lawless*, however, stand vastly out of line with the natural and ordinary meaning of the phrase 'public emergency threatening the life of the nation'.[36] While a 'secret army operating within the state engaged in unconstitutional activities' may sound like solid grounds for declaring a state of emergency, it should be noted that the IRA generally targeted its actions against the UK rather than the institutions of the Irish state. To say, therefore, that the IRA posed a threat to the life of the Irish nation is highly questionable. Instead, the real concern was the impact the IRA's actions had on the UK, hence the inclusion of the further justification, 'deteriorating relations between Ireland and its neighbour'. On this issue, however, Oren Gross and Fionnuala Ní Aoláin particularly criticise the notion that the deterioration of foreign relations with another state could amount to a 'threat to the life of the nation'.[37]

Gross and Ní Aoláin argue that the language used by the ECtHR shows that a state enjoys a certain margin of appreciation or 'measure of discretion' when deciding whether an emergency exists or not.[38] The ECtHR therefore defers to the national authorities as these are considered best placed to answer this question. Nevertheless, the ECtHR did expressly declare that it had jurisdiction to review the existence of an emergency.[39] Thus, while the issue is a legal one, the margin

[34] *Lawless* (n 32) [28]. The earlier decision of the Commission also found an emergency existed; however, it was divided by a majority of nine to five on this issue.

[35] ibid.

[36] See 'The Siracusa Principles on the Limitation and Derogation Provisions in the International Covenant on Civil and Political Rights' (1985) 7 *Human Rights Quarterly* 3, 7; Richard Lillich, 'The Paris Minimum Standards of Human Rights Norms in a State of Emergency' (1985) 79 *American Journal of International Law* 1072, 1073; See also text to n 78 in ch 1 regarding how international human rights treaties define emergencies.

[37] Oren Gross and Fionnuala Ní Aoláin, *Law in Times of Crisis: Emergency Powers in Theory and Practice* (Cambridge University Press, 2006) 271.

[38] Oren Gross and Fionnuala Ní Aoláin, 'From Discretion to Scrutiny: Revisiting the Application of the Margin of Appreciation Doctrine in the Context of Article 15 of the European Convention on Human Rights' (2001) 3 *Human Rights Quarterly* 623, 631–34. The 'margin of appreciation' doctrine was subsequently expressly referred to in *Ireland v UK*, Judgment of 18 January 1978, 25 EurCtHR (ser A, 1978).

[39] See Dickson (n 32) 37.

of appreciation doctrine shows that the ECtHR recognises that it is, nevertheless, a highly politicised legal issue.[40] Relatedly, as *Lawless* was its first decision, the Court's legitimacy could have been seriously threatened were it to undermine the decision of a democratic sovereign state.[41] *Lawless* presents the image of a judicially active court, declaring its jurisdiction to review the decision of a sovereign state as to the existence of an emergency. In reality, this is substantially tempered by the wide margin of appreciation afforded to a state when assessing whether an emergency exists or not. In other words, what constitutes an emergency may be a notionally legal question but whether that condition actually exists is a functionally political one. As a result, *Lawless* sets the severity threshold that a crisis must cross in order to justify a state of emergency extremely low, potentially encompassing mundane phenomena that do not threaten the existence of the state. Thus, despite appearing to assess whether a state of emergency exists or not, the ECtHR's approach in *Lawless* renders the first limb of Article 15 redundant, as serious scrutiny of whether such a state exists is not undertaken. The ECtHR's rationale in *Lawless* has been subject to substantial criticism, yet the decision has never been overruled, but rather, has been repeatedly endorsed.[42] In *Ireland v UK* the Court stated that:

> National authorities are in principle in a better position than the international judge to decide both on the presence of such an emergency and on the nature and scope of the derogations necessary to avert it. In this matter article 15 paragraph 1 leaves the authorities a wide margin of appreciation.[43]

Consequently, the vulnerable legitimacy of an international court in its infancy in *Lawless* cannot continue to excuse the Court's deferential approach to this question. Rather, the same factors influencing judicial deference on issues of national security at the domestic level are also operating at the international level.

The United Kingdom

While the margin of appreciation is a factor that should not necessarily affect domestic courts when reviewing the existence of a state of emergency, the similarities between domestic courts and the ECtHR on this issue is striking. This is typified by the almost identical approach of the UK and ECtHR in the aftermath of 9/11. In *A v UK (Belmarsh)*, the margin of appreciation doctrine was utilised both by the House of Lords and the ECtHR when asked to rule on whether a state of emergency existed in the UK following the attacks on the United States

[40] Gross and Ní Aoláin (n 38) 631–34.

[41] See Dickson (n 32) 37.

[42] See, for example, Oren Gross, '"Once More Unto the Breach": The Systematic Failure of Applying the European Convention on Human Rights to Entrenched Emergencies' (1998) 23 *Yale International Law Journal* 437, 460–64. *Ireland v the United Kingdom* (n 38).

[43] *Ireland v United Kingdom* (n 38).

on 11 September 2001.[44] In *Belmarsh*, the ECtHR declared that: '[T]he national authorities are, in principle, better placed than the international judge to decide ... on the presence of such an emergency.'[45] Accordingly, a wide margin of appreciation should be left to the national authorities. The House of Lords had earlier conflated the margin of appreciation with classic justifications in domestic law for courts recognising that certain matters 'fall within the discretionary area of judgment properly belonging to the democratic organs of the state'.[46] Consequently, while the margin of appreciation as a concept may have undermined the ECtHR as a useful comparator with domestic courts on national security questions, its conflation with classic justifications of deference assuages this.

The result was that declaration of a state of emergency by the UK was not challenged, despite the fact that it was the only state to derogate from the Convention following 9/11. Indeed, Spain did not declare a state of emergency in accordance with Article 15 ECHR following a significant terrorist attack on a train in Madrid on 11 March 2004.[47] In *Belmarsh*, the ECtHR simply asserted that as terrorism constituted legitimate grounds for derogating in *Lawless*, so too could it justify an emergency in this instance.[48] Such reasoning, however, completely avoids any engagement with the concept of terrorism and its varying degrees of magnitude and manifestations as discussed in chapter two.[49] To isolate particular instances of terrorism from their contextual specificities, time and magnitude eviscerates the complexities and disagreements as to the nature of terrorism, instead conceptualising it as a relatively uniform phenomenon. It would not be hyperbole to describe such an approach as manifestly incorrect.

Consequently, the ECtHR essentially mirrored the majority approach of the House of Lords which briefly stated that terrorism can constitute an emergency, although some members of the majority did express scepticism as to whether an emergency did actually exist.[50] Lord Hoffmann, however, went further, finding that no emergency existed and arguing that al-Qaeda did not pose a 'threat to the life of the nation'.[51] Lord Hoffmann contrasted the contemporary threat to that of the Spanish Armada or Nazi Germany, which he argued did threaten the life of the nation, not because of the loss of life their actions would entail but because they would overthrow British rule and make its institutions subject to the rule of others.[52] Al-Qaeda, in contrast, did not pose such a threat. Lord Hoffmann did

[44] *A v Secretary of State for the Home Department* 2 WLR 87 (2005) (House of Lords); *A and Others v United Kingdom* (hereinafter '*Belmarsh*'), Judgment of 19 February 2009, 3455 (ECtHR). This case concerned the legality of the indefinite detention of the applicants in Belmarsh Prison, London under s 23 of the Anti-Terrorism, Crime and Security Act 2001.

[45] ibid, [173].

[46] ibid, [37].

[47] ibid, [24].

[48] *A v UK* (n 44) [177]–[181].

[49] See text to nn 148–58 in ch 2.

[50] *Belmarsh* (n 44) [154] (Lord Scott).

[51] ibid, [96] (Lord Hoffmann).

[52] ibid.

concede that the IRA posed a threat to the life of the nation as it was an organisation dedicated to and had the potential to threaten the territorial integrity of the UK.[53] However, this is not an endorsement of the ruling in *Lawless*, which referred to a state of emergency declared by Ireland, not the UK. Instead, Lord Hoffmann contended that the Attorney General's submissions of al-Qaeda's ability to cause severe destruction of life and property did not necessarily entail a threat to the 'life of the nation'.[54] Lord Hoffmann's reasoning on what constitutes a threat to the life of the nation thus separates the existence of the state which is a metaphysical institution from the life of its citizens.

Judicial Push Back?

Lord Hoffmann's judgment in *Belmarsh* is remarkable due to its status as an outlier in the judicial record on reviewing the existence of a state of emergency and other questions of national security. Fiona de Londras, however, questions whether this poor record of judicial review on questions of national security is universal. While past instances of courts in the US and UK during World War II would suggest that the judicial record has been poor, de Londras argues that judicial review post 9/11 has been much more robust.[55] In the United States, for example, the Supreme Court eventually declared that detainees in Guantanamo Bay could challenge their detention by way of habeas corpus petitions. Firstly, in *Rasul v Bush*, the Supreme Court held that Guantanamo Bay detainees were within the jurisdiction of federal courts.[56] While the Supreme Court did not overturn the constitutional reasoning in *Johnson v Eisentrager*—the constitutional precedent upon which Guantanamo Bay was founded to exploit—the Court did find that the statutory interpretation in that case no longer applied, thus deciding the case on the narrowest possible grounds.[57] Congress responded to *Rasul* by introducing a jurisdiction-stripping clause in section 1005(1)(e) of the Detainee Treatment Act 2005; however, in *Hamdan v Rumsfeld* the US Supreme Court found that this clause did not have retrospective effect and so pending claims such as Hamdan's could be heard. Both these cases, however, turned on the question of statutory interpretation, leaving the constitutional question as to its jurisdictional applicability in Guantanamo unanswered.[58] Finally, in *Boumediene v Bush; Al Odah v United States*, the Supreme Court found the jurisdiction-stripping provision unconstitutional on the grounds that it violated Article III and the right to habeas

[53] ibid.

[54] ibid, [110] (Lord Bingham).

[55] Fiona de Londras and Fergal Davis, 'Controlling the Executive in Times of Terrorism: Competing Perspectives on Effective Oversight Mechanisms' (2010) 30 *OJLS* 19, 39–41.

[56] *Rasul v Bush* (2004) 542 US 466.

[57] Fiona de Londras, *Detention in the War on Terror: Can Human Rights Fight Back?* (Cambridge University Press, 2011) 251; *Johnson v Eisentrager* (1950) 339 US 763.

[58] *Hamdan v Rumsfeld* (2006) 548 US 557.

corpus.[59] This series of cases may be seen as reflecting Sunstein's approach to constitutional minimalism with the Supreme Court in each case doing the minimal amount necessary to get the desired outcome.

De Londras does not, however, laud *Boumediene* as 'entirely unproblematic'; 'quite the opposite is true, in fact'.[60] In particular, de Londras emphasises the unclear guidance given to lower courts regarding how they should deal with habeas corpus petitions from Guantanamo Bay detainees. Ultimately, this warning has proved prescient with the supposed fortitude of the Supreme Court in *Boumediene* not matched by the lower courts. Jules Lobel argues that cases such as *Boumediene* married lofty principled rhetoric with practical guidance on how the rights of Guantanamo Bay detainees should be vindicated.[61] This guidance fell short of the standards evoked by *Boumediene* and it has been this aspect of the Supreme Court's judgments, rather than the lofty rhetoric, that has been followed by the lower courts. The Supreme Court has thus paved the way for its prima facie robust judicial scrutiny to legitimise the subsequent overly deferential position of the lower courts, ultimately culminating in a rather pyrrhic victory for many Guantanamo Bay detainees.[62]

De Londras also considers *Belmarsh* to be an example of the judiciary pushing back against claims from the political branches as to the necessity of measures in the name of national security.[63] While both the House of Lords and the ECtHR in *Belmarsh* effectively refused to scrutinise the existence of an emergency in the UK post-9/11, both courts did instead focus on the second limb of Article 15—on whether the measures were proportionate to the exigencies of the situation. Following the same reasoning as the Special Immigration Appeals Commission which first reviewed the claimants' detention, the House of Lords found by a majority of nine to six that the measures enacted by the British government were disproportionate and discriminatory, as they differentiated arbitrarily between non-nationals suspected of international terrorism, and UK citizens who were considered to present the same threat qualitatively.[64] Lord Walker dissented, as he endorsed the position of the UK Court of Appeal and the Attorney General's submission that on matters of national security, courts should defer to the executive and legislature as these were questions of a political nature.[65] The ECtHR took an almost-identical position to the majority, focusing little attention on whether

[59] *Boumediene v Bush; Al Odah v United States* (2008) 553 US 723.

[60] De Londras (n 57) 260.

[61] Jules Lobel, 'The Rhetoric and Reality of Judicial Review of Counter-Terrorist Actions: The United States Experience' in Fergal F Davis and Fiona de Londras, *Critical Debates on Counter-Terrorism Judicial Review* (Cambridge University Press, 2014) 97, 109–17.

[62] At the time of writing, there are currently 41 detainees held at Guantanamo Bay. See 'Guantánamo by the Numbers' *Human Rights First* (23 March 2017) <www.humanrightsfirst.org/sites/default/files/gtmo-by-the-numbers.pdf> accessed 38 August 2017.

[63] De Londras and Davis (n 55) 41–42 (per de Londras).

[64] *Belmarsh*, (n 44) [96]–[97].

[65] ibid, [209].

an emergency existed and concentrating instead on whether the measures enacted were proportionate to the exigencies of the situation. However, the ECtHR differed from the House of Lords in respect of who constitute the 'national authorities' capable of declaring a state of emergency.[66] The ECtHR considered the House of Lords as competent to review the decision of declaring emergency, and as the latter was satisfied that the executive acted legitimately, so too was the ECtHR. This, however, was despite the fact that the House of Lords, with the exception of Lord Hoffmann's dissenting judgment, proffered little scrutiny of the decision to declare a state of emergency, but also deferred to the executive's assessment of the situation.[67]

Belmarsh has been lauded as a high point of judicial power in the United Kingdom, with courts now no longer willing merely to acquiesce to claims of national security and non-justiciability, shifting instead to review based on deference and proportionality.[68] Fundamental to this shift has been the passing of the Human Rights Act 1998 (HRA), equipping the British courts with the capacity to review legislative and executive acts for their conformity with the UK's international human rights obligations.[69] However, while *Belmarsh* did result in both the House of Lords and the ECtHR finding the measures in violation of the UK's human rights obligations, it nevertheless endorsed the assessment of the political branches that an emergency existed. *Belmarsh* presents both the ECtHR and the House of Lords as focusing only on whether the measures enacted are proportionate to the exigencies of the situation. Such is the foreseeable consequence of *Lawless*, which sets a minimal threat severity threshold for a state of emergency, and defers to the national authorities on this question. To date, there is only one example—the *Greek Case*—in which a declaration of emergency was rejected by the now defunct European Commission on Human Rights; the case never made it before the ECtHR.[70] However, Gross and Ní Aoláin argue that this decision has more to do with the fact that it was an anti-democratic regime that declared a state of emergency in Greece, rather than an objective analysis of whether or not a serious threat was posed to the state by the Greek communist opposition.[71]

Belmarsh can therefore be read as an exercise in minimalism by both the House of Lords and the ECtHR, with the courts finding a breach on as narrow a ground as possible. While ultimately the UK's indefinite detention without trial did come to an end, the courts' refusals to review the decision to declare a state of emergency effectively endorsed its existence. Thus, the then Home Secretary Charles Clarke continued to insist that the UK was in a state of emergency and this formed the

[66] Dyzenhaus (n 4) 179.
[67] ibid.
[68] Aileen Kavanagh, 'Constitutionalism, Counterterrorism, and the Courts: Changes in the British Constitutional Landscape' (2011) 9 *ICON* 172, 191.
[69] ibid.
[70] *The Greek Case* (1969) 12 *YB* 1; Gross and Ní Aoláin (n 37) 273–76.
[71] *The Greek Case*, ibid.

fundamental lynchpin around which the control order regime—the UK's response to the *Belmarsh* judgment—was justified.[72] Thus, while the judicial record on national security may be improving in some aspects, on the issue as to the existence of a state of emergency, it remains stubbornly overly deferential.

Fortifying the Rule of Law? Human Rights and Legal Grey Holes

The above discussion of the judicial record on national security issues—particularly on the question of whether a state of emergency exists—would appear to corroborate Dyzenhaus's concerns regarding the danger of legal grey holes legitimising permanent states of emergency through overly deferential review. Legal grey holes therefore present a robust challenge to the assertion that invoking the idea of constituent power to demonstrate that the decision to declare a state of emergency must be amenable to judicial review can respond to the Schmittian Challenge. Dyzenhaus's thesis instead has the potential to invert this, arguing that the potential for legal grey holes arising from overly deferential judicial review and paying lip service to the rule of law poses the greatest danger for these suspended constitutional norms.

Dyzenhaus thus rejects an overly formalist conception of the rule of law, seeking instead to imbue it with more substantive values in order to confront the Schmittian Challenge.[73] Dyzenhaus's 'thicker' conception of the rule of law is one that reflects Lon Fuller's idea of the 'inner morality of law', fortifying it as a concept and thus making it a more formidable normative value against which a provision should be tested against.[74] Although Dyzenhaus is not precise in what his thicker conception of the rule of law would look like, more substantive conceptions of the rule of law tend to incorporate formalist values such as certainty, equality and generality and then go further, including certain substantive content that laws must abide by in order to be compatible with the rule of law.[75] The closest we get to Dyzenhaus's understanding of the rule of law is the following:

> In summary, my position is that legislation must be capable of being interpreted in such a way that it can be enforced in accordance with the requirements of due process;

[72] Rachel Sylvester, 'Suspects' Families Will also Face Tight Controls' *The Telegraph* (28 January 2005) <www.telegraph.co.uk/news/uknews/1482210/Suspects-families-will-also-face-tight-controls.html> accessed 24 August 2017.

[73] Dyzenhaus (n 4) 42.

[74] ibid, 61–62; Lon Fuller, *The Morality of Law* (Yale University Press, 1969).

[75] Thus, Benjamin James Lozano contends that Dyzenhaus argues that judges are compelled by 'duty' to uphold the rule of law but he does not set out what concrete substance of this inner morality of law entails. Benjamin James Lozano, 'Book Review: The Constitution of Law: Legality in a Time of Emergency by David Dyzenhaus' (2008) 4 *Law, Culture and the Humanities* 456, 458.

> the officials who implement it can comply with a duty to act fairly, reasonably and in a fashion that respects the equality of all those who are subject to the law and independent judges are entitled to review the decisions of these officials to check that they do so comply. I will also argue that our understanding of concepts such as fairness, reasonableness, and equality is inevitably influenced by our evolving view of the individual who is subject to the law, the legal subject in short, and thus in recent times by the claim that the legal subject has to be regarded primarily as the bearer of human rights.[76]

In light of this, Benjamin James Lozano argues that Dyzenhaus's rule of law requires a commitment to individuals' rights to due process and freedom from arbitrary government action.[77] While these are the rights that Dyzenhaus focuses most on in *The Constitution of Law*, it is doubtful that these are the sole values that Dyzenhaus would consider a law must respect in order to satisfy his thick version of the rule of law. Rather, these are the values that, based in his analysis of the case law on emergency powers, tend to be infringed upon most. Instead, as Dyzenhaus's substantive conception of the rule of law is expressly influenced by the work of Fuller and Ronald Dworkin it is reasonable to speculate that his conception of the rule of law would match closely that of Dworkin or other substantive rule of law theorists.

For Dworkin, the rule of law requires positive laws and state actions to recognise and respect the moral and political rights of individuals.[78] If a law does not do this, then it violates the rule of law, regardless of its formal legitimacy.[79] Similarly, Judith N Shklar, like Dyzenhaus, expressly contends that formalist conceptions of the rule of law can lead one to antagonistic positions towards human rights. Shklar argues that the rule of law originally had two distinct meanings: it referred either to a way of life, a formulation she attributed to Aristotle; or it referred merely to specific public institutions, as stated by Montesquieu.[80] Shklar argues that Aristotle's rule of law as the 'rule of reason' is perfectly compatible with slavery as it can allow a dual state in which two different sets of law applies to two different sets of peoples. This is achieved by simply declaring one group of people subhuman. Consequently, Aristotle's formulation of the rule of law can still allow grave evils.

Montesquieu, in contrast, saw the rule of law as having only one aim: to protect the ruled against the aggression of those who rule and consequently to realise 'freedom from fear'. Thus, while its range was much narrower in the sense that it was directed only against those who ruled, its goal embraced and impacted upon

[76] ibid; Dyzenhaus (n 4) 12–13; See also Thomas Poole, 'Constitutional Exceptionalism and the Common Law' (2009) 7 *ICON* 247, 264.

[77] Lozano (n 75).

[78] Ronald Dworkin, 'Political Judges and the Rule of Law' (1978) 64 *Proceedings of the British Academy* 259, 262.

[79] ibid; Brian Tamanaha, *On the Rule of Law: History, Politics, Theory* (Cambridge University Press, 2004) 102–04.

[80] Judith N Shklar, *Political Thought and Political Thinkers*, ed Stanley Hoffmann (University of Chicago Press, 1998) 21–22.

all people. Shklar argues that in order to realise this, all that was needed was not an exceptional degree of virtue (unlike Aristotle's syllogistic judge)[81] but

> a properly equilibrated political system in which power was checked by power in such a way that neither the violent urges of kings nor the arbitrariness of legislatures could impinge directly upon the individual in such a way as to frighten her and make her feel unsecure in her daily life.[82]

Shklar then suggests that AV Dicey's formulation of the rule of law was influenced by Montesquieu in the sense that he saw the rule of law amounting to men all following the same body of rules; however, Dicey took this to mean uniform institutions which also required one national order.[83] It follows from this formulation that a multiplicity of rules or institutions would only lead to liberty being decreased due to decreased certainty in the law. Shklar critiques this as 'trivialising the rule of law', stating that: 'No wonder that Dicey thought England's law and freedoms were already gravely threatened.' Shklar thus argues that Dicey ignores Montesquieu's fundamental assertion that the rule of law's goal was to reduce fear, instead seizing upon its elements of clarity and certainty and turning them against both the administrative state and Irish home rule. Dicey's conception was, in turn, the framework for FA Hayek's vision of the rule of law. This was then used as a sledgehammer against the establishment of the welfare state based on the delegation of power and complex administrative decision-making to unaccountable bodies using open-ended legal norms.[84] Shklar thus argues that there is no point in countenancing the rule of law if its function to protect individuals from fear is only to be conceptualised as 'the rules that govern courts or as a football in a game between friends and enemies of free-market liberalism'.[85]

Nevertheless, Dyzenhaus does attempt to reconcile Dicey's conception of the rule of law with that of his own. Dyzenhaus finds in Dicey a deep scepticism of the royal prerogative or inherent executive power.[86] Dyzenhaus thus contends that Dicey puts faith in Parliament and statutes. While this may ostensibly pave the way for 'rule by law' with a valid statute potentially enabling anything, Dyzenhaus argues that under Dicey's conception of the rule of law, one cannot have rule by law without rule of law as there eventually comes a point whereby rule by law is incapable of guiding behaviour.[87] It is difficult, however, to see what exactly is 'thick' about this conception of the rule of law. It is thick in the sense that it views law as not merely a mechanism through which state power flows; that stated, Raz's formalist conception also stresses the importance of the rule of law in guiding

[81] See text to n 52 in ch 4.

[82] Shklar (n 80) 22.

[83] ibid. Hence Dicey's objections to Irish home rule. See AV Dicey, 'Speech of Professor Dicey at the Liberal Unionists Meeting in the Music Hall, Birkenhead, 10 December 1887' (1997) *Bristol Selected Pamphlets*, (University of Bristol Library) www.jstor.org/stable/60243925, accessed 10 August 2017.

[84] See Friedrich August Hayek, *The Road To Serfdom* (Routledge, 1944).

[85] Shklar (n 80); see text to n 21 in ch 4.

[86] Dyzenhaus (n 4) 58–60; Dyzenhaus (n 7) 2031–32.

[87] Dyzenhaus (n 4) 6–7.

behaviour.[88] Nevertheless, Dyzenhaus elaborates by calling for 'appreciating the paradox that a concession that a statute is a valid one is not necessarily a concession that it has legal authority'.[89] While Dyzenhaus and Shklar differ in their interpretation of Dicey's account of the rule of law, both would, however, most likely agree that if the rule of law is recognised as an essential element of constitutional government generally and of representative democracy particularly, then it has an inherent value. For this reason, Shklar argues that the rule of law ought to be imbued with certain substantive content:

> If it is to avoid these conditions, the Rule of Law must take certain types of human conduct entirely out of public control, because they cannot be regulated or prevented without physical cruelty, arbitrariness and the creation of unremitting fear in the population. … The Rule of Law is meant to put a fence around the innocent citizen so that she may feel secure in these and all other legal activities. This implies that public officials will be hampered by judicial agents from interfering in these volatile and intensely personal forms of conduct.[90]

In light of these thicker conceptions of the rule of law, theories regarding the constitutional justification of judicial review may often be based, not on democracy or accountability but on the normative value of human rights. We saw in chapter four that as rights are not self-applying—someone must enforce them[91]—it generally falls on the judiciary to legally enforce such norms due to the judiciary's apparent elevation above the slings and arrows of politics.[92] Even in states where traditionally the scope of judicial review has been minimal, leaving the vindication of rights to the political branches, a more prominent role for judicial review has nevertheless been advocated for. David Feldman, prior to the enactment of the HRA, argued that the scope of judicial review in the UK could potentially be expanded and not be incompatible will the principle of parliamentary sovereignty. Feldman argued that parliamentary sovereignty was fundamentally justified by democratic legitimacy and so, it followed, that judicial review ought to be possible where it would improve democracy or not be in conflict with democracy.[93] This would potentially have been similar to John Hart Ely's justification for judicial review in the United States; however, as noted in chapter four, Dworkin demonstrated that this theory collapsed due to the instability of Ely's distinction between procedural and substantive rights.[94] Dworkin therefore justifies judicial review based on the

[88] Joseph Raz, *The Authority of Law*, 2nd edn (Oxford University Press, 2009) 210; see also text to n 23 in ch 4.

[89] Dyzenhaus (n 7) 2036.

[90] Shklar (n 80) 22.

[91] Tamanaha (n 79) 195.

[92] See text to n 42 in ch 4.

[93] See David Feldman, 'Democracy, the Rule of Law and Judicial Review' (1990) 19 *Federal Law Review* 1.

[94] See John Hart Ely, *Democracy and Distrust: A Theory of Judicial Review* (Harvard University Press, 1980); Ronald Dworkin, 'The Forum of Principle' (1981) 56 *New York University Law Review* 469, 516. See text to n 111 in ch 4 of this book.

normative value of a broad, substantive conception of the rule of law. The difficulty with this approach, however, is the consequentialist pressure that emergencies place on human rights which may make them an unstable base upon which to justify judicial review of emergency powers.

National Security and Human Rights

Much of the literature on emergency powers and judicial review is devoted to this consequentialist pressure that national security places on human rights. Scrutinising the relationship between security and human rights or 'liberty' is not a recent avenue of academic inquiry, with Kant, Locke and Hobbes, for example, all having dwelt on this issue. While they all reached the prima facie paradoxical conclusion that there cannot be liberty without security, the dominant paradigm today tends to consider liberty and security to be in a more antithetical relationship.[95] This 'security–liberty trade-off thesis', as stated by Eric Posner and Adrian Vermeule in *Terror in the Balance*, posits state security and liberty in a hydraulic relationship creating a situation whereby a measure taken in favour of state security tends to sacrifice liberty, and vice versa.[96] While this relationship is not automatic—eg increasing security necessarily results in decreasing liberty[97]—they argue that nevertheless a certain modicum of inverse change is generally present whenever security or liberty interests are advanced. Using this model, Posner and Vermeule argue that all counter-terrorism measures can be represented, or conceptualized, as 'constrained by a security–liberty possibility frontier' and mapped onto a hypothetical Cartesian plane with security and liberty on respective axes.[98] Measures that cannot be represented on this frontier are policies that cannot be attained due to existing technological constraints or limited resources.[99] This frontier is not fixed, however; it can change over time as threats 'wax and wane'.[100] Addressing subsequent criticisms of *Terror in the Balance*, Vermeule is keen to stress that the security–liberty trade-off thesis is not a normative argument advocating security over liberty. Instead, it is the second part of *Terror in the Balance* containing their 'deference thesis' based on consequentialist or utilitarian reasoning that makes

[95] Isiah Berlin, 'Two Concepts of Liberty' in *Four Essays on Liberty* (Oxford Paperbacks, 1969) 123–24; Steven J Heyman, 'Positive and Negative Liberty' (1992–93) 68 *Chicago-Kent Law Review* 81, 82.

[96] Eric Posner and Adrian Vermeule, *Terror in the Balance: Security Liberty and the Courts* (Oxford University Press, 2007).

[97] Vermeule describes as a 'misunderstanding the statement that whenever liberty is curtailed, security is automatically increased. Adrian Vermeule, 'Security and Liberty: Critiques of the Tradeoff Thesis', Harvard Public Law Working Paper No 11-19 (18 July 2011) <https://ssrn.com/abstract=1888334 or http://dx.doi.org/10.2139/ssrn.1888334> accessed 30 August 2017.

[98] Posner and Vermeule (n 96) 26–30.

[99] Vermeule (n 97) 3; Posner and Vermeule (n 96) 33–36.

[100] Posner and Vermeule (n 96) 27.

such an argument.[101] Vermeule further argues that the trade-off thesis is also not an empirical claim that 'any given security policy or the whole set of polices lies on the frontier' of the security–liberty trade-off as it may also lie behind this frontier;[102] however, this is not to say that it is not an empirical framework.

While the security–liberty trade-off thesis is not a normative argument, it nevertheless dominates the normative framework surrounding emergency powers. This dichotomy between security and liberty has created a dialectic in which emergency responses or controls may be defended on utilitarian grounds that they better advance security interests, or, conversely, they are critiqued from a deontological perspective that prioritises the protection and vindication of human rights.[103] Measures may also be attacked on similar grounds that they do not give adequate weight to security or liberty concerns. The security–liberty trade-off thesis therefore frames the normative debate on emergency powers with opposing sides arguing that the state *ought* to advance security concerns or conversely, *ought* to protect individual liberty. Indeed, the security–liberty trade-off has come to dominate the discourse on emergency powers, almost to the exclusion of other normative considerations.[104] This is reflected in Kent Roche's assertion that debates about emergency powers are not actually about emergencies but are instead about rights.[105]

While Posner and Vermeule use the language of liberty, it is not just this right alone that may be constrained by advancing security concerns; other rights, such as the right to privacy, expression, or rights pertaining to a fair trial may also be compromised when security is prioritised. This, too, is not an exhaustive list. 'Human rights' encompasses a large number of different principles and ideologies. Not all human rights will be forsaken in a period of emergency. Rather, it is those rights that a state feels most restricts its ability to act effectively that are derogated from and this will vary depending on the nature of the emergency. The role of rights as 'trumps', constraining the state from acting in a certain manner, illustrates how rights can impact upon state power, prioritising the individual over the alleged communal good.[106] It is those rights identified as 'civil and political rights' as distinct from 'social and economic rights' that are most likely to act as trumps

[101] Vermeule (n 96) 4–5.

[102] ibid, 2–3.

[103] Stephen Holmes describes this as 'the master metaphor dominating discussions on the war on terror'. Stephen Holmes, 'In Case of Emergency: Misunderstanding Tradeoffs in the War on Terror' (2009) 97 *California Law Review* 301, 313.

[104] An exception to this, however, would be the movement to find what Benjamin J Goold and Liora Lazarus term 'a language of reconciliation' between human rights and the rule of law. Liora Lazarus and Benjamin J Goold, 'Security and Human Rights: The Search for a Language of Reconciliation' in Benjamin J Goold and Liora Lazarus, *Security and Human Rights* (Hart Publishing, 2007) 3.

[105] Kent Roche, 'Ordinary Laws for Emergencies and Democratic Derogations from Rights' in Victor V Ramraj (ed), *Emergencies and the Limits of Legality* (Cambridge University Press, 2008) 231–34.

[106] See Ronald Dworkin, *Taking Rights Seriously* (Harvard University Press, 1977); Ronald Dworkin, 'Rights as Trumps' in Jeremy Waldron (ed), *Theories of Rights* (Oxford University Press, 1984) 153–67.

on state action, and consequently, are most likely to be put under strain during national security emergencies. Socioeconomic rights may instead be viewed as imposing positive duties or obligations on the state to act in a certain manner, as opposed to 'trumps' prohibiting state action or interference with the individual.[107] That stated, socioeconomic rights may also come under pressure in a state of emergency, particularly emergencies triggered by economic crises.[108] Relatedly, budgetary resources that may have been allocated towards the realisation of a right to education, for example, may instead be diverted towards military expenditure in a time of emergency. Budgetary pressures may also impact on the delivery of civil and political rights—for example, inhuman and degrading treatment arising from poor prison conditions.[109] The focus of the relation between security and liberty in the literature therefore masks the broad nature of phenomena that can trigger an emergency and the similarly broad nature of the emergency responses and laws that may be enacted.

Civil and political human rights are generally justified from a deontological point of view.[110] These deontological values become harder to cling onto, however, in situations where utilitarianism may offer a more 'persuasive' or politically palatable view of what may be ethical, or what action ought to be taken. In normalcy, doctrines such as 'proportionality' reject the trumping effect of human rights in instances where the public good to be achieved is commensurate to, or less than the impact on, an individual's right.[111] Emergency situations hyperbolise this consequentialist or utilitarian conception of the good to such an extent that arguments pertaining to the 'lesser of two evils' become potentially irresistible. To counter the extreme utilitarian pressures of emergencies, human rights treaties such as the ICCPR, ECHR and ACHR contain a number of rights that may not be derogated from, even during a period of emergency. These non-derogable rights include, amongst others, the right not to be subject to torture or cruel and unusual punishment, freedom from slavery and the right not to be subject to retrospective criminal legislation.[112] These 'absolute' norms ought to apply in all instances, corroborating their deontological justification, regardless of consequentialist pressures.[113]

[107] Inga Markovits, 'Socialist vs Bourgeois Rights—An East–West German Comparison' (1978) 45 *University of Chicago Law Review* 612, 621–623.

[108] See Ben Warwick, 'Socio-Economic Rights during Economic Crises: A Changed Approach to Non-Retrogression' (2016) 65 *ICLQ* 249; UN Counter-Terrorism Implementation Task Force Working Group Protecting Human Rights while Countering Terrorism, 'Expert Seminar on the Impact of Terrorism and Counter-Terrorism Measures on the Enjoyment of Economic, Social and Cultural Rights (ESCR)' (Geneva, 5–8 November 2008) <www.un.org/en/terrorism/ctitf/pdfs/wg_protecting_human_rights.pdf> accessed 10 August 2017.

[109] See, for example, *Peers v Greece* App No 28524/95 (19 April 2001), where the ECtHR found a breach of Art 3 ECHR due to the conditions in which the applicant was subject to in detention.

[110] George Letsas, 'Two Concepts of the Margin of Appreciation' (2006) 26 *OJLS* 705, 714.

[111] ibid.

[112] Art 15.2 ECHR; Art 4.2 ICCPR; Art 27.2 ACHR.

[113] For a detailed discussion of the concept of 'absoluteness', see Natasa Mavronicola, 'What Is an Absolute Right? Deciphering Absoluteness in the Context of Article 3 of the European Convention on Human Rights' (2012) 12 *HRLR* 723.

The events of 9/11, however, challenged even these fundamental norms, particularly the prohibition of torture which was considered objectively immoral and therefore a *jus cogens* norm of international law. The subsequent US-led 'war on terror' saw the United States use torture as a counter-terrorist technique, despite its moral repugnance and universal condemnation. What was once considered a settled debate was reopened with scholars invoking ticking time-bomb scenarios to stress-test the deontological justification for the absolute prohibition on torture by subjecting it to extreme utilitarian pressure.[114] Novel procedural 'safeguards', such as Alan Dershowitz's 'torture warrants', were conjured up[115] and the definition of torture was itself manipulated and recalibrated downwards in an attempt to exclude certain acts.[116] Declassified memos from the US Department of Justice show how the US definition of torture was interpreted by legal counsel advising the CIA and US military on conducting interrogations.[117] The interpretation of torture advanced by the Department of Justice was set at such a high threshold for an act to satisfy it that interrogators were able to subject detainees to severe treatment that would otherwise have constituted torture.[118] Key to this was the judgment of the ECtHR and its finding in *Ireland v UK* that methods of extreme interrogation used by British soldiers during the conflict in Northern Ireland amounted to 'inhuman and degrading treatment' but not torture.[119] An unintended consequence of this 'minimalist' approach of the ECtHR therefore was its utilisation to facilitate the elaborate torture regime operated by the United States post-9/11. The public–private divide was also exploited with much of the sophisticated rendition apparatus put in place by the US government delivered by the private sector.[120]

Thus, even if one manages to cling to a deontological justification for human rights, the language of human rights may itself be manipulated to recalibrate downwards treatment of individuals so as not to breach the right in question. Relatedly, the language of rights may be interpreted to encompass new rights such as that of the 'right to security or safety', which in turn can be used to 'trump' other rights

[114] Oren Gross, 'Are Torture Warrants Warranted? Pragmatic Absolutism and Official Disobedience' (2004) 88 *Minnesota Law Review* 1481, 1497–1500.

[115] See Alan Dershowitz, *Why Terrorism Works: Understanding the Threat, Responding to the Challenge* (Yale University Press, 2003).

[116] For a discussion of the 'recalibration' of rights in the UK and US during the 'war on terror', see de Londras (n 54) ch 3.

[117] 18 USC §§2340–2340A.

[118] Jay Bybee, 'Memorandum for A Gonzales … [Re:] Standards for Conduct for Interrogation under 18 USC 2340–2340A', United States, Department of Justice, Office of Legal Counsel (1 August 2002).

[119] *Ireland v UK* (n 38). In 2014, Ireland submitted a petition to the ECtHR to reopen this case in light of new information regarding the UK government's knowledge of the interrogation methods used by the British armed forces in Northern Ireland. See Henry McDonald, 'Ireland to Clash with UK at Human Rights Court over Hooded Men Judgment' *The Guardian* (2 December 2014) <www.theguardian.com/world/2014/dec/02/ireland-european-court-hooded-men> accessed 10 August 2017.

[120] See Fiona de Londras, 'Privatised Sovereign Performance: Regulating in the "Gap" between Security and Rights?' (2011) 38 *Journal of Law and Society* 96.

such as liberty and privacy.[121] Indeed, Article 3 of the United Nations Universal Declaration of Human Rights (UDHR) boldly states that: 'Everybody has the right to life, liberty and security of the person.'[122] While this traditionally meant that a person had a right to security *from* state action, it is now being re-interpreted as bestowing a positive obligation on a state to pursue the security interests of its citizens.[123] These arguments harken back to the original finding of Locke, Hobbes and Kant that one cannot have liberty without security. Liora Lazarus, however, argues that if a right to security does exist it must be defined in the narrowest sense possible. That is, it must protect that which is not already vindicated by other rights that already exist. Lazarus stresses the dangers in framing security issues in rights language, arguing that vesting individuals with enforceable rights to security is 'at odds with the inherently collective and polycentric pursuit of safeguarding security in society'.[124] Relatedly, if an individual's right to security is enforced, will this undermine the security of others? And finally, if a right to security is recognised, would it be one that could trump almost every other right?[125] Consequently, while it was earlier suggested that the security–liberty trade-off identified by Posner and Vermeule could be expanded to be described as the security–human rights trade-off, one must remember that human rights themselves can be used to impact upon other rights. Notwithstanding this, however, one can state that security concerns in a state of extreme necessity produce a strong utilitarian argument in favour of constricting classic civil and political human rights norms. Who decides as to what balance ought to be struck between security and human rights is, however, a markedly different question.

Legal Grey Holes and Constituent Power

The result of this is that a 'thicker' understanding of the rule of law imbued with values such as human rights may open up the judiciary to accusations of making overtly political decisions given the lack of agreement as to what such rights entail. In essence, it can potentially delegitimise the judiciary when reviewing issues of national security. Moreover, it potentially makes the rule of law vulnerable to the security–liberty thesis in a manner that a more formalist conception of the rule of law may be insulated from. That stated, my argument is certainly *not* that these values are not worth preserving in a state of emergency. Nor is it my contention

[121] Jeremy Waldron, *Torture, Terror and Trade-offs: Philosophy for the White House* (Oxford University Press, 2010) ch 2.

[122] Art 3 Universal Declaration of Human Rights (1948).

[123] Liora Lazarus and Benjamin J Goold, 'Security and Human Rights: The Search for a Language of Reconciliation' in Goold and Lazarus (n 104) 19.

[124] ibid.

[125] Liora Lazarus, 'Mapping the Right to Security' in Goold and Lazarus (n 104) 327–38.

that those advocating the protection and vindication of human rights in a period of emergency are pursuing a fruitless inquiry. In fact, my contention is quite the opposite. Rather, I contend that these values need assistance. This can potentially be done by shifting the debate away from concepts where there is considerable disagreement as to the scope of norms back to one where there the legitimacy of judicial review is on more solid ground: namely, a restatement of the justification of judicial review on a straightforward vindication of a narrower conception of the rule of law and keeping decision-makers within the bound of their discretion—that is, by invoking the concept of constituent power to demonstrate that all emergency powers must be conceptualised as 'constituted powers' in order to resist the Schmittian Challenge. In this way I seek to provide judges with 'a better justificatory basis to scrutinise'[126] while at the same time insulating the judiciary from accusations of politicisation that may affect more substantive conceptions of the rule of law. Consequently, this requires focus, not just on the second limb of the Schmittian Challenge—the measures taken in lieu of a declaration of an emergency—but on the existence of an emergency in the first instance. Indeed, as I shall now argue, the first limb may be more important than the second as focus on the second allows for the first to be disregarded.

The Two Limbs of the Schmittian Challenge

To reiterate, the Schmittian Challenge is that both the decision to declare a state of emergency and act in an emergency cannot be circumscribed by law. Once again, the *Belmarsh* judgment is an excellent example of the importance of both limbs of Schmitt's challenge, in particular Lord Hoffmann's dissent which stands as a striking outlier of judicial fortitude in the jurisprudence regarding the existence of a state of emergency. Indeed, Lord Hoffmann's fortitude was particularly surprising in light of his earlier judgment on issues of national security in *SSHD v Rehman*.[127] *Rehman* concerned a Pakistani national with temporary leave to stay in the UK challenging a decision of the Home Secretary to deport him from the UK on the grounds that his deportation would be conducive to the public good in the interests of national security.[128] Lord Hoffmann held that while what is meant by 'national security' is a question of law, the question of whether something is 'in the interests' of national security is not. Rather it is a 'matter of judgment and policy' entrusted to the executive.[129] Lord Hoffmann relies on *Chandler v DPP* to reach this conclusion, arguing that the finding in that case that whether having nuclear bombers was conducive to the safety of the state was a matter for the decision of the executive.[130] Lord Hoffmann's deference on this question thus

[126] Dyzenhaus (n 4) 180.
[127] *SSHD v Rehman* [2001] UKHL 47; [2002] 1 All ER 122.
[128] ibid, 124.
[129] ibid, 139 [50] (Lord Hoffmann).
[130] *Chandler v DPP* [1962] 3 All ER 142; ibid 139 [50].

strays into the area of non-justiciability, recognising certain matters pertaining to national security as political questions.

While Lord Hoffmann's judgments in *Rehman* and *Belmarsh* seem inherently irreconcilable, Dyzenhaus contends that there is a degree of ideological and doctrinal consistency connecting both. Dyzenhaus argues that in both *Belmarsh* and *Rehman*, Lord Hoffmann accepted the second limb of Schmitt's challenge—'that the executive is entitled to decide how to respond to an emergency, if in fact there is an emergency'.[131] Dyzenhaus thus contends that Lord Hoffmann is perfectly happy with legal black holes so long as they are correctly formed. Dyzenhaus may, however, be being somewhat harsh on Lord Hoffmann's reasoning in *Belmarsh*. Dyzenhaus argues that while Lord Hoffmann was robust on the existence of a state of emergency, he accepted the second limb of Schmitt's challenge—that the executive is entitled to decide how to respond to an emergency if in fact there is an emergency. The difficulty with this analysis, however, is that it is predicated upon Lord Hoffmann's refusal to review whether the measures where proportionate to the exigencies of the situation. However, as Lord Hoffmann had already found that an emergency existed, there was no need to review this second question, with Lord Hoffmann expressly stating that:

> I would prefer not to express a view on this point. I said that the power of detention is at present confined to foreigners and I would not like to give the impression that all that was necessary was to extend the power to United Kingdom citizens as well. In my opinion, such a power in any form is not compatible with our constitution.[132]

This may imply that Lord Hoffmann did think that all that was necessary was to extend the provision to detain British citizens too; however, he then emphasises that such a power *in any form* would not be compatible with the British Constitution. Although he is silent as to whether Parliament *could* do this given the at times ambiguous distinction between 'legality' and 'constitutionality' in British public law, Lord Hoffmann is acutely aware of the transformative nature of permanent emergencies:

> [T]he real threat to the life of the nation … comes not from terrorism, but from laws such as these. They are the true measure of what terrorism may achieve. It is for Parliament to decide whether to give the terrorists such a victory.[133]

Lord Hoffmann's key difficulty in *Belmarsh* is that he considered parliamentary sovereignty to be the constitutional bedrock against which law had no recourse to. His reasoning therefore is *not* that he is comfortable with the executive acting as it sees fit once a black hole is correctly created by Parliament. Rather, his understanding of the British Constitution focuses on the potential of Parliament to do as it sees fit, creating zones beyond the reach of courts—something that

[131] Dyzenhaus (n 4) 181.
[132] *Belmarsh* (n 44) 135.
[133] ibid.

Dicey's conception of the rule of law seems comfortable with too.[134] It is for this very reason that Lord Hoffmann warns that: 'It is for Parliament to decide whether to give the terrorists such a victory.'[135] Hence it is Parliament, not the executive, that Lord Hoffmann is concerned with. Moreover, it was for this reason that Lord Hoffmann sought refuge in the text of the HRA—a creation of Parliament itself. Under Lord Hoffmann's conception of the British Constitution, there is no distinction between supreme legislative power of parliament and constituent power. The 'radical incoherence' of Lord Hoffmann in *Belmarsh* and *Rehman* therefore is not necessarily due to Lord Hoffmann's own judicial philosophy of constitutional interpretation but due to the Scmittian Challenge to norms such as human rights and the rule of law in a constitutional order vindicating the absolute sovereignty of Parliament.[136]

The difference between Lord Hoffmann's reasoning in *Belmarsh* and *Rehman* may also, in fact, be due to what de Londras describes as judicial push-back. *Belmarsh* was decided by the House of Lords in 2005, some four years after 9/11 and, in particular, shortly after the invasion of Iraq and what Lord Hoffmann described as 'the fiasco over Iraqi weapons of mass destruction'.[137] The truth may be therefore that *Rehman* and *Belmarsh* are not reconcilable; rather, *Belmarsh* is a 'Road to Damascus' moment for Lord Hoffmann following the Iraq war and the consequences of blind trust in the executive's assessment of the threat to national security. Unfortunately, Lord Hoffmann was very much in the minority on this issue.

Dyzenhaus, however, also criticises the majority in *Belmarsh* for conceding to the first ground of Schmitt's challenge: the existence of a state of emergency. Dyzenhaus argues that judges were not wrong to defer to the executive in principle on the question as to the existence of a state of emergency; rather, they were wrong to defer because an inadequate case for deference was made.[138] As we have seen, with the exception of Lord Hoffmann no judge in either the House of Lords or the ECtHR engaged in any effective scrutiny of whether there existed a public emergency threatening the life of the nation. While Dyzenhaus does argue for scrutiny of *both* decisions, a thicker substantive conception of the rule of law with an emphasis on protecting values such as human rights will, nevertheless, harken back to the security–liberty divide, placing the judiciary on the back foot. It creates a dichotomy between the two concepts that judges are expected to choose between with the system stacked in favour of security. This framing is understandable when the derogation is included in a human rights treaty or a domestic bill of rights. That stated, even in times of normalcy, justifications for judicial review

[134] See text to n 86 above.
[135] *Belmarsh* (n 44) 135.
[136] See text to nn 131–72 in ch 6 for a discussion of parliamentary sovereignty and constituent power.
[137] *Belmarsh* (n 44) 134.
[138] Dyzenhaus (n 4) 179.

from human rights perspectives may also put the judiciary on the defensive as such arguments open up space for debate regarding law and disagreement; on who should decide and accusations that judges are merely carrying out politics by other means.[139]

This broad, substantive conception of the rule of law may therefore have the opposite of its intended effect and, somewhat ironically, could potentially result in a minimalist approach. It encourages the judiciary to view the entire question as one of proportionality and, in turn, its own function as one of gauging proportionality. It collapses the existence of a state of emergency into the second limb of whether the measures are proportionate, opening the door for the potential of permanent measures. It is for this reason that the ECtHR felt comfortable with declaring that nowhere in Article 15 ECHR does it say that emergencies must be temporary, ignoring the tricky question as to the existence of a state of emergency and falling back on the more familiar surroundings of the proportionality of the measures.[140] It is only through Lord Hoffmann's approach of emphasising the transformative aspect of the state of emergency that the dangers of permanence are evident. This can only be done by stressing the importance of reviewing the existence of a state of emergency in the first instance, rather than merely falling back to the relative security and familiarity of the second limb.

Indeed, if courts were to take a minimalist approach to the question as to the existence of an emergency and the measures taken in lieu of a declaration of emergency, it is difficult to see how the existence of a state of emergency could ever be challenged. *Belmarsh* illustrates how emergency measures are dependent upon the existence of a state of emergency; however, the existence of a state of emergency is not necessarily dependent upon an individual measure but rather all the measures taken. Thus, the existence of an emergency is the keystone legitimising all subsequent emergency powers.[141] This response could entail numerous different measures. A minimalist judge therefore would focus only on each individual measure rather than on the broader question as to the existence of a state of emergency so as not to undermine the entire emergency regime as a whole. The result is that the existence of a state of emergency can never be questioned by the minimalist judge. Moreover, a human rights approach may potentially lead to such a minimalist approach by encouraging the judiciary to focus on the proportionality question rather than the question as to the existence of a state of emergency. However, by stressing the transformative nature of permanent states of emergency and highlighting the potential they have to act as a claim for the constituent power, a court's constitutional duty to review the existence of a state of emergency is revealed as fundamental to ensuring this power is a constituted power.

[139] See text to nn 100–12 in ch 4.
[140] *A v UK* (n 44) [178].
[141] See text to nn 177–93 in ch 1.

Beyond Human Rights Norms

A further limitation to a human rights approach is that it its scope is limited to emergency powers that affect these norms only. Certainly, the most egregious impact of emergency powers is invariably on human rights with the aforementioned discussion on torture a particularly acute example.[142] Nevertheless, permanent states of emergency affect other constitutional norms: for example, those pertaining to the separation of powers; norms regulating the relation between federal and regional governments in a federal constitutional order; and even what may, prima facie, appear to be purely procedural norms. In addition, even when human rights are concerned, legal arguments may centre on other issues raised by the case. For example, much of the legal advice concerning the torture of detainees in the war on terror was focused on the separation of powers doctrine in the US Constitution and the inherent executive power of the president to interrogate detainees.[143] This was reflected in the dissenting judgment of Thomas J in *Hamdi v Rumsfeld* that 'judicial interference in these areas [national security] destroys the purpose of vesting primary responsibility in a unitary Executive'.[144] A difficulty arises, therefore, in how a human rights approach could justify judicial scrutiny of these powers.

Ireland: Beyond the Security–Liberty Divide

An example of this can again be seen from Ireland's entrenched emergency from 1939 and 1995. Between 1939 and 1995, when Ireland was in a period of official emergency, the scope of Article 28.3.3° was entirely dependent upon the interpretation of the phrase 'Nothing in this constitution' contained in the first line of the constitutional provision. In *Re McGrath and Harte*, the applicants sought relief via habeas corpus from their sentence of death following their conviction of murder by a military court established by the Emergency Powers (Amendment) (No 2) Act 1940.[145] The barrister for the petitioners, Seán Mac Bride, proposed three possible constructions of the phrase 'Nothing in this constitution':

1. They refer to those declaratory statements of right (a) of a non-specific nature (b) which are contained in the constitution and (c) which had no independent existence prior to the enactment of, or apart from the Constitution, or (d) which are not expressly or impliedly, maintained under all emergencies short of actual war or rebellion.
2. They refer to those declaratory statements of right (a) which are contained in the constitution and (b) which are not expressly or impliedly maintained under all emergencies short of actual war or armed rebellion.

[142] See text to n 113 above.

[143] Bybee (n 118) 31–39.

[144] *Hamdi v Rumsfeld* (2004) 542 US 507, 582.

[145] *Re McGrath and Harte* [1941] IR 68. This validity of this act was dependent upon a declaration of emergency under Art 28.3.3°.

3. They refer to all the rights and institutions created by the constitution (a) whether or not they had an independent existence prior to or a part from the constitution and (b) whether or not they are maintained expressly or impliedly by other provisions of the constitution at all times short of actual war or armed rebellion.[146]

For Mac Bride, constructions 1 and 3 represented opposite extremes. He concluded that 'a large number of intermediate constructions could be found'.[147] The case was decided against the petitioners, with Sullivan CJ finding that:

> [O]n the construction of the article itself none of the suggested alternative constructions proposed by counsel can have any foundation in view of the clear language of the article which, in the times and circumstances contemplated, makes it impossible to invoke other articles of the constitution to invalidate acts passed by the Oireachtas and expressed to be for the purpose of securing the public safety and the preservation of the state within the terms of the article.[148]

Following this judgment, the Attorney General and, consequently, the Irish government considered that the third interpretation, the broadest—permitting the suspension of essentially every article of the Constitution–was the correct meaning of the phrase 'Nothing in this constitution'.[149]

Archival sources also show that the Taoiseach sought specific advice from the Attorney General relating to whether the life of the current Dáil could be extended beyond the limit of seven years set by Article 16.5.[150] Following the widest possible interpretation proposed by the Attorney General in the aftermath of *Re McGrath and Harte*, the Attorney General concluded that such an extension of the life of the Dáil was permissible under Article 28.3.3°. The Attorney General did, however, suggest that such an extension should be done via legislation rather than an emergency order, before clarifying that 'although there is no sufficient reason, of which I am aware why this step could not be taken by an emergency order'.[151] Advocating a legislative mechanism was therefore a matter of optics and a more politically acceptable approach, rather than being legally required.

Support for this widest possible interpretation can also be found in the drafting of the Constitution. Early drafts of the Constitution considered listing the specific articles of the proposed constitution that could be suspended during a period of emergency, rather than a general suspension of the entire Constitution.[152]

146 These arguments are not explicitly enumerated in the Court's judgments; however, they are contained in a letter the barrister for the petitioners in *Re McGrath and Harte* submitted to the Taoiseach in which he expressed concern regarding the scope of Art 28.3.3°. 'Letter from Sean Mac Bride to an Taoiseach', 8 January 1941 NAI/TAOIS S12172; see also Greene, 'Declaring a State of Emergency' (n 22) 383–86.

147 'Letter from Sean Mac Bride', ibid; Greene, ibid.

148 ibid; *Re McGrath and Harte* (n 145) 76; 'Letter from Attorney General to an Taoiseach', 16 January 1941, NAI/TAOIS S12172.

149 'Letter from Attorney General to an Taoiseach', ibid.

150 ibid.

151 ibid, [4].

152 Greene, 'Historical Evolution' (n 22) 121–24.

However, there was a conflict between this provision and subsequent provisions that provided for the general suspension of the Constitution. This was resolved by opting for the broader, general suspension clause. Indeed, Mac Bride himself notes that there is nothing in the Constitution to support a narrow interpretation of 'Nothing in this constitution' and no guidance to be gleaned from the Constitution to help identify which rights are capable of suspension and which are absolute.[153] Early drafts of the Irish Constitution included the emergency provisions either in a separate headed provision, or within the articles dealing with fundamental rights.[154]

One could perhaps adopt a teleological approach to the issue, which is essentially what Mac Bride did when discerning his respective definitions; however, given the 'clear language' of Article 28.3.3° any interpretation, other than the literal meaning of 'Nothing in this constitution' when parsed into 'nothing' is satisfactory.[155] The unpredictable nature of emergencies would also make it difficult to identify what provisions could be safely excluded from the scope of Article 28.3.3°. The Taoiseach's question regarding the life of the Dáil shows that not just articles dealing with personal rights may be suspended, but also articles regarding the separation of powers.[156] Indeed, MacBride noted that: 'Every article of the constitution contains a constitutional declaration and an equivalent right to have that declaration observed.'[157] If one were therefore to follow the literal definition of 'Nothing in this constitution', every article of the Constitution would be liable to suspension, including Article 46, enabling amendment of the Constitution without a referendum.

Thus, if the Irish Government were to follow through with the proposal to extend the duration of Dáil Éireann beyond the seven years stipulated by the Constitution, for example by issuing an executive order saying that elections would be held every ten years, and this order were to remain in place indefinitely, the constitutional provision of seven years would no longer be effective. In turn, this lack of effectiveness would then call into question the validity of the constitutional provision. Moreover, the interpretation of Article 28.3.3° suggested by the Attorney General could potentially legitimise a move by the government to suspend elections indefinitely. A challenge to this could be made from a human rights perspective, for example, by conceptualising democracy as a human rights issue or elaborating upon a substantive conception of the rule of law that includes democratic values. However, it may be difficult to do so in the context of an extension of the period between elections from seven to ten years. A substantive conception of the rule of law would therefore find it difficult to challenge such an

[153] 'Letter from Sean Mac Bride' (n 146); Greene, 'Declaring a State of Emergency' (n 22) 384–85.
[154] Greene, ibid, 383–89.
[155] ibid.
[156] 'Letter from Attorney General' (n 148).
[157] 'Letter from Sean Mac Bride' (n 146).

emergency provision, notwithstanding its draconian and authoritarian implications. However, by distinguishing between constituent and constituted power, one can demonstrate that this interpretation of Article 28.3.3° is more in line with the former than the latter. This interpretation thus amounts to a claim to the constituent power and therefore is ultra vires the legislature as constituted by the Irish Constitution. Such a claim, as demonstrated in chapter three, must be rejected.

Article 48 of the Weimar Constitution: Beyond the Security–Liberty Divide

A human rights approach would also find it difficult to challenge, for example, an indefinite state of emergency that impacted on the separation of powers between national and regional governments in a federal constitution. As discussed in chapter one, states of emergency often result in a concentration of power in one branch of government—usually the executive. This consolidation comes not just at the expense of the legislature or judiciary but from the local to the national, or from the regional to the federal.[158] Carl Schmitt's own analysis of the infamous Article 48 of the Weimar Constitution expressly acknowledges and embraces this.[159] The second paragraph of Article 48 empowered the Reich President in a state of emergency to take the measures necessary for their restoration, intervening, if necessary, with the aid of the armed forces.[160] Article 48 then listed Articles 114, 115, 117, 118, 123, 124 and 153 as those which the Reich President could 'temporarily abrogate in whole or in part'. At first glance, one would assume that 'necessary measures' in the first sentence of this paragraph was necessarily qualified by the express articles mentioned in the following sentence of the same paragraph. It should follow that any other provision of the constitution was inviolable and, indeed, this was the dominant and widely accepted interpretation of Article 48 in the early years of the Weimar Constitution. This interpretation, as set out by Richard Grau, was defended on historical, logical-grammatical and systematic grounds.[161] At the first annual conference of the Association of German Constitutional Lawyers in Jena in 1924, however, Schmitt took direct aim at this 'doctrine of inviolability'. While aspects of his argumentation centred on Grau's historical analysis of the drafting of Article 48 and so is contextually specific to Article 48, Schmitt also argues that emergency measures taken before 1924 had infringed other constitutional norms.[162] Schmitt argued that these infringements were not unconstitutional; rather they were just a necessary application of the power contained in Article 48. For example, emergency powers conferred on the Reich President would invariably infringe upon the constitutional norms

[158] Posner and Vermeule (n 96) 16.

[159] Carl Schmitt, *Dictatorship*, trans Michael Hoelzl and Graham Ward (Polity Press, 2014) 183–86.

[160] Art 48 Weimar Constitution.

[161] Marc de Wilde, 'The State of Emergency in the Weimar Republic: Legal Disputes over Article 48 of the Weimar Constitution (2010) 78 *Legal History Review* 135, 141.

[162] Schmitt (n 159) 183–86.

regulating the federal powers between the federal government and the constituent states.[163]

Schmitt's analysis does not, however, envisage that the President had unlimited authority under Article 48. Rather, he stated that such powers had to be necessary 'for the restoration of public safety and order'.[164] In addition, the President could not violate what Schmitt termed the 'organisational minimum' of the Constitution and could only make 'measures' as distinct from enacting a new civil code.[165] Had this been the entirety of Schmitt's analysis of Article 48, his conclusions may have correlated with his earlier 1921 thesis on commissarial dictatorship. Schmitt's idea of an 'organisational minimum' of the constitutional order could then be said to be similar to the discussion in chapter three of the Indian courts' distinction between amending the constitution and abolishing its 'essential features'.[166] However, Schmitt's analysis does not end here. He also notes that paragraph 5 of Article 48 envisaged a statute being passed that would further clarify the powers of the President under Article 48. Article 48 was thus intended as a transitory provision.[167] Such a statute had not been passed, however, and so as it was left open, allowing Schmitt an opportunity to unleash his more radical interpretation of Article 48. It thus paved the way for Schmitt to interpret Article 48 as containing the residue of constitution-making power, ie the constituent power. This is not to say, however, that had this paragraph 5 not been included, Schmitt would have argued that Article 48 was a limited power. Schmitt's *Political Theology* was published a year earlier in 1922 and thus he had already abandoned his distinction between commissarial and sovereign dictatorship.[168] Paragraph 5 therefore merely provided Schmitt with the necessary formal text in which he could unleash his more radical theory.

The Weimar Constitution therefore illustrates problems similar to those faced by the Irish Constitution, notwithstanding the fact that the former had expressly enumerated the rights that could be suspended during a state of emergency. What both these examples reveal is that emergencies have an impact on the constitutional order far beyond human rights provisions. Consequently, it is difficult to see how imbuing the rule of law with substantive values such as human rights in Weimar could establish judicial review on constitutional questions involving the division of powers between federal and regional governments. However, by stressing the potential permanence of such emergency powers and the impact this can

[163] ibid.

[164] ibid, 190–91.

[165] de Wilde (n 162) 144.

[166] See text from nn 112–26 in ch 3.

[167] de Wilde (n 161) 144–45; Schmitt (n 159) 200–08. Rosalind Dixon and Tom Ginsburg refer to constitutions leaving certain matters open for future decision-makers as 'deciding not to decide'. See Rosalind Dixon and Tom Ginsburg, 'Deciding not to Decide: Deferral in Constitutional Design' (2011) 9 *ICON* 636.

[168] Carl Schmitt, *Political Theology: Four Chapters on the Concept of Sovereignty*, trans G Schwab (University of Chicago Press, 2005).

have on the validity of these norms, the true nature of the Schmittian Challenge is revealed. It is a claim to the constituent power of the state, a claim that is ultra vires that of the legislature or executive. It is a claim that the judiciary must reject if it is to establish the constitution truly as a constitution and distinguish the constituent power from the constituted power.

Beyond National Security Emergencies

The constitutional impact of emergencies beyond human rights norms raises a further difficulty with justifications of judicial review grounded in human rights and the existing literature which overemphasises national security emergencies. This is typified by the security–liberty divide and, in particular, Kent Roche's assertion that emergencies are actually about rights.[169] To recall, in chapter one, I argued that constructing a typology of emergency powers based on the phenomenon that triggers them may be of limited use due to the propensity of one crisis triggering or morphing into another crisis.[170] That stated, the emergency measures bespoke to each individual crisis may look radically different from other emergencies. Again, the measures taken in response to an economic crisis will invariably be different to those enacted to tackle a national security emergency.

On this question of economic measures, Lon Fuller, whom Dyzenhaus draws upon for his substantive conception of the rule of law, is sceptical of the role of judicial review in adjudicating upon what he termed 'polycentric disputes'.[171] Polycentric disputes 'comprise a large and complicated web of interdependent relationships, such that a change to one factor produces an incalculable series of changes to other factors'.[172] The resolution of these disputes therefore should not be for courts but for the political branches. Fuller's own conception of the rule of law therefore saw a diminished role for courts on these issues. I have argued elsewhere that the nature of polycentric disputes over economic measures calls into question the standard emergency response of legislative—as distinct from judicial—deference to executive claims of necessity and expertise.[173] However, the permanence of the measures or processes surrounding the implementation of the measures decided upon to resolve such polycentric disputes can raise concerns as to the effectiveness, and consequently the validity, of constitutional norms as those raised by national security emergencies. Again, Article 48 of the Weimar Constitution illustrates this point as its use was often to enable extraordinary powers to

[169] Kent Roche, 'Ordinary Laws for Emergencies and Democratic Derogations from Rights' in Victor V Ramraj (ed), *Emergencies and the Limits of Legality* (Cambridge University Press, 2008) 231–34.

[170] See text to n 123 in ch 1.

[171] See Lon Fuller, 'The Forms and Limits of Adjudication' (1978) 92 *Harvard Law Review* 353.

[172] JA King, 'The Pervasiveness of Polycentricity' [2008] *PL* 101, 101–02; Fuller, ibid, 395.

[173] See Alan Greene, 'Questioning Executive Supremacy in an Economic State of Emergency' (2015) 35 *LS* 594.

tackle economic crises such as hyperinflation; crises that the Reichstag, paralysed by the antagonistic communists and National Socialists, was incapable of dealing with. The constitutional norms circumvented by the use of Article 48 in this manner were thus those pertaining to the separation of powers, rather than human rights norms. One could perhaps focus on impact of such economic measures on, for example, socioeconomic rights or the delivery of civil and political rights which require state resources.[174] Again, however, Fuller's own substantive conception of the rule of law saw a limited role for courts on such issues, even if their human rights impact it stressed. However, by stressing the distinction between constituent and constituted powers and assessing the impact such permanent emergency powers may have on the validity and effectiveness of the constitutional norms in question, judicial review can be justified. Moreover, this is done using a narrower conception of the rule of law than that envisaged by Dyzenhaus or Fuller, thus insulating this justification from accusations of politicisation that may affect these more substantive conceptions of the rule of law.

Conclusions

In order to respond to the Schmittian Challenge, both the decision to declare a state of emergency and the emergency measures enacted must be scrutinised. However, this second question—the necessity of the measures taken—is necessarily dependent upon the first question—the existence of a state of emergency. In order to assess whether a state of emergency has rendered certain norms ineffective is to assess the measures taken in lieu of a declaration of a state of emergency. Thus, it follows that a permanent state of emergency cannot invalidate constitutional norms through the process of desuetude if the emergency powers enacted do not invalidate constitutional norms. This was the case of Ireland's entrenched emergency from 1939 to 1995 where there were no emergency powers in operation at all and the emergency therefore was purely notional. As noted in chapter three, the key issue, however, is the potentiality for a permanent state of emergency. It is this potentiality that reveals the distinction between constituent and constituted power—between limited and unlimited power. Constitutionally providing for a state of emergency is not to succumb to the first limb of Schmitt's challenge if these emergency powers are treated as constituted powers.

As Dyzenhaus argues, such review ought to be meaningful, however, or this control would act merely as legitimating emergency powers by providing a 'thin veil of legality' and creating a legal grey hole.[175] This risk is dwarfed, however, in

[174] See text to n 109.
[175] Dyzenhaus (n 4) 41–43.

comparison to the consequences of a non-justiciable decision to declare a state of emergency. Relatedly, it is possible that the courts, while being initially deferential to the political branches, may then begin to reassert themselves as the emergency drags on; such an outcome would not be possible if the courts were to hold that the decision to declare a state of emergency is non-justiciable.[176] The risk of a legal grey hole is dwarfed in comparison to the dangers to the legal order that would be the result of considering the decision to declare a state of emergency to be a purely political question.

The normative value of human rights in and of themselves is vulnerable to utilitarian pressures that may arise in periods of emergency. These pressures to constrain human rights may be fanned by further constitutional pressure from the democratic branches, accountable to a fearful or retributive public. Human rights need a helping hand in emergencies and so the normative framework surrounding emergencies and controls of emergencies ought to look beyond security and human rights. The rule of law has the capacity to perform this function, and so adds an additional value that ought to be taken into account when assessing whether the judiciary ought to defer to the executive during an emergency. This formulation of the rule of law can be formalistic, in the sense that it does not prima facie incorporate human rights concerns, as to collapse human rights into the rule of law brings with it all the baggage that weakens the human rights approach. However, it ought to be 'thicker' than a 'rule by law' approach such as that taken by the ECtHR towards the first limb of Article 15. Schmitt himself admitted this when arguing that a state of emergency cannot be accommodated by law as it cannot be described accurately enough to satisfy the demands of clarity and certainty.

The result therefore is that the decision to declare a state of emergency is one that should be amenable to judicial review, notwithstanding the prudential difficulties with judicial review of such issues, concerns as to the democratic legitimacy of the judiciary, and contentions from a substantive conception of the rule of law that this may result in overly deferential review, thus doing more harm than good. However, what of constitutions that do not expressly provide for emergency powers; is this, perhaps, a better solution to the Schmittian Challenge? Moreover, is this a better way of dealing with extreme crises without embracing the flawed assumption of the normalcy–emergency dichotomy? It is these questions that I shall address in the following chapter.

176 De Londras and Davis (n 55).

6

Alternatives to Constitutional States of Emergency

Introduction

Dangers are inherent when providing for constitutional emergency powers. In one sense, this may be seen as capitulating to the first limb of the Schmittian Challenge and admitting that there are certain situations which the ordinary bounds of the constitution cannot accommodate. On the other hand, failing to account for emergency powers may lead either to officials acting expressly in contravention of the constitution, or the ordinary parameters of the constitution may be recalibrated and reinterpreted to permit the exceptional. The purpose of this chapter is to explore the idea of refusing to countenance emergency powers in a constitutional order, unpacking the specific details in line with this. Constitutions that vindicate the sovereignty of parliament will also be addressed as these orders present their own particular challenges to the normalcy–emergency dichotomy. I contend that both these 'business as usual' constitutions and constitutions which vindicate the sovereignty of parliament must, nevertheless, address the question of emergencies and, in particular with regards to the latter, the question of constituent power. Moreover, the 'recalibration of normalcy' also affects what has been termed legislative accommodation—confronting emergencies through exceptional legislation rather than constitutional provisions. These models therefore must also be scrutinised with a view to assessing whether they provide an alternative solution to providing for emergency powers in a constitution. Finally, proposals to confront emergencies 'extra-legally' will be discussed. Ultimately, I will contend that expressly providing for emergency powers, nevertheless, remains the best approach to confronting extreme crises.

Why Emergency? The Problem with 'Business as Usual'

Providing for a state of emergency is an express admission that there are situations with which the ordinary legal system cannot deal.[1] These responses often envis-

[1] See text to nn 142–93 in ch 1 of this book.

age the temporary jettisoning of the very values that give the constitutional order its identity. Not all constitutions, however, expressly recognise this normalcy–emergency dichotomy. 'Monism'[2] or 'business as usual'[3] models of crisis confrontation reject this notion that emergencies justify any alteration of the formal constitutional legal system. The constitutional order is instead perceived as able to accommodate any situation that it faces. An emergency thus creates no distinct legal opportunity for additional power that the state may use to defend itself. A prima facie reading of these monist constitutions would appear to suggest that the executive and other branches of government are afforded no more power or discretion than in ordinary times to promote and protect the common good. The rationalisations for an emergency response—flexibility, urgency and necessity—are not considered to warrant a deviation from the ordinary constitutional order.

Such a prima facie reading of US Constitution would suggest that it is an example of a 'business as usual' approach to crises.[4] Apart from the provision that Congress may suspend the writ of habeas corpus in a time of war, the US Constitution is largely silent on emergency powers.[5] This is, perhaps, somewhat striking given the influence of Roman republican thought on the founders of the US Constitution. Surprisingly little attention in the *Federalist Papers*, however, is devoted to providing for emergency powers. Much concern instead seems to centre on curtailing the abuse of executive power. Thus in *Federalist No 48*, James Madison highlights the danger of a hereditary monarchy, which should not come to fruition in a 'representative republic where the executive magistracy is carefully limited'.[6] Fear as to the destructive capacity of dictatorship was also evident with Alexander Hamilton noting in *Federalist No 70* how often the Roman Republic had to resort to dictatorship.[7] Notable anti-federalists were also averse to the idea of a constitutional dictatorship, with the third US President, Thomas Jefferson, writing on the drafting of the constitution of Virginia, rejecting the idea of an emergency dictatorship. Jefferson drew a clear connection between the decline of the Roman Republic with the abuse of dictatorship and liberation of its potential to become tyrannical.[8] Jefferson stressed that the Roman Republic was, in essence, 'the government … of a heavy-handed, unfeeling aristocracy', implying its distinction from the US manifestation of a republic as a manifestation of the people.[9]

[2] Ian Zuckerman, 'One Law for War and Peace? Judicial Review and Emergency Powers between the Norm and the Exception' (2006) 13 *Constellations* 522, 524.

[3] See Oren Gross, 'Chaos and Rules: Should Responses to Violent Crises always be Constitutional?' (2003) 112 *Yale Law Journal* 1011; Oren Gross and Fionnuala Ní Aoláin, *Law in Times of Crisis: Emergency Powers in Theory and Practice* (Cambridge University Press, 2006) Ch 2.

[4] Gross and Ní Aoláin ibid 89.

[5] Article 1, § 9 United States Constitution.

[6] Alexander Hamilton, John Jay and James Madison, *The Federalist Papers*, ed George W Carey and James McClellan (Liberty Fund, 2001) 256 <http://files.libertyfund.org/files/788/0084_LFeBk.pdf> accessed 31 August 2017.

[7] ibid, 362.

[8] ibid, 156.

[9] Thomas Jefferson, 'Notes on the State of Virginia, Query 13, 121–29' in Philip B Kurland and Ralph Lerner (eds), *The Founders' Constitution* (University of Chicago Press and the Liberty Fund) http://press-pubs.uchicago.edu/founders/documents/v1ch17s20.html, accessed 22 August 2017.

This strength in belief in the value of US republicanism as a manifestation of the will of the people did not, however, stop Jefferson from owning thousands of slaves himself.[10]

With no other express provisions regarding government in a time of crisis, the US Supreme Court in *Ex parte Milligan* held that 'the same law applies in war as in peace'.[11] That an emergency could create additional powers for the executive or other branches of governance was rejected by Justice Davis, arguing that this would lead to the usurpation of liberty by those more interested in power than in benevolent rule.[12] Justice Davis therefore rejected the notion that constitutional provisions could be abrogated, suspended or reduced even during a period of war.[13] On a prima facie level, one could thus envisage the 'business as usual' approach as offering a more robust defence of human rights and other constitutional norms than the state of emergency model which permits derogations from prescribed norms against which an aggrieved individual has no recourse.

Notwithstanding this apparent precedent set down in *Ex parte Milligan*, the US Supreme Court subsequently held in *Korematsu* that the removal and internment of all Japanese–US citizens living along the US Pacific coast was constitutional. [14] Concurring with the majority, Frankfurter J stated:

> The provisions of the Constitution which confer on the Congress and the President powers to enable this country to wage war are as much part of the Constitution as provisions looking to a nation at peace. ... Therefore, the validity of action under the war power must be judged wholly in the context of war.[15]

The principal difference between the two cases is that *Korematsu* was decided at the height of World War II, whereas the forceful language of the US Supreme Court in *Ex parte Milligan* was decided in 1864, once the guns of the US civil war were silent and the Union secure.[16] The 'business as usual' model may therefore be criticised as naïve and hypocritical, standing vastly out of line with reality.[17] Judicial oversight of the executive appears to be tempered during periods of extreme crisis, ie a level of flexibility is afforded the executive, and political branches that are entrusted to wage war, regardless of what the law insists.[18] The risks that this poses

[10] See Lucia C Stanton, *"Those who Labour for my Happiness": Slavery at Thomas Jefferson's Monticello* (University of Virginia Press, 2012).

[11] *Ex parte Milligan* (1866) 71 US (4 Wall) 2, 120–21. The applicant in this case sought a writ of habeas corpus following a death sentence handed down by a military court in Indiana established under the authority of President Lincoln. Milligan was convicted of aiding the Confederates by conspiring to free Confederate prisoners. The Supreme Court unanimously held that the US President had no power to establish military tribunals in areas where the ordinary courts were still functioning.

[12] ibid, 125.

[13] Gross and Ní Aoláin (n 3) 92.

[14] *Korematsu v United States* (1944) 323 US 214.

[15] ibid, 224–25 (Frankfurter J).

[16] Gross and Ní Aoláin (n 3) 96.

[17] ibid, 95.

[18] Mark Tushnet, 'Controlling Executive Power in the War on Terrorism' (2005) 18 *Harvard Law Review* 2673, 2675.

to the constitution and the values espoused therein were summarised in Jackson J's famous dissent:

> [O]nce a judicial opinion rationalizes such an order to show that it conforms to the Constitution, or rather rationalizes the Constitution to show that the Constitution sanctions such an order, the Court for all time has validated the principle of racial discrimination in criminal procedure and of transplanting American citizens. The principle then lies about like a loaded weapon, ready for the hand of any authority that can bring forward a plausible claim of an urgent need. Every repetition imbeds that principle more deeply in our law and thinking and expands it to new purposes.[19]

'Business as Usual' and the 'Shielding Effect' of Emergency Powers

'Business as usual' constitutions may therefore find that other norms may be reinterpreted so as to validate actions or powers that previously they had not been attached to. Jules Lobel states that originally when presidents, such as Jefferson in completing the Louisiana Purchase, acted without any explicit legal validation, they recognised that what they did was without constitutional authority but nevertheless continued in their actions and hoped that the people would be forgiving.[20] The unconstitutionality of such actions was therefore expressly admitted. Today, however, the approach taken is to interpret certain constitutional norms as validating inherent emergency powers. The three clauses of the US Constitution that are usually used to argue that the president has certain emergency powers are the executive power clause, the commander-in-chief clause and the implied power in foreign affairs clause.[21] US presidents today now claim that their unilateral actions have a legal grounding.[22] This pressure to ensure the security of citizens may in turn have a knock-on effect on human rights obligations. In the absence of provisions permitting derogations from such norms, they may instead be revised downwards. As this flexibility itself becomes law, it sets a precedent that fundamentally alters the base of US constitutional law. The perceived necessity of draconian measures can result in emergency powers becoming cloaked in a 'veil of normalcy',[23] leading to the 'normalisation of the exception'.[24] Consequently,

[19] *Korematsu* (n 14) 246 (Jackson J).

[20] J Lobel, 'Emergency Power and the Decline of Liberalism' (1989) 98 *Yale Law Journal* 1385, 1397–99.

[21] ibid, 1404; Art II US Constitution.

[22] See generally, Richard M Pious, 'Inherent War and Executive Powers and Prerogative Politics' (2007) 37 *Presidential Studies Quarterly* 66. In addition, Barack Obama's administration claimed the US President has the power to order drone strikes on targets without the need for congressional approval. See Steve Hollan and Susan Heavey, 'Memo Justifies Drone Kills even with Patchy Intelligence' *Reuters* (5 February 2013) <www.reuters.com/article/2013/02/05/us-usa-drones-idUSBRE9140X120130205> accessed 11 August 2017.

[23] Gross and Ní Aoláin (n 3) 103.

[24] Zuckerman (n 2) 532–33; Jean Cohen, 'Whose Sovereignty? Empire or International Law?' (2004) 18 *Ethics and International Affairs* 1.

instead of human rights in a period of emergency being afforded the same level of protection as in normalcy, those during normalcy are diminished to the same level as in an emergency. Andrew Arato thus argues that despite the US founding fathers' best efforts, the spectre of dictatorship has not been banned from the US constitutional order.[25] Refusing to expressly comprehend emergency powers in a legal system, therefore, ignores the role that declaring a state of emergency can play in restricting encroachments on constitutional norms.

As I argued in chapter one, states of emergency can be described as a sword and a shield as they both legitimise the infringement of constitutional norms but also prevent their infringement when conditions do not amount to a state of emergency. Considering this critique of a 'business as usual' approach, a clear separation between normalcy and emergency should be the approach taken when accommodating emergencies, quarantining extraordinary measures to extraordinary times, and preventing such measures from seeping into the ordinary legal system, or lying around 'like a loaded gun'[26] waiting to be used.

The Deepening of Emergency Powers: Legislative Accommodation

'Business as usual' constitutional orders may instead provide for emergency powers through legislation and, in this manner, vindicate the normalcy–emergency dichotomy. Indeed, John Ferejohn and Pasquale Pasquino argue that even in advanced democracies with emergency powers, these powers are not used and, instead, a legislative response within the ordinary bounds of the constitution is now more commonly enacted.[27] Such crisis-specific legislation enables a bespoke response necessary to confront the threat at hand;[28] yet it does so without a constitutional declaration of a state of emergency. Nevertheless, as such legislation and the response it permits is conceptualised or represented as beyond that ordinarily permissible, it is accurate to describe this legislation as 'emergency legislation'. The inclusion of time-limits or 'sunset clauses' may also reinforce the legislation's temporary and exceptional status, illustrating that the goal of this legislation is the same as a constitutional state of emergency: the restoration of the status quo that existed prior to the emergency.[29] Consequently, the fundamental assumptions of the emergency paradigm remain the same; however, from a constitutional perspective, a state of normalcy remains.

[25] See Andrew Arato, 'The Bush Tribunals and the Specter of Dictatorship' (2002) 9 *Constellations* 457.
[26] Per dissent in *Korematsu* (n 14).
[27] John Ferejohn and Pasquale Pasquino, 'The Law of the Exception: A Typology of Emergency Powers' (2004) 2 *ICON* 210, 215.
[28] ibid, 215–21; see Gross and Ní Aoláin (n 3) 66–72.
[29] See generally, John Ip, 'Sunset Clases and Counterterrorism Legislation' [2013] *PL* 74.

However, this also means that the same problems that afflict the 'business as usual' model—recalibration downwards of constitutional norms and human rights protections, and the lack of a 'shielding effect' of declaring a state of emergency—may also afflict the legislative model. A brief discussion of how such legislative accommodation has operated in the United Kingdom and the United States illustrates how this normalcy–emergency dichotomy is reified though legislation, but also how the practical application of this approach has failed to prevent the entrenchment of such emergency powers. In fact, legislative accommodation may exacerbate the normalisation of emergency powers.

Legislative Accommodation: United States

'I think of it as the new normalcy', declared US Vice-President Richard Cheney on 26 October 2001.[30] Cheney was referring to his belief that the Patriot Act signed into law that day would become a permanent feature on the legal landscape.[31] In addition, the 'target hardening' of certain public buildings, increased security and encroachments on civil liberties that appeared shortly after the attacks on the United States on 11 September 2001 would not be a temporary aberration from the norm, but would become the norm themselves.[32] Cheney's prediction, so far, has been accurate. The Patriot Act originally contained 16 temporary provisions due to expire on 31 December 2005.[33] Of these, 14 were made permanent and provisions relating to roving wiretaps, permitting investigators to seize 'any tangible things' and the so called 'lone wolf' terrorist suspect, were given a new four-year extension. In February 2010 these provisions were extended for an additional year.[34] On 17 February 2011, ahead of the looming sunset date, the three provisions were extended for an additional 90 days.[35] Subsequently, on 26 May 2011, the US Senate voted to extend the wiretap provision in the Patriot Act for another four years until June 2015.[36] In June 2015, this was again extended to December 2019.

Emergency accommodation through legislation in the United States did not just start once the Twin Towers fell, however. A report by the Special Committee on the Termination of the National Emergency, chaired by US Senators Charles Mathias and Frank Church in 1973, commences with the line: 'Since March 9, 1933,

[30] 'Richard B Cheney Delivers Remarks to Republican Governors Association', *FDCH Political Transcripts* (25 October 2001).

[31] Or the Uniting and Strengthening America by Providing Appropriate Tools Required to Intercept and Obstruct Terrorism Act of 2001 to give it its full title.

[32] Target hardening is the idea of reducing crime by taking steps to make it more difficult to commit crime, eg through the use of technology such as locks, security cameras and alarms. See Jonathan Simon, *Governing Through Crime: How the War on Crime Transformed American Democracy and Created a Culture of Fear* (Oxford University Press, 2009) 210–14, 271–72.

[33] S 224 'Sunset' Patriot Act.

[34] 'Patriot Act Elements Extended' *New York Times* (25 February 2010).

[35] SA Miller, 'Patriot Act Gets Extension' *New York Post* (18 February 2011).

[36] C Savage, 'Senators Say Patriot Act Is Being Misinterpreted' *New York Times* (26 May 2011); 'MD Shear, 'Obama Uses Autopen to Sign Patriot Act Extension' *New York Times* (27 May 2011).

the United States has been in a state of declared national emergency.'[37] In fact, there were actually four simultaneous states of emergency in existence: President Roosevelt's declaration in 1933 to deal with the 'Great Depression'; President Truman's declaration to deal with the Korean War; and two declarations by President Nixon—to deal with a strike by postal service workers, and secondly to meet an international monetary crisis.[38] These emergency decrees gave effect to 470 provisions of federal law that, according to the authors, conferred enough powers on the president to be able to rule the country without reference to normal constitutional processes.[39] The US legislative landscape, therefore, consists of numerous statutes that were enacted on the basis that they would be temporary conferrals of power on the executive by the legislature; however, such powers have become normalised through repeated use and renewal.

Legislative Accommodation: United Kingdom

A similar story can be seen from the United Kingdom's experience of counter-terrorist legislation. Like the US, the UK's experience of legislative responses to deal with an emergency originated long before 9/11. The governmental powers necessary to conduct World War II, for example, were enabled by the Emergency Powers (Defence) Act 1939 and the Emergency Powers (Defence) (No 2) Act 1940. This followed a similar pattern to the UK's response to World War I, key to which was the enactment of the Defence of the Realm Act 1914 (DORA). Whereas the 1939 and 1940 acts were eventually repealed by the Emergency Laws (Repeal) Act 1959, DORA was amended on a number of occasions with a number of provisions subsequently made permanent in the Emergency Powers Act 1920. These powers were to remain on the statute books until the enactment of the Civil Contingencies Act 2004, which, in turn, conferred considerable powers on the executive to act in an emergency.[40] Certain provisions of DORA were also mirrored in the Restoration of Order in Ireland Act 1920 (ROIA) to deal with the war of independence in Ireland. This was not repealed until 1953.[41] Indeed, Ireland has been something of a legal laboratory for legislative emergency powers being deployed to confront a terrorist threat, particularly in Northern Ireland following partition. In addition to ROIA, the Civil Authorities (Special Powers) Act (Northern Ireland) 1922,

[37] US Senate Special Committee on the Termination of the National Emergency, 'Report of the Special Committee on the Termination of the National Emergency' (19 November 1973) 93-549, II.

[38] HC Relyea, 'National Emergency Powers', *Congressional Research Service* (updated 30 August 2007) 98-505 GOV,

[39] 'Foreword' in US Senate Special Committee on the Termination of the National Emergency (n 37).

[40] Ben Anderson and Peter Adey, 'Governing Events and Life: "Emergency" in UK Civil Contingencies' (2012) 31 *Political Geography* 24. The extent of the potential powers contained in the Civil Contingencies Act has resulted in it being described by Statewatch UK as 'Britain's Patriot Act'. See Statewatch, 'UK: The Civil Contingencies Bill—Britain's "Patriot Act"' *Statewatch* (14 November 2003) <www.statewatch.org/news/2003/nov/14civilcont.htm> accessed 11 August 2017.

[41] Statute Law Revision Act 1953.

for example, permitted the imposition of curfews, the banning of certain publications and imprisonment without trial (internment).[42] The act contained a yearly renewal clause, signalling the wish of the legislature that such powers be temporary and 'special'. They were accordingly renewed yearly until 1928 when they were extended for five years. In 1933, they were made permanent.[43]

The escalation of the conflict in Northern Ireland in the 1970s triggered a reciprocal escalation in the legislative response. Although the 1922 Act already permitted internment without trial, the Northern Ireland (Emergency Provisions) Act 1973 (EPA 1973) introduced a new model for processing internment and of trials for certain scheduled terrorist offences—the so-called Diplock Courts.[44] The EPA 1973 was amended in 1978, 1987, 1991 and 1996 before being replaced by the Terrorism Act 2000 (2000 Act).[45] The 2000 Act, rather than repealing many of the provisions contained in the EPA 1996, re-enacted them under Part VII, subject to annual renewal. It could not, however, be renewed after five years—an effective sunset clause on the renewal clause. Part VII lapsed on 31 July 2007, ending the 34-year life of the so-called 'emergency provisions'.[46]

In conjunction with the EPA, police and security forces also had a number of powers at their disposal under the Prevention of Terrorism (Temporary Provisions) Act 1974 (PTA 1974). The PTA 1974 was enacted in response to the IRA bombing of a bar in Birmingham that killed 21 people and injured over 180.[47] The PTA 1974 introduced the offence of being a member of an illegal organisation, the classification of such organisations being left to the executive with no scrutiny by Parliament or the judiciary.[48] The PTA 1974 also permitted the power to arrest and detain, and allowed search-and-seizure raids without a warrant.[49] The PTA was subject to a sunset clause and was therefore subject to review by Parliament. It was renewed every five years including amendments in 1976, 1984 and 1989. Following the collapse of the IRA ceasefire and the bombing of Canary Wharf in 1996, the Prevention of Terrorism (Additional Powers) Act 1996 (PTA 1996) was enacted which gave the authorities the power to declare areas 'special zones'.[50]

[42] For a detailed discussion of the Special Powers Act in Northern Ireland, see Laura K Donoghue, 'Regulating Northern Ireland: The Special Powers Acts, 1922–1972' (1998) 41 *Historical Journal* 1089.

[43] Brice Dickson, *The European Convention on Human Rights and the Conflict in Northern Ireland* (Oxford University Press, 2010) 10.

[44] The Diplock Courts were seen to be a solution to the effective arbitrary detention by the will of the executive the 1922 Act permitted. Nevertheless, the Diplock Courts still excluded the judicial sphere from assessment as to the validity of detention of an individual and so fall far short from what could be considered due process. The Diplock Courts were non-jury courts where only one judge would hear a case. See John Jackson and Seán Doran, 'Conventional Trials in Unconventional Times: The Diplock Court Experience' (1993) 4 *Criminal Law Forum* 503; John Jackson and Seán Doran, *Judge without Jury: Diplock Trials in the Adversary System* (Clarendon Press, 1995).

[45] Part VII Terrorism Act 2000.

[46] See Dickson (n 43) 161–65.

[47] ibid, 107–08.

[48] Part I PTA.

[49] Section 7 PTA.

[50] Part IVB PTA.

Within these 'special zones' persons could be subject to body searches even in the absence of suspicion. It, too, was replaced by the Terrorism Act 2000, which applied the provisions therein to the whole of the UK, not just Northern Ireland. In 2010, these stop-and-search provisions were ultimately held to be in breach of the right to respect of privacy contained in Article 8 ECHR by the Grand Chamber of the ECtHR.[51] These powers were subsequently repealed and reformed in light of this judgment by the Protection of Freedoms Act 2012. The Terrorism Act 2000 was itself largely a response to the Omagh bombing in Co Tyrone in 1998 which killed 28 people.[52] Despite the ratification of the Belfast Agreement and the hope of a restoration of a semblance of normalcy in Northern Ireland, the 'draconian and fundamental'[53] changes contained in the Terrorism Act 2000 were intended to be permanent and not subject to parliamentary renewal.

11 September 2001 was to signal the start of a perceived new terrorist threat: that of Islamic fundamentalism. Despite being in existence for just a year, the UK government felt the Terrorism Act 2000 was not sufficient to confront this new threat.[54] The Anti-Terrorism, Crime and Security Act 2001 (ATCSA 2001) applied to the UK as a whole and permitted indefinite detention without trial of non-British terrorist suspects, pending deportation. This power under Part IV was due to expire in 15 months from the date of enactment; however, the Secretary Of State could extend the expiry date for a period of 12 months. He could not, however, extend it beyond 10 October 2006 without legislative approval.[55] As noted in chapter five, however, in December 2004, the UK House of Lords declared Part IV to be incompatible with Article 15 of the ECHR; however, the provision remained in force until repealed by the Prevention of Terrorism Act 2005 (PTA 2005).[56] The PTA 2005 replaced Part IV of the ATCSA 2001 with control orders, a mechanism by which a court could attach restrictions on a suspected terrorist suspect's liberty without trial or imprisonment.[57] Helen Fenwick and Gavin Phillipson have thus described this lifting of the de jure state of emergency but subsequent introduction of exceptional legislation as amounting to a 'covert derogation'.[58] The control order regime was subject to a 12-month sunset clause; however, it was renewed yearly until it was replaced by the new Terrorism Prevention and Investigation Measures (TPIMs) in 2011.[59] TPIMs recalibrated the balance somewhat between

[51] *Gillan and Quinton v UK*, ECtHR 12 January 2010.

[52] Ian Cuthbertson, 'Whittling Liberties: Britain's Not-so-Temporary Antiterrorism Laws' (2001/02) 18 *World Policy Journal* 27.

[53] ibid, 30.

[54] Fiona de Londras, *Detention in the War on Terror: Can Human Rights Fight Back?* (Cambridge University Press, 2011) 122–25. See also Adam Tomkins, 'Legislating Against Terror' [2002] *PL* 205; Helen Fenwick, A Proportionate Response to 11 September? (2002) 65 *MLR* 724.

[55] Section 29 Part IV ATCSA 2001.

[56] *A v Secretary of State for the Home Department* [2005] 2 WLR 87; see also text to n 44 in ch 5.

[57] See de Londras (n 54) 197–200.

[58] See Helen Fenwick and Gavin Phillipson, 'Covert Derogations and Judicial Deference: Redefining Liberty and Due Process Rights in Counterterrorism Law and Beyond' (2011) 46 *McGill Law Journal* 863.

[59] Terrorism Prevention and Investigation Measures Act 2011.

security and liberty in favour of the latter by, for example, increasing the burden of proof from reasonable suspicion to reasonable belief and amending the scope of liberty-restricting measures an individual could be subject to. TPIMs have, however, have been branded as 'control orders-lite' by human rights group Liberty, which argues that they replicate the worst excess of the control order scheme.[60] Furthermore, on 1 September 2011, the UK government published the Enhanced Terrorism Prevention and Investigation Measure Bill (Draft ETPIM Bill).[61] Enhanced TPIMs were described by the then Independent Reviewer of Counter-terrorism Legislation David Anderson as an example of '[a] liberalisation of counter-terrorism law [that] has been accompanied by a draft Bill which, if Parliament should choose to enact it, will go some way to restoring the previous powers'.[62] Anderson describes such approaches as keeping bills in reserve so that should an emergency arise, the bill can be presented expeditiously to Parliament.[63] However, this also reflects the difficulties in restoring normalcy through the use of counter-terrorist legislation. While some liberalisation may occur, the 'restoration' of the prior 'emergency' regime is never far away but hovers in the background, ready to be used should it be considered necessary. The ETPIM Bill has never been enacted and, indeed it is unlikely to be. This is not due to some new-found faith in human rights but due to amendments made to TPIMs in 2015, reintroducing the powers to relocate individuals, thus rendering ETPIMs largely redundant.[64] Relocation powers have, therefore, been reintroduced without the enhanced safeguards that ETPIMs would have required.

It should also be noted that 'extraordinariness' is not just limited to the public or criminal legal sphere but is also increasingly 'creeping' into civil procedures in the UK. This is most apparent in evidentiary matters during court proceedings. The Justice and Security Act 2013 (JSA) introduced closed material procedures (CMPs) into civil procedures in cases involving national security issues. CMPs permit courts in civil proceedings to consider evidence the disclosure of which would be 'damaging to the interests of national security' without the non-government

[60] Liberty, 'TPIMS: Terrorism, Prevention and Investigation Measures' <www.liberty-human-rights.org.uk/human-rights/terrorism/control-orders/index.php> accessed 27 February 2013. See also Helen Fenwick, 'Designing ETPIMS around ECHR Review or Normalisation of 'Preventive' Non-Trial-Based Executive Measures?' (2013) 76 *MLR* 876.

[61] See Helen Fenwick, 'Designing ETPIMs around ECHR Review of Normalisation of "Preventive" Non-Trial-Based Executive Measures?' (2013) 76 *MLR* 876.

[62] David Anderson, 'First Report of the Independent Reviewer on the Operation of the Terrorism Prevention and Investigation Measures Act 2011' (The Stationery Office, 2013) 29 <https://terrorismlegislationreviewer.independent.gov.uk/wp-content/uploads/2013/04/first-report-tpims.pdf> accessed 11 August 2017. A similar example can be seen following the then Labour government's defeat in the House of Lords when trying to introduce legislation to allow pre-trial detention of suspected terrorists for up to 42 days. While the Bill was defeated, the then government indicated that a similar bill would nevertheless be drawn up and kept in reserve should the need ever arise in future. See de Londras (n 54) 159–61.

[63] ibid.

[64] Counter-Terrorism and Security Act 2015, Part II.

side seeing such evidence.[65] CMPs have therefore been described by Tom Hickman as 'a carve-out from basic principles of equality of arms and open justice'.[66]

The 'Deepening' Effect of Legislative Accommodation

In chapter two I argued that a key contributing factor to the permanent state of emergency was the 'broadening' of the scope of emergency to encompass more banal, 'quotidian' phenomena not perhaps envisaged by the drafters of such emergency powers.[67] Relatedly, emergency powers may become much more difficult to quarantine when they are enacted by ordinary legislation. The perceived advantage of legislative accommodation over constitutional accommodation is that it should not result in the suspension of constitutional norms and so the powers available under legislative accommodation should not be antithetical to the constitutional order. An additional advantage to the legislative approach is that its conformity with a higher normative order (ie the constitution) necessarily entails that judicial review of such emergency powers is available and therefore that the ordinary constitutional structure remains intact.[68] Crucially, however, like the 'business as usual' approach, in order to prevent conflict with a higher constitutional norm, rather than curtailing the legislative provisions, the higher constitutional norm may be reinterpreted to permit the legislative emergency powers.[69] Such an interpretation would be permanent, permitting the emergency powers to be likewise permanent. Legislative accommodation therefore has a structural vulnerability to entrenchment.

Legislative accommodation also facilitates the entrenchment of emergency powers by focusing scrutiny upon individual measures in isolation, rather than a 'hyperopic' view of the emergency response and the existence of a state of emergency in general. A case-by-case assessment of the necessity of each power in question subjectively mitigates the cumulative impact of these emergency legislative provisions. States of emergency require a broad or hyperopic view of the interrelated networks and responses that constitute the state and the nature of the threat facing it. The courts, by focusing only on the proportionality of a specific measure, avoid this hyperopic view. So too, however, does responding to an emergency by enacting crisis-specific legislation without the need for a declaration of an emergency.

[65] Justice and Security Act 2013, Part II.

[66] Tom Hickman 'Turning Out the Lights? The Justice and Security Act 2013' *UK Constitutional Law Blog* (11 June 2013) <https://ukconstitutionallaw.org/2013/06/11/tom-hickman-turning-out-the-lights-the-justice-and-security-act-2013/> accessed 11 August 2017; see John Jackson, 'The Role of Special Advocates: Advocacy, Due Process and the Adversarial Tradition' (2016) 20 *International Journal of Evidence and Proof* 343.

[67] See text to n 141 in ch 2.

[68] See text to n 83 below regarding this argument in the context of a constitution that asserts the sovereignty of parliament.

[69] Lobel (n 20) 1397–99; Fenwick and Phillipson (n 58) 867.

The symbolic act of crisis-specific legislation also satisfies the need for an emasculated government 'to be seen to be doing something' while at the same time avoids the checks and balances, and increased scrutiny that can—or should—follow a declaration of a state of emergency.[70] While the body in the constitutional order best placed to conduct this hyperopic view is the legislature, sunset clauses potentially hamper this by providing an opportunity for renewal for that specific piece of legislation only. It too avoids a broader view of the state's emergency response as a whole while at the same time enabling the democratic relegitimation of the legislation in question. Sunset clauses are often included as a means of overcoming parliamentary opposition to hastily enacted legislation, reassuring sceptical legislators that they will get a chance to have their say on the legislation in question in future.[71] Sunset clauses therefore act as a means of facilitating legislative deference to the executive.[72] However, these debates on the renewal of sunsetting legislation may be poorly attended and brief, with no real substantive engagement with the issue raised by the renewal of exceptional powers.[73]

The use of sunset clauses in the UK and the US, and the failure of time-limits in general to stymie the perpetuation of emergency powers, appear to lend credence to the argument that emergencies are incapable of temporal limitation. The responses that were once considered 'special' and 'emergency' eventually over time become normalised or indeed insufficient to deal with a new threat. A 'ratcheting' effect occurs, where each subsequent attack leads to a further, more draconian response by the authorities, gradually eroding civil liberties.[74] Like the exception becoming the rule, the temporary altering of the legislative field, becomes permanent.

A further difficulty with the lack of a constitutional declaration of a state of emergency is that it negates any stigma that may be attached to an official declaration of an emergency. As constitutional emergency powers permit derogation from higher constitutional norms, these higher norms ought to be accorded respect commensurate to their position in the constitutional order. Suspension of these norms should, therefore, attract a stigma; this stigma may act as a constitutionalist control on emergency powers, coaxing those of a constitutionalist disposition into ending the state of emergency. It is for this 'increased scrutiny'

[70] See text to n 132 in ch 2.

[71] Jessie Blackbourn, 'Independent Reviewers as Alternative: An Empirical Study from Australia and the United Kingdom' in Fergal Davis and Fiona de Londras (eds), *Critical Debates on Counter-Terrorism Judicial Review* (Cambridge University Press, 2014) 161, 161.

[72] This contrasts with how sunset clauses historically evolved, with Antonios Kouroutakis demonstrating that sunset clauses were originally used in the UK by a Parliament growing in ambition as a means to extract concessions from the all-powerful monarch. See Antonios Kourourtakis, *The Constitutional Value of Sunset Clauses: A Historical and Normative Analysis* (Routledge, 2017) ch 2.

[73] John Finn, 'Sunset Clauses and Democratic Deliberation: Assessing the Significance of Sunset Provisions in Antiterrorism Legislation' (2009–10) 48 *Columbia Journal of Transnational Law* 442.

[74] See Andrew Ashworth, 'Crime, Community and Creeping Consequentialism' [1996] *Criminal Law Review* 220; Gross (n 3) 1090–92.

reason that international human rights treaties such as the ECHR and ICCPR contain the express obligation to lodge a notice of derogation with the respective treaty-monitoring bodies.[75] In addition, even if the legitimacy of enumerated constitutional norms in general may be challenged from a democratic perspective,[76] constitutional emergency powers should, nevertheless, be construed as even less legitimate from a democratic perspective. The legitimacy of constitutional emergency powers should therefore be closely bound to their exceptionality, more so than legislative measures which can potentially appeal to a higher degree of democratic legitimacy.[77]

For this reason, legislative accommodation should be viewed with heightened scrutiny in constitutions that already provide for emergency powers and, most importantly, when this legislative accommodation occurs following the official termination of a state of emergency. France is an excellent illustrative example of this. France declared a state of emergency in November 2015 following a terrorist attack on various locations in Paris that left 130 people dead.[78] The emergency powers triggered by this declaration dated back to 1955 and France's last declaration of a state of emergency to deal with Algeria's struggle for independence. These powers—outlined in legislation, not the French Constitution—gave French police the power to search homes without a warrant, ban protests and other public gatherings, and could potentially ensure control of the press and radio; although these latter provisions were never triggered. That stated, the power to ban protests and other public gatherings was utilised almost immediately, with climate change activists subject to house arrest and other restrictions during the 2015 UN Paris Climate Conference in November 2015.[79] These emergency powers were significantly expanded on 22 July 2016 following an attack using a vehicle on a crowd celebrating Bastille Day in Nice a week earlier, killing 86 people.[80]

While then French President François Hollande had sought to amend the French Constitution and transpose the emergency legislation in question into the Constitution, the election of President Emmanuel Macron saw a shift in the French

[75] See text to n 78 in ch 1.

[76] Thus, Thomas Jefferson argued that a constitution can lack democratic legitimacy by allowing a previous generation to bind a subsequent generation without their consent. Thomas Jefferson, 'Letter to James Madison' (6 September 1789) <http://classicliberal.tripod.com/jefferson/mad02.html> accessed 11 August 2017.

[77] See text to n 102 in ch 4 for a discussion on political constitutionalist theories and the belief that democratic legitimacy and accountability ought to be maximised in a constitutional order.

[78] 'Paris Attacks: What Happened on the Night' *BBC News* (9 December 2015) <www.bbc.co.uk/news/world-europe-34818994> accessed 11 August 2017.

[79] Arthur Nelson, 'Paris Climate Activists put under House Arrest Using Emergency Laws' *The Guardian* (27 November 2015) <www.theguardian.com/environment/2015/nov/27/paris-climate-activists-put-under-house-arrest-using-emergency-laws> accessed 11 August 2017.

[80] 'France's National Assembly Votes to Extend State of Emergency' *The Guardian* (20 July 2016) <www.theguardian.com/world/2016/jul/20/frances-national-assembly-votes-to-extend-state-of-emergency> accessed 11 August 2017.

approach to emergency powers.[81] Macron sought to end the state of emergency; however, restoration of the status quo that existed prior to the November 2015 attacks was not envisaged. Rather Macron terminated the constitutional state of emergency on 31 October 2017 but also entrenched the emergency powers in question in permanent legislation.[82] In so doing, the de jure state of emergency was converted into the de facto, creating merely a façade of normalcy. France has thus followed a similar pattern to other states' experiences of legislative experimentation with emergency powers.

Permanent States of Emergency and Parliamentary Sovereignty

We have seen that by failing to expressly provide for emergency powers, courts operating in a 'business as usual' constitutional order may capitulate to national security claims and recalibrate rights and other constitutional provisions downwards to accommodate these newly enacted powers, rather than finding such measures unconstitutional. This is done without quarantining these recalibrations to exceptional circumstances as would have occurred under the emergency paradigm. Such problems also afflict legislative approaches to emergency powers. 'Business as usual' and 'legislative accommodation' arguably reach their 'apotheosis' in constitutional orders where courts do not have the power to strike down legislation as unconstitutional and constitutional norms are not clearly enumerated in a codified document. In this regard, the unique constitutional structure of the UK presents a challenge for typologies of emergency powers. Lacking a codified constitution in the conventional sense, constraints on state power tend to be political rather than legal. The UK's normal, therefore, relative to other states that have more express legal constraints on power, is exceptional, rendering it difficult to describe the UK constitutional order as recognising a clear dichotomy between normalcy and emergency. Parliamentary sovereignty thus poses a unique challenge to the normalcy–emergency dichotomy: if everything is permissible under

[81] Angelique Chrisafis, 'French MPs Vote for Enshrining Emergency Powers in Constitution' *The Guardian* (10 February 2017) www.theguardian.com/world/2016/feb/10/french-mps-to-vote-on-controversial-changes-to-constitution> accessed 11 August 2017; Joseph Bamat, 'France's Macron to End State of Emergency but Keep its Anti-Terror Powers' *France 24* (9 June 2017) <www.france24.com/en/20170609-france-state-emergency-macron-police-powers-civil-liberties-terrorism> accessed 11 August 2017; Samuel Osborne, 'France Declares End to State of Emergency almost Two Years after Paris Terror Attacks' *The Independent* (31 October 2017) <www.independent.co.uk/news/world/europe/france-state-of-emergency-end-terror-attacks-paris-isis-terrorism-alerts-warning-risk-reduced-a8029311.html> accessed 31 October 2017.

[82] Projet de loi renforçant la sécurité intérieure et la lutte contre le terrorisme (INTX1716370L) <https://www.legifrance.gouv.fr/Droit-francais/Actualite/22-juin-2017-securite-interieure-et-lutte-contre-le-terrorisme> accessed 11 August 2017.

normal conditions, there is no need to declare a state of emergency. That stated, it is possible to discern certain elements of the emergency paradigm in the UK.

Prerogative Powers in a State of Emergency

Much like the British Constitution itself, the UK emergency regime is a tapestry of legislation delegating specific powers to the executive or agents of the executive, and creating prerogative powers—legal attributes belonging to the Crown which derive from common law, not statute, and which still survive.[83] Prerogative powers are difficult to define but the key indicative characteristic is that their authority is not derived statute.[84] The existence of prerogative powers raises fundamental questions regarding the relationship between state power and the legal order, particularly so in a period of emergency. As briefly noted in Chapter 3, John Locke was particularly exercised by the nature of exceptional power in the English constitutional order.[85] Locke conceptualised the prerogative as 'the power to do good without a rule and sometimes even against this', thus leaving an area of state power beyond the legal order.[86] From a rule of law perspective, this raises questions as to the legitimacy of this power and its accountability, as if the monarch is above or beyond the law, he cannot be accountable to it. On this issue, Locke said that this could only take the form of public acquiescence. If the public did disagree with the approach taken by the holder of the prerogative, they had no recourse except to throw their arms to heaven.[87] There are obvious parallels to be drawn between Locke's concept of the prerogative and Carl Schmitt's articulation of sovereignty. By placing the prerogative and therefore the sovereign beyond the law, this separates the legal order from the state, making the latter a prerequisite for the former to exist. In essence, it is a vindication of Schmitt's assertion that the sovereign is he who decides upon the exception, and this decision itself is a zone beyond the law.[88]

The circumstances in which the prerogative operates has, however, evolved considerably since Locke's day.[89] The exercise of the prerogative is amenable to judicial review;[90] furthermore, no new prerogative powers can be created and the scope of existing prerogative powers can be limited through statute. For this reason, Poole argues that the classic exceptionalism dichotomy of law versus the prerogative is outmoded.[91] Consequently, the key difficulty with regards to emergency powers in

[83] Colin Munro, *Studies in Constitutional Law* (Oxford University Press, 1999) 256.
[84] See Thomas Poole, 'The Royal Prerogative' (2010) 8 *ICON* 147.
[85] See text to n 28 in ch 3.
[86] John Locke, *Second Treatise of Government*, ed CB McPherson (Hackett, 1980) 84–88.
[87] ibid.
[88] See Carl Schmitt, *Political Theology: Four Chapters on the Concept of Sovereignty*, trans G Schwab (University of Chicago Press, 2005) 1; see text to n 52 in ch 3.
[89] Thomas Poole, 'Constitutional Exceptionalism and the Common Law' (2009) 7 *ICON* 247, 258.
[90] See text to n 64 in ch 4.
[91] Poole (n 89) 252–58.

the UK is not the justiciability of executive power or even the fact that this check on power may be substantially tempered by judicial deference;[92] rather, it is the reviewability of statutes conferring such emergency powers and, indeed, legislation in general.

Common Law Constitutionalism and Parliamentary Sovereignty

As UK courts are incapable of striking down legislation, this raises the question of what legal limits there are on what Parliament can do in both normalcy and emergency.[93] Despite this prima facie weak position of the British courts, we saw in chapter four that judges in the UK and other common law countries do have some robust tools at their disposal to rein in executive and administrative decision-makers, and, by implication, Parliament.[94] Judges can legitimately go to considerable lengths to interpret legislation in such a way that it is compatible with other 'fundamental constitutional norms such as the rule of law and common law values'.[95] Such constructions may go against the literal interpretation of the statute itself, particularly where the statute purports to oust judicial review over certain administrative decisions.[96] The law therefore is not helpless in the 'face of the legislative sovereignty of Parliament'.[97] It was also noted in Chapter 4, however, that ground-breaking judgments such as *Anisminic* were not easily reconcilable with the classic ultra vires theory of the constitutional justification for judicial review which viewed courts as merely keeping decision-makers within the bounds of their discretion as laid down by Parliament. This challenge to the ultra vires justification of judicial review ultimately resulted in the evolution of what has been termed 'common law constitutionalism'.[98]

[92] What David Dyzenhaus refers to as 'legal grey holes', as discussed in detail in ch 5.

[93] UK public law makes a distinction between primary and secondary legislation. Primary legislation is the product of the Westminster Parliament and consists of Acts of Parliament and statutes. Secondary legislation refers to delegated legislation, for example to the devolved institutions such as the Scottish Parliament and the Northern Irish and Welsh Assemblies. It is only the validity of primary legislation that is non-reviewable and therefore this section uses 'legislation' as shorthand for 'primary legislation'. Human Rights Act 1998, s 6.

[94] See text from nn 67–71 in ch 4.

[95] See, for example, *Evans v AG* [2015] UKSC 21; TRS Allan, 'Law, Democracy and Constitutionalism: Reflections on *Evans v Attorney General* (2016) 75 *Cambridge Law Journal* 38, 46–47. Mark Elliott, however, is critical of *Evans*, arguing that while courts can interpret statutory provisions by applying constitutional provisions, parliamentary sovereignty is not 'infinitely elastic'. Mark Elliott, 'A Tangled Constitutional Web: The Black Spider Memos and the British Constitution's Relational Architecture' [2015] *Public Law* 539, 548.

[96] *Evans v AG*, ibid; *Anisminic v Foreign Compensation Commission* [1969] 2 AC 147; see also text from nn 17–19 in ch 4.

[97] TRS Allen 'Legislative Supremacy and the Rule of Law: Democracy and Constitutionalism' (1985) 44 *Cambridge Law Journal* 111, 112, quoting Sir Leslie Scarman, 'English Law—The New Dimension' (*The Hamlyn Lectures, 26th Series*) 15 <https://socialsciences.exeter.ac.uk/media/universityofexeter/schoolofhumanitiesandsocialsciences/law/pdfs/English_Law_the_New_Dimension.pdf> accessed 11 August 2017.

[98] Mark Elliott, *The Constitutional Foundations of Judicial Review* (Hart Publishing, 2001) ch 4.

Key to common law constitutionalism is the idea that the common law is a fount of values such as the rule of law and 'civil liberties'. Poole contends that such arguments asserting the common law as a source of fundamental values of the political community justify this in three separate ways: through philosophy, adjudication and history.[99] Common law constitutionalism thus lauds the ability of the common law through courts to protect rights, and hold the executive and administrative state within the bounds of their legal and constitutional authority. Consequently, TRS Allen states that Dicey's understanding of the British Constitution consisted of two pillars: parliamentary sovereignty and the rule of law, with subsequent interpretations of Dicey emphasising the former over the latter.[100] Common law constitutionalism therefore seeks to rebalance this relationship between parliamentary sovereignty and a substantive conception of the rule of law by providing the constitutional justifications for a muscular judiciary capable of innovative interpretations of legislative enactments.[101]

In undertaking this more muscular role, common law courts have reached similar conclusions to their continental counterparts and judiciaries that have the express authority to declare legislation unconstitutional: namely, the identification of a hierarchy of norms as a guide to legal interpretation.[102] Additionally, judges may be expressly empowered to interpret legislation compatibly with human rights norms under a 'bill of rights' such as the Human Rights Act 1998 in the UK or the New Zealand Bill of Rights Act 1990. Thus, the British legal order is not merely a tapestry of different statutes whereby, for example, the Dangerous Dogs Act 1991 has the same constitutional status as the HRA or the Scotland Act 1998. The hierarchy of statutes within this legislative landscape has developed to the extent that some statutes are considered to possess a 'constitutional' status.[103] This has concrete legal implications with, for example, courts holding that ordinary rules of statutory interpretation such as *lex posterior derogat legi priori* do not apply when later-enacted non-constitutional statutes come into conflict with prior-existing constitutional statutes.[104] The uncodified British Constitution therefore exhibits symptoms of a hierarchy of norms.

Fundamental to this development of a hierarchy of norms is the aforementioned common law constitutionalist contention that public law constitutes a set of higher-order principles and rights that are derived from the common law.[105] Poole further suggests that the moral superiority of these norms should

[99] Thomas Poole, 'Questioning Common Law Constitutionalism' (2005) 25 *LS* 142, 150.

[100] Allan (n 97) 112.

[101] For further discussion of 'muscular' judicial review in the context of counter-terrorism, see Fiona de Londras, 'Counter-Terrorism Judicial Review as Regulatory Constitutionalism' in Davis and Londras (n 71) 35.

[102] See text to n 109 in ch 3.

[103] See *Thoburn v Sunderland City Council* [2002] EWHC 195 (Admin); [2003] QB 151; *R (HS2 Action Alliance Ltd) v Secretary of State for Transport* [2014] UKSC 3.

[104] See *R v Secretary of State for Transport Ex p Factortame Ltd (No1)* [1990] 2 AC 85; *R v Secretary of State for Transport Ex p Factortame Ltd (No2)* [1991] 1 AC 603.

[105] Poole (n 99) 153.

necessarily entail the constitutional superiority of the branch of government best placed to vindicate these rights over the other branches, ie the judiciary's supremacy over the legislature and executive.[106] Poole thus argues that common law constitutionalism appears to invert the hierarchical relationship between courts and Parliament which previously operated in the UK.[107] There have been some judicial intimations to this effect, most famously in *Jackson v Attorney General* where Lord Steyn obiter dicta argued that:

> The classic account given by Dicey of the doctrine of the supremacy of Parliament, pure and absolute as it was, can now be seen to be out of place in the modern United Kingdom. Nevertheless, the supremacy of Parliament is still the general principle of our constitution. It is a construct of the common law. The judges created this principle. If that is so, it is not unthinkable that circumstances could arise where the courts may have to qualify a principle established on a different hypothesis of constitutionalism. In exceptional circumstances involving an attempt to abolish judicial review or the ordinary role of the courts, the Appellate Committee of the House of Lords or a new Supreme Court may have to consider whether this is a constitutional fundamental which even a sovereign Parliament acting at the behest of a complaisant House of Commons cannot abolish.[108]

Despite Lord Steyn's emphasis on the HRA as a justification for this contention, the inversion of the hierarchal relationship between Parliament and the courts may, arguably, have been somewhat stymied, rather than accelerated, by the passage of the HRA.[109] Instead, the rise of constitutional dialogue as a means of mediating between courts and Parliament has, for the most part, halted the apparently inevitable process of this inversion of the hierarchical relationship between courts and parliament. The relationship under the dialogic model is thus more horizontal than hierarchal but ultimately, it remains the case that parliamentary sovereignty still stands at the epoch of the hierarchy of norms.[110] Moreover, the justification of

[106] Intimations to this effect have been made by Lord Justice Laws and Jeffrey Jowell. Allison Young further suggests that this is the logical conclusion of common law constitutionalism.

[107] Poole (n 99) 154.

[108] *Jackson v Attorney General* [2005] UKHL 56 [102] (Lord Steyn). Similar intimations to this effect were made by Lord Hodge in *Moohan v Lord Advocate* [2014] UKSC 67 [65], where he stated obiter dictum that: 'While the common law cannot extend the franchise beyond that provided by parliamentary legislation, I do not exclude the possibility that in the very unlikely event that a parliamentary majority abusively sought to entrench its power by a curtailment of the franchise or similar device, the common law, informed by principles of democracy and the rule of law and international norms, would be able to declare such legislation unlawful.' For a criticism of *Jackson* and a defence of Parliamentary Sovereignty, see Michael Gordon, *Parliamentary Sovereignty in the UK Constitution: Process, Politics and Democracy* (Hart Publishing, 2015) ch 5.

[109] That stated, a number of high-profile judgments have suggested a 'resurgence' in common law rights, particularly in relation to the development of fair procedures in administrative hearings. See *Osborn v Parole Board* [2013] UKSC 61; *A v BBC* [2014] 2 WLR 1243. For further discussion of this resurgence, see Roger Masterman and Se-shauna Wheatle, 'A Common Law Resurgence of Rights Protection?' [2015] *EHRLR* 57; Scott Stephenson, 'The Supreme Court's Renewed Interest in Autochthonous Constitutionalism' [2015] *PL* 394.

[110] See Roger Masterman and Jo Murkens, 'Skirting Supremacy and Subordination: The Constitutional Authority of the United Kingdom Supreme Court' [2013] *PL* 800.

the courts' new review role under the HRA is tied back to giving effect to legislative intention rather than common law constitutionalism.[111]

Courts have vindicated these common law values through creative legislative interpretation;[112] nevertheless, despite the obiter dicta in *Jackson* and *Moohan*[113] the challenge still remains that common law constitutionalism tends to articulate a defence of a constitutional system that still allows almost the unlimited potential of Parliament to legislate as it sees fit.[114] Despite the normative values espoused in common law constitutionalism, it still, prima facie, leaves space for Parliament to run roughshod over these values with an emergency-type situation being the prime candidate for conditions that may trigger this. The question therefore remains unanswered: if everything is possible in a state of normalcy, how then can a constitution espousing the sovereignty of parliament respond to the Schmittian Challenge?

Common Law Constitutionalism and Emergency Powers

In *The Constitution of Law*, David Dyzenhaus attempts to provide such an answer.[115] As outlined in Chapter 5, Dyzenhaus is scathing in his critique of judges who pay mere lip-service to the rule of law.[116] These judges may do more harm than the judge who expressly acknowledges that she is incapable of holding the political branches to account on national security issues and labels the decision non-justiciable. The judge who rejects this approach but then is hyper-deferential to the executive's assessment of the situation cloaks these draconian powers in the 'thin veil of legality' to the extent that it legitimises the decision in a manner that the judge who declares the decision non-justiciable does not.[117] Dyzenhaus's answer to this is to insist that judges uphold the rule of law in a state of emergency and that the common law can provide a framework for this. Dyzenhaus's framework argues for a value-laden conception of the rule of law and states that a judge is entitled to interpret a grant of discretion to the executive 'in the light of the fundamental values of legal order, values which are nowhere more important than at a time when

[111] Thus Lord Hoffmann in *Belmarsh* was comfortable in robustly reviewing the existence of a state of emergency precisely because he was empowered to do so under the HRA. See text to n 135 in ch 5.

[112] Thus, in *Evans v AG* (n 95) a majority of the Supreme Court used a substantive conception of the rule of law that vindicated a strong role for courts to interpret s 53(2) of the Freedom of Information Act 2000 regarding the Attorney General's veto over the disclosure of information which he could block on 'reasonable grounds'. In *Evans*, the majority found that 'it is not reasonable for an accountable person to issue a section 53 certificate simply because, on the same facts and admittedly reasonably, he takes a different view from that adopted by a court of record after a full public oral hearing' (per Lord Nuberger at [89]).

[113] *Moohan* (n 108).

[114] Again, see the comments of Mark Elliott that parliamentary intention is not 'infinitely elastic': Elliott (n 95).

[115] David Dyzenhaus, *The Constitution of Law: Legality in a Time of Emergency* (Cambridge University Press, 2006).

[116] See text to n 4 in ch 5.

[117] Dyzenhaus (n 115) 41–43.

the legal order is under severe political stress'.[118] This is a paradigmatic application of the role of judges envisaged by common law constitutionalism. Interpretation cannot, however, resolve every constitutional dispute and Parliament may enact a statute that is unambiguous in terms of its effect—for example, realising Lord Steyn's dystopian vision in *Jackson* and abolishing or ousting the role of courts in the review of certain draconian emergency powers.[119] Dyzenhaus, however, also stops short of completing the inversion of the relationship between the courts and legislature. Rather, Dyzenhaus envisages judges playing a 'weatherman' role, ready to 'alert the public to the storm clouds on the horizon'.[120] This alert would have a similar effect to a declaration of incompatibility under section 4 of the HRA, ie the infringing provision would remain valid; however, by flagging its infringement of these values inherent in the rule of law, it condemns, rather than legitimizes, the offending provision.[121] Dyzenhaus's model is thus a restatement of the dialogic model that evokes a horizontal relationship between courts and Parliament but still preserves the supremacy of Parliament. Indeed, Dyzenhaus is expressly critical of the contention that judges operating under written constitutions with the power to strike down legislation can be more effective in emergencies and, certainly, the historical record would tend to corroborate this latter point.[122]

As Thomas Poole argues, however, Dyzenhaus's common law 'tells us nothing about where the chosen values come from, save that they are inherent in the very notion of legality, which, given that this is precisely the subject in dispute, rather begs the question'.[123] Poole thus argues that Dyzenhaus's theory suffers from the same defects as theories of common law constitutionalism more generally, namely that we are told there are some deep transcendental values in the common law, but when we look for them, we do not know quite where to find them or of what they might consist of.[124] While Dyzenhaus's conception of the values inherent in the common law are quite hard-edged to the extent that he is sceptical of formalised values in written constitutions, Poole argues that given the 'continuity of change' inherent in common law constitutions, the normative content is 'reasonably soft-edged'. Thus, if the common law is soft-edged and procedural rather than resolutely normative, 'the notion that a value-laden rule of law derived from common law sources can determine what counts as exceptional (and ipso facto invalid) seems unsound'.[125] In this regard, the historical account of the common law has, in particular come under attack as a highly romanticised notion of how the common law has actually operated. Values supposedly loved by the British and

[118] ibid, 98.
[119] *Jackson* (n 108).
[120] Dyzenhaus (n 115) 11, 233.
[121] David Dyzenhaus, 'Deference, Security and Human Rights' in Benjamin J Goold and Liora Lazarus (eds), *Security and Human Rights* (Hart Publishing, 2007) 125, 144–46.
[122] Dyzenhaus (n 115).
[123] Poole (n 89) 264.
[124] ibid, 226.
[125] ibid, 269.

espoused and vindicated through the common law through centuries can only be identified through a highly selective reading of history.[126] Invariably, this involves ignoring sources that contradict this romanticised version of the common law.

The nebulous nature of common law values raises further difficulties with regards to assessing the 'validity and effectiveness' of these common law norms. Indeed, this criticism can be levied at many constitutional norms in general. As stated in Chapter 3, Hans Kelsen's description of the relation between validity and effectiveness of a legal norm is that effectiveness is a necessary condition of, but not synonymous with, validity.[127] While the effectiveness of a legal rule may be relatively straightforward to identify and a matter of empiricism, the effectiveness of legal principles as understood by much of common law constitutionalism inspired by Ronald Dworkin may be more difficult.[128] Dworkin's key distinction between rules and principles is that the former apply in an 'all or nothing' fashion, whereas the latter act more as signposts guiding a decision-maker in the direction of the correct answer.[129] The validity of a principle, therefore, is much more tenuously connected to its effectiveness as there is greater flexibility for it to be followed. Consequently, while I argued in Chapter 3 that a permanent state of emergency that perpetually suspended a legal norm in a written constitution could be conceptualised as a proxy-constitutional amendment and therefore a claim for the constituent power due to the fact that it denies the norm in question of the necessary effectiveness to ensure its validity, this argument faces a direct challenge by conceptualising the norm in question as a 'principle' rather than a rule.

Consequently, by conceptualising common law values as principles rather than rules (which indeed, it would be more accurate to do), one could confront the argument that their lack of effectiveness over an extended period of time, for example through the enactment of perpetual emergency measures, does not affect their validity. It would follow that a permanent emergency under a common law constitution, or indeed, any constitution which enumerates vague principles rather than hard and fast norms, does not act as a proxy-constitutional amendment and therefore is not a claim for the constituent power. This argument would not, however, confront the Schmittian Challenge; rather it would be to capitulate to it. It would be to fall into the trap outlined in chapter three of stretching the rule of law so far as to empty it of any meaningful content.[130] Indeed, such an argument would be turning common law constitutionalism against itself and give in to what Ellen Kennedy calls the 'most unsettling and in retrospect ominous' aspect of Schmitt's work: his contention that 'rights as legal institutions can remain even when these are not secured to the individuals or groups who bear them'.[131]

[126] Conor Gearty, *On Fantasy Island: Britain, Europe, and Human Rights* (Oxford University Press, 2016) 17–33.

[127] See text to n 134 in ch 3.

[128] See Ronald Dworkin, 'The Model of Rules' (1967) 35 *University of Chicago Law Review* 14.

[129] ibid.

[130] See text to n 25 in Chapter 3.

[131] Ellen Kennedy, *Constitutional Failure: Carl Schmitt in Weimar* (Duke University Press, 2004) 174.

Conceptualising common law or any constitutional norms as principles, therefore, in order to confront challenges to their validity posed by a permanent state of emergency does not address the Schmittian Challenge and should be rejected.

Parliamentary Sovereignty and Constituent Power

As stated previously, key to the legitimacy of common law constitutionalism is its philosophy, namely the inherent normativity of the values it purports to vindicate. In this regard, Dyzenhaus argues that legal theory should focus on 'the question of legal authority as one internal to a legal order, with its authority dependent upon the normative value of the order itself'. It follows that Dyzenhaus is also critical of the concept of 'constituent power' due to its 'deep ambivalence about whether authority is located within or without the legal order'.[132] For normative legal theories, such as common law constitutionalism, the question of constituent power does not arise. In this regard, Dyzenhaus's analysis, as we saw in chapter five, once again focuses on human rights provisions in constitutional orders. Dyzenhaus does expressly acknowledge, albeit in a footnote, that 'a written constitution can of course confine itself to setting out the division of powers in a federal system of government or combine such a division with a statement of entrenched rights'; however, he then continues, 'for simplicity's sake assume for the most part that the relevant document is a bill of rights'.[133]

In addition to the critique outlined in chapter five regarding this overreliance on the normativity of human rights norms and ignoring other constitutional norms, a further weakness in this argument is that it already takes as established the constituted legal order.[134] Consequently, Loughlin describes such normativism as 'a peculiarly inadequate expression of constitutional thought'; as 'constitutional thought in blinkers'.[135] Indeed, by rejecting the concept of constituent power, common law constitutionalism ignores the juristic potential that it may have in complementing and advancing the norms that it espouses.[136] Consequently, Dyzenhaus's *The Constitution of Law* presents a highly persuasive argument in favour of robust judicial review in a period of emergency under common law constitutionalist orders; however, even this judiciary, armed with a substantive conception of the rule of law, eventually baulks in the face of parliamentary sovereignty. His judge is reduced to a 'weatherman', forecasting the dangers to the rule of law posed by the emergency legislation in question but incapable of halting it. By separating the validity of the law from its conformity with his substantive conception of the

132 David Dyzenhaus, 'Constitutionalism in an Old Key: Legality and Constituent Power' (2012) 1 *Global Constitutionalism* 229.

133 ibid, 230 fn 5.

134 See text from nn 126–75 in ch 5.

135 Martin Loughlin, 'The Concept of Constituent Power' (2014) 13 *European Journal of Political Theory* 218, 223.

136 See text from nn 126–75 in ch 5.

rule of law, Dyzenhaus places faith in the fact that this judicial warning will, over time, reassert itself and provide an opportunity for the emergency power in question to be reviewed and ultimately repealed. Indeed, in order to do so, Dyzenhaus further elaborates on the idea of a 'culture of justification' where judicial deference is earned and all branches of government are collaborators in the rule of law project.[137] And hopefully, under Dyzenhaus's model, most emergencies would end in such a manner; however, if the day were to ever come when courts were placed in a position whereby they must decide whether they have the power to strike down a piece of legislation by Parliament, it would most likely be in an emergency situation, when the exigencies of this situation have placed the courts in such a position in the first instance and all avoidance techniques and other avenues of inquiry are exhausted. This will be the ultimate test for common law constitutionalism and, at present, the answer is left 'blowing in the wind'.[138]

Even if one were to reject the common law constitutionalist approach, constitutions that affirm the sovereignty of the Crown in Parliament, nevertheless, pose a robust challenge to the idea of using constituent power as a concept in judicial interpretation and controlling emergency powers. In this regard, the notion of constituent power in the UK was, until recently, conspicuous by its absence.[139] Martin Loughlin does argue that 'the concept of constituent power was explicitly expressed during the [English] revolutionary debates of the mid-seventeenth century'.[140] Loughlin's discussion of the political philosophy and debates of the Levellers' is particularly persuasive on this point; however, the somewhat ambiguous outcome of the English Civil War which confirmed the sovereignty of Parliament but subsequently restored the Crown resulted in these more radical ideas being forgotten.[141] Thus Loughlin argues that constituent power now serves no juristic function having been 'entirely absorbed into the doctrine of the absolute authority of the Crown-in-Parliament to speak for the British nation'.[142] Westminster has, therefore, been described by Alexis de Tocqueville as 'at once a legislative and constituent assembly'.[143] The constituted power of Parliament therefore is indistinguishable from the constituent power. Joel Colón-Ríos reaches a similar conclusion, attributing the ambivalent nature of constituent power in the UK to parliamentary sovereignty as the constituent power was not needed in a system where Parliament can alter any legal norm it wishes.[144]

137 Dyzenhaus (n 121); see text to n 15 in ch 7.

138 In this regard, Dyzenhaus takes Bob Dylan's 'Subterranean Homesick Blues' as inspiration for his judge as 'weatherman'. Dyzenhaus (n 115). Here, I refer to Dylan's earlier work from *The Freewheelin' Bob Dylan*.

139 Joel I Colón-Ríos, 'Five Conceptions of Constituent Power' (2014) 130 *LQR* 306.

140 Martin Loughlin, 'Constituent Power Subverted: From English Constitutional Argument to British Constitutional Practice', in Martin Loughlin and Neil Walker (eds), *The Paradox of Constitutionalism* (Oxford University Press, 2007) 28.

141 ibid, 35–38.

142 ibid.

143 ibid; Alexis de Tocqueville, *Democracy in America* (American Library, 1956) 74.

144 Joel I Colón-Ríos, *Weak Constitutionalism: Democratic Legitimacy and the Concept of Constituent Power* (Routledge, 2012) 89.

Subsequent work by Colón-Ríos, however, notes that prior to Dicey's dominance, British constitutional theory did in fact utilise the idea of constituent power in a number of areas, particularly regarding the administration of its overseas colonies.[145] Thus, the Imperial Parliament was often considered to possess the constituent power to found the constitutional orders of the overseas colonies of the British Crown. Indeed, Colón-Ríos identifies five separate conceptions of constituent power that can be seen throughout British history: constituent power as parliamentary sovereignty; the Crown and Parliament as sources of constituent power; constituent power as the right of the people to instruct their elected representatives; constituent power as the right of resistance; and constituent power as popular sovereignty. If there is a common thread running through these five conceptions, it is an attempt to explain the relation between Parliament and 'the people' and, related to this, to understand the omnipotent paradox that lies at the heart of parliamentary sovereignty, namely an all-powerful Parliament that can do anything, yet it cannot limit itself.

In relation this latter issue, Jeffrey Goldsworthy, writing about Peter Oliver's exploration of the limitations of parliamentary sovereignty and former British colonies, states that Oliver uses the term constituent power or constituent process to 'denote the power or process by which the most fundamental norms—which is to say, the constitution—of a legal system can be changed'.[146] Giving the example of the US Constitution, Goldsworthy argues that:

> [W]hatever the original constituent power that enacted or created the constitution—and often it would have been an extra-legal, perhaps revolutionary, power—while that constitution persists, the only constituent power by which it may be lawfully changed is the amendment procedure that it itself prescribes.[147]

This, however, mistakenly conflates the power to amend the Constitution with the constituent power as the amendment power under Article 5 of the US Constitution is clearly a constituted power. In turn, Goldsworthy states that: 'Parliament can be said to have constituent power to change every part of the unwritten constitution except, arguably, that which grants its own law-making authority.'[148] According to Goldsworthy, therefore, 'whether Parliament has constituent power to limit or abdicate parts of its own sovereignty is just another way of asking whether its sovereignty is continuing or self-embracing'.[149] However, stating that Parliament has constituent power but that this power is limited is actually an admission that Parliament does not possess constituent power at all. Such an interpretation appears to view Parliament as possessing the power to amend any constitutional

[145] Colón-Ríos (n 139).
[146] Jeffrey Goldsworthy, *Parliamentary Sovereignty: Contemporary Debates* (Cambridge University Press, 2010) 110.
[147] ibid.
[148] ibid, 111.
[149] ibid.

norm except the norm of parliamentary sovereignty which would amount to what Colón-Ríos refers to as the 'fundamental core' of the constitution. As any amendment of this 'fundamental core' can only be achieved by the exercise of constituent power, it follows that Parliament does not possess the constituent power. This interpretation would ultimately appear to suggest that Parliamentary sovereignty can only be maintained if constituent power is conceptualised as 'closed', exhausted at the moment of the constitution's foundation.

There are, therefore, a number of authorities that appear to point to the fact that Parliament in the UK possesses constituent power and that this is often conflated with the idea of parliamentary sovereignty. However, these assertions run into difficulty when trying to constrain this so-called constituent power in order to prevent Parliament limiting itself in future. One could potentially argue that vesting Parliament with the capacity to exercise constituent power is merely an extension of constituent power being vested in the people as the legitimacy of parliament stems from its democratic mandate. A difficulty with this, however, is that only one chamber—the House of Commons—has any sort of claim to a democratic mandate.[150] While Sieyès stresses that constituent power rests in the people, the context of the French Revolution and searching for a principle that legitimated and justified the revolution was key to Sieyès's motivation in this regard.[151] The supposed 'divine right of kings' as emanating from God may also provide a legitimating principle for monarchical rights and so a monarch may possess constituent power. Loughlin gives imperial Japan as such an example, noting how power was exercised through the emperor and that the emperor possessed more than just a veto over legislation.[152] While the same may be the case in the UK, the apparent omnipotent status of the monarch or 'the Crown' in the British constitutional is a legally formalistic one. In reality, this power is substantially tempered by politics and custom so that the monarch is ultimately merely a figurehead. In emphasising this, Loughlin reveals the importance of custom and 'facticity' with regard to the idea of public law.[153] Loughlin therefore concludes that constituent power in the UK rests with 'the people'.[154] Yet again this does alone not answer the question of how the people exercise this power or of what the relationship between the constituent power and parliamentary sovereignty is.

[150] However, even this can be challenged due to the often weak democratic mandate the executive has when measured according to its vote share as distinct from the number of seats in the House of Commons the governing party has won. Moreover, the executive dominance of the British parliamentary system led Lord Hailsham to describe the UK as an 'elective dictatorship'. See Lord Hailsham, 'Elective Dictatorship', *BBC: The Richard Dimbleby Lecture*, 14 October 1976.

[151] Emmanuel-Joseph Sieyès, *What Is the Third Estate?* [1789] <http://pages.uoregon.edu/dluebke/301ModernEurope/Sieyes3dEstate.pdf> accessed 11 August 2017.

[152] Martin Loughlin, *Foundations of Public Law* (Oxford University Press, 2010) 223–24.

[153] Martin Loughlin, *The Idea of Public Law* (Oxford University Press, 2003) ch 6.

[154] Loughlin (n 152) 224.

Relational Constituent Power

Consequently, there is a fundamental conceptual difficulty in saying that constituent power resides in a constituted entity such as a parliament or that constituent power is vested in the Crown in Parliament even though Parliament cannot fetter itself. Andres Kalyvas thus argues that constituent power poses a challenge to parliamentary sovereignty:[155] 'Parliamentary sovereignty finds in the constituent power its own impossibility. It is exposed as a usurpation of the constituent power by a constituted power, which reduces popular sovereignty to parliamentary representation and to the powers of elected officials.'[156] A 'closed model' of constituent power therefore limits parliamentary sovereignty by making it clear that Parliament is a constituted rather than a constituent assembly. Indeed, parliamentary sovereignty also challenges the idea of 'constituent power' itself, as if constituent power is 'constitution-making power' and everything is on the agenda under parliamentary sovereignty, it follows that the constituted power looks very much like the constituent power.[157]

It is this ambivalence as to where constituent power in the UK lies and its relationship with parliamentary sovereignty that much of Loughlin's work is concerned with and it is, perhaps, for this reason that the idea of an 'open constituent power' or 'relational constituent power' has taken root in British constitutional theory.[158] In particular, this centres on the paradox of constituent power and understanding the constituent moment: how constituent power can simultaneously be vested *in* the people but also that constituent power must *constitute* the people.[159] Key to this puzzle is the 'relation' between the people in whom constituent power is vested, and their representatives. Loughlin follows Schmitt in stating that the people cannot decide; at best they can affirm or reject a decision that has already been taken. However, Loughlin differs from Schmitt in the need for an all-powerful sovereign arguing that 'political power is generated only when "the people" is differentiated from the existential reality of a mass of particular people'.[160] With the transfer of power from prince to people, Loughlin argues that the sovereign is lost but the space of sovereignty is retained: the space of the political.[161] In order to preserve the democratic potential of this space, Loughlin argues that it must be 'recognised as incorporating an unresolved dialectic of determinacy and indeterminacy'. Loughlin thus attempts

[155] Andres Kalyvas, 'Popular Sovereignty, Democracy and the Constituent Power' (2005) 12 *Constellations* 223, 229.

[156] ibid. See text to n 167 below regarding the recent proliferation in the use of referendums in the UK and the implications this has for the locus of constituent power in the UK.

[157] Kalyvas (n 155) 229.

[158] Martin Loughlin, 'The Concept of Constituent Power' (2014) 13 *European Journal of Political Theory* 218, 227–31.

[159] See Hans Lindahl, 'Constituent Power and Reflexive Identity: Towards and Ontology of Collective Selfhood' in Loughlin and Walker (n 140) 10.

[160] Loughlin (n 158) 228.

[161] ibid.

to solve the paradox of constituent power by arguing that constitutional ordering is dynamic, never static. Thus constituent power 'expresses a dialectical relation between "the nation" posited for the purpose of self-constitution and the constitutional form through which it can speak authoritatively'.[162] For Loughlin, the constituent power is not only engaged (and exhausted) only at the founding moment; rather, it continues to operate and function within an established regime 'as an expression of the open, provisional, and dynamic aspects of constitutional ordering'.[163] Constituent power thus acts as an irritant, driving forward dynamic constitutional development without end.[164] Ultimately, Loughlin leaves the question as to where the locus of constituent power lies. Indeed, he must as he argues that:

> [L]egitimacy must be claimed in the name of the people, and the question of who represents that people remains the indeterminate question of modern politics. The function of constituent power is to keep that question open, not least because 'the people-as-on'" is the hallmark of totalitarianism.[165]

Parliamentary Sovereignty and Constituent Power: Conclusions

There are many, therefore, who 'claim the authentic voice of constituent power', and certainly, a parliament unbridled by a written constitution could make a strong claim. In this regard, Poole argues that the majority in Supreme Court decision in *Miller v Secretary of State for Exiting the European Union* appears to recognise Parliament's claim.[166] The case concerned whether it was for Parliament to trigger Article 50 of the Treaty on European Union (TEU) commencing the process by which the UK would withdraw from the EU, or whether the government could do so by exercise of the prerogative. For Poole, the key paragraph in the judgment is the following:

> We cannot accept that a major change to UK constitutional arrangements can be achieved by ministers alone; it must be effected in the only way that the UK constitution recognises, namely by Parliamentary legislation.[167]

Poole thus argues that *Miller* draws a distinction between 'constituent authority' and 'legislative capacity', arguing that it was perfectly coherent for EU law to have primacy over ordinary law but not the fundamentals of the constitutional order.[168] Poole thus embraces de Tocqueville's assertion that 'Parliament is at once

[162] ibid, 229.
[163] Martin Loughlin and Neil Walker, 'Introduction' in Loughlin and Walker (n 140) 1–8.
[164] Loughlin (n 158) 233–34.
[165] ibid, 234.
[166] *Miller v Secretary of State for Exiting the European Union* [2017] UKSC 5; Thomas Poole, 'Devotion to Legalism: On the Brexit Case' (2017) 80 *MLR* 685.
[167] *Miller*, ibid, [82]; Poole, ibid, 700.
[168] Poole (n 166) 702.

a legislative and constituent assembly.'[169] Again, however, the difficulty remains in attributing the constituent power to an assembly such as a parliament with its regulated procedures regarding the creation of legislation and membership. Poole expressly acknowledges this, arguing that 'Parliament is not and cannot be the fundamental source of political authority.'[170] Rather, Poole argues that Parliament exercises *derived* constituent power with *original* constituent power vested in the people.[171] More importantly, however, only one chamber possesses any modicum of democratic legitimacy and thus can claim to speak for 'the people'. *Miller*, in particular, illustrates this potential clash between Parliament and the people as the case was taken in lieu of a referendum where 'the people' voted by a majority of 52 per cent to 48 per cent to leave the EU; however, the Supreme Court shied away from according the referendum any constitutional or legal significance.[172] Nevertheless, Poole suggests that future constitutional reform in the UK could entail '"we the people" acting through constituent agents, whether prosaically through our Parliaments or more ambitiously by engaging a more bespoke constituent process'.[173]

Additionally, Loughlin expressly raises the issue of the growth of constitutional jurisdiction of courts with some claiming that they speak directly in the name of the sovereign people and as the authentic voice of constituent power. Key to Loughlin's model, however, is the capacity to challenge those claiming to speak for the people. Thus, a claim for the constituent power in the name of the people is subject to challenge by the people. Similarly, Goldsworthy is keen to point out that a change in the rule of recognition does not come about by a branch of government such as Parliament or the courts stating that 'the rule of recognition has changed'. Rather, what is key to its change is the *acceptance* that it has changed by high-ranking government officials, including courts. In this regard, an equivalence can be drawn between Loughlin's notion of 'facticity' and Goldsworthy's emphasis on officialdom acceptance in the change of the rule of recognition.[174] However, while Goldsworthy puts express faith in officialdom, Loughlin is concerned with 'the people' more broadly drawn.

Loughlin does not give any concrete examples of situations in which those claiming to exercise constituent power have been challenged. However, a state of emergency may be a prime candidate for this. Thus, if one were to take the example given by Lord Steyn in *Jackson* of 'exceptional circumstances involving an attempt to abolish judicial review or the ordinary role of the courts', such a monumental constitutional change may expose the underlying tension between the people and their representatives in the Commons. This space could potentially be filled by a court

[169] ibid, 703; see text to n 142.
[170] ibid, 704.
[171] ibid. Poole takes this idea of 'derived constituent power' from Yaniv Roznai, *Unconstitutional Constitutional Amendments* (Oxford University Press, 2017) ch 4.
[172] Poole (n 166) 704–05.
[173] ibid, 706.
[174] See text to n 154.

using the constituent power vested in the people to justify striking down such powers as unconstitutional and thus clearly establishing Parliament as a constituted power. However, what both Loughlin and Goldsworthy make clear is that this would merely be the start of constitutional tumult and would certainly not be conclusive. Nevertheless, constituent power may offer a complementary justification for common law constitutionalist claims regarding the relation between parliament and the rule of law.

The Extra-Legal Measures Model

The most extreme examples of violations of the rule of law during an emergency are measures taken by officials that are unsanctioned by the law and that cannot ex ante trace their legitimacy from any legal norm or authority. These actions are extra-legal (not ex-ante validated by law/outside the law) or may be illegal (in violation of the law).[175] The justification (or excuse depending upon one's perspective) for such recourse is generally based on the necessity of the measures taken—that the official had no choice but to undertake the unlawful action in question. A famous example of this is Abraham Lincoln, who, upon the outbreak of the US Civil War and with no lawful authority, enlarged the army and navy beyond the legally acceptable levels, suspended habeas corpus, called forth the militia, and imposed blockades on southern ports—all without the legal backing of Congress.[176] When Congress did convene, it had no choice but to rubberstamp and endorse Lincoln's actions rather than repeal them.[177]

Lincoln, however, was not the first to grapple with the conundrum of protecting the state by using extra-legal means. The infamous phrase *inter arma enim silent leges*—in times of war, the law falls silent— is attributed to Cicero who himself resorted to unlawful measures in order to protect the Roman Republic. Upon the discovery of the Second Catilinarian Conspiracy, Cicero, in his role as Consul, implored the Senate to order the execution of several of the conspirators without trial. As noted in chapter one, this was a clear violation of the right of appeal (*provocatio*) sacred to the Roman citizen and thus evocative of the monarchical tyranny which the Republic ousted. Cicero justified his unlawful actions on the grounds of necessity; nevertheless, they remained unlawful. Cicreo was subsequently forced into exile from Rome once his arch rival Publius Clodius Pulcher,

175 David Dyzenhaus, 'The State of Emergency in Legal Theory' in Victor V Ramraj, Michael Hor and Kent Roach (eds), *Global Anti-Terrorism Law and Policy* (Cambridge University Press, 2005) 83–84. Dyzenhaus states that the humanitarian arguments against torture are so strong that it could never be considered 'extra-legal' but will always be 'unlegalizable' and therefore always illegal.

176 See Clinton Rossiter, *Constitutional Dictatorship: Crisis Government in the Modern Democracies* (Transaction Publishers, 2002) 224–30.

177 ibid.

was elected a tribune of the plebs and passed a law threatening exile to anyone who executed a Roman citizen without a trial.[178] Following Pompey's return from Rome, however, Cicero's exile was lifted.

This episode in the dying days of the Roman Republic is used by Oren Gross as an illustrative example of what he terms the 'extra-legal measures model' (ELM).[179] Like the 'business as usual' model, ELM does not envisage a separate legal regime that operates in time of crisis. However, this approach also recognises that there may be instances in which the state cannot adequately respond to acute crises while remaining within the rule of law. In such extreme cases, the executive or public official should act extra-legally out of necessity, in order to protect the security of the state. Such extra-legal or unlawful actions may then be potentially ex-post facto approved or condemned. Cicero, for example, was subsequently condemned and exiled but then ultimately condoned and allowed return to Rome. This process of approval or condemnation may, according to Gross, be done through a variety of different mechanisms: from those within the legal system, to measures that are expressly political. Nevertheless, there remains no ex-ante legal norm to validate such action in the first place. ELM, therefore, is based on 'three essential components': official disobedience, disclosure and ex-post ratification.[180]

Gross presents ELM as a solution to the naïvety of constitutions that refuse to countenance emergency powers, and the all-too-frequent 'seepage' of exceptional emergency powers into the ordinary legal system and the resultant permanent state of emergency that results in those states that do.[181] As a result, the logical conclusion reached by Gross is that while the rule of law is incapable of accommodating every crisis that it faces, the seepage of emergency powers into the ordinary legal system means that a dualist approach (attempting to maintain a normalcy–emergency dichotomy) of enacting emergency powers in legal norms must also be rejected.[182] To prevent this seepage, emergency actions should be extra-legal and this acceptance of illegality on behalf of the actor should constrain her actions to the extent that is absolutely necessary.[183] Furthermore, Gross stresses that ELM would be less likely to become entrenched due to the uncertainty surrounding whether or not the unlawful action in question would be ex-post-facto validated. ELM may therefore be resorted to much less frequently than emergency powers that are ex-ante authorised.[184]

[178] Oren Gross, 'Extra-Legality and the Ethic of Political Responsibility' in Victor V Ramraj (ed), *Emergencies and the Limits of Legality* (Cambridge University Press, 2008) 60, 69–71.

[179] See Gross (n 3) 1096–130.

[180] Oren Gross, 'Stability and Flexibility: A Dicey Business' in Ramraj, Hor and Roach (n 175) 90, 93.

[181] Gross (n 178) 1089–95.

[182] ibid; Mark Tushnet, 'Defending Korematsu? Reflections on Civil Liberties in Wartime' (2003) *Wisconsin Law Review* 273, 303–307.

[183] Gross (n 3) 1123.

[184] Gross (n 178) 71–75.

ELM and the Source of Legal Authority

A fundamental challenge to ELM, however, is that it fails to adequately explain the source of an official's authority to act extra-legally. Logic would dictate that an official acting extra-legally does not have the official authority to do so, meaning that their power cannot be an exercise of a public function. In which case, the official is acting in his private, rather than public capacity. ELM, therefore, appears to rely heavily on the public–private divide; however, this is not wholly clear. Dyzenhaus argues that this issue also afflicts Locke's theory of the prerogative—which Gross also cites as an inspiration for ELM—as he 'vacillates in his answer to the question whether the executive, personified in the figure of the prince, exercises the prerogative in his natural capacity or in his artificial role as the public official at the apex of the hierarchy of a state'.[185]

This reliance on the public–private divide raises a number of difficulties, however. Firstly, while the distinction may work for low-ranking officials, eg the member of the security forces who resorts to torture to extract information from a suspect, it becomes more difficult to maintain for higher-ranking officials, particularly those who personify the office they hold, ie a president or prime minister. For such officials, it becomes almost impossible to maintain the public–private distinction as the opportunity to act only arises by virtue of their public position. Ultimately, this is the case with all officials. This reliance upon the public–private divide is also problematic when the ex-post-facto ratification effectively endorses a permanent change in the legal and constitutional landscape of the state. While Gross does argue that ELM should never result in permanent change, he also offers Jefferson's actions in conducing the Louisiana Purchase as such an event. It did effect permanent and dramatic constitutional change in the United States, expanding its territory and ultimately resulting in the creation of some thirteen new states in the union.[186]

This reliance on the separation of the public and private may also encourage states to further abuse this distinction. The 'war on terror' has demonstrated how this divide has already been exploited, with private companies heavily involved in the extraordinary rendition programme operated by the United States. This tension between the public and private may, therefore, encourage the exact opposite of what the extra-legal measures model seeks to achieve: transparency, accountability and the protection of the existing legal order.

[185] David Dyzenhaus, 'The Compulsion of Legality' in Ramraj (n 178) 33, 42–43. Clement Fatovic, however, argues that this is not ambivalence on Locke's part but an advantage of his theory of the prerogative. See Clement Fatovic, 'Constitutionalism and Contingency: Locke's Theory of the Prerogative' (2004) 25 *History of Political Thought* 276, 288–290.

[186] Gross and Ní Aoláin (n 13) 123–25.

ELM and the Authority of Affirmation

A further difficulty with ELM is that even if it can attribute the official's extra-legal actions to his private self, the authority of the constitutional or legal actor that passes judgment ex post facto is also not clear. Much of this is due to the fact that ELM stresses the various ways in which the extra-legal measures taken can be condoned or expressed, each of which raise different implications for the source of this authority and, in turn, the degree of damage done to the rule of law.

Relying on prosecutorial discretion, for example, does do damage to the rule of law through the creation of a black hole. Gross contends that ELM does not create a legal black hole by arguing that that the violated rule in question still applies to other situations and, more importantly, is 'not even overridden in the concrete case at hand'.[187] In this manner, ELM could potentially circumvent the validity–effectiveness difficulty that afflicts constitutional norms that are subject to permanent states of emergency, as discussed in chapter three. However, by relying on prosecutorial discretion to decide whether or not to prosecute, ELM does, nevertheless, create a legal black hole: the space in which the prosecutor decides to make their decision on whether or not to prosecute. Ultimately, therefore, such an approach does damage to the rule of law and the principle of legality—something that ELM is supposed to prevent in the first instance. All ELM does is shift the black hole from the official who acted unlawfully to the prosecutor deciding whether or not to prosecute.

A further example that illustrates the unclear authority of the ex-post-facto validation is Gross's interpretation of AV Dicey's description of an Act of Indemnity. Gross argues that Dicey's conception of Acts of Indemnity is that they 'legalise illegality' with the official breaking the law and trusting for protection to an Act of Indemnity.[188] Dyzenhaus, however, contests this by arguing that Dicey viewed an Act of Indemnity as a statute that 'indemnifies action that could and should have been authorised in advance, had there been time'.[189] For Dyzenhaus, the Act of Indemnity is meant to secure the rule of law, not undermine it. Thus, the principle of non-retroactive legislation that is inherent in even formal concepts of the rule of law is sacrificed in favour of the more important principle of the rule of law that all state power is exercised through law.[190] Dyzenhaus's interpretation of Dicey's Act of Indemnity, therefore, is that it is merely an exercise of the legislative power, albeit the legislative power of a sovereign power. Dicey himself makes this clear, stating that:

> An Act of Indemnity, again, though it is the legalisation of illegality, is also, it should be noted, itself a law. It is something in its essential character, therefore, very different

[187] Gross (n 178) 63.
[188] Gross (n 180) 8; AV Dicey, *Law of the Constitution*, 10th edn (MacMillan, 1959) 233.
[189] Dyzenhaus (n 185) 47.
[190] ibid, 47–48.

> from the proclamation of a state of siege, or any other proceeding by which the executive government at its own will suspends the law of the land. It is no doubt an exercise of arbitrary sovereign power; but where the legal sovereign is a Parliamentary assembly, even acts of state assume the form of regular legislation, and this fact of itself maintains in no small degree the real no less than the apparent supremacy of law.[191]

That stated, Gross draws parallels between Parliament passing and Act of Indemnity and Locke's concept of the prerogative as 'the power to do good without a rule and sometimes against it'. Locke's 'litmus test' for assessing the exercise of the prerogative—whether it was directed at promoting the public good—is essentially what Parliament does when it considers passing the Act of Indemnity.[192] In this model, Parliament is cast in the role of Locke's public; however, while Locke viewed the public as only being able to 'throw their eyes up to heaven' or acquiesce, or even take up arms and rebel, Gross emphasises the importance of ex-post-facto scrutiny and express ratification of the extra-legal measures taken. While this may suggest that Gross rejects Locke's conception of the prerogative as something outside of the legal order, this only raises the question as to the nature of the power of affirmation. If, however, this is simply an exercise of the legislative power, Dyzenhaus argues that there is nothing extra-legal about it, notwithstanding the fact that it is the legislative function of a sovereign parliament.

Ultimately, Gross stresses that: 'Society retains the role of making the final determination whether the public official who acted extra-legally ought to be punished and rebuked, or rewarded and commended for their actions.'[193] Again, however, ELM is unclear as to the nature or source of this power being vested in 'society' or how this determination is made. A direct appeal to 'society' evokes the idea of 'the people' deciding, which could, perhaps, be intimating at the idea of the constituent power being exercised to pass judgment on the official in question. The closer we get to attributing the validation of extra-legal measures to 'the people' through the exercise of their constituent power, the closer we get to Schmitt's contention that: 'Sovereign is he who decides on the exception.' Rather than create a rule of law, ELM may create the space for a 'zone beyond law' which, as was argued in chapter five, is much more sinister than the legal black hole.

Extra-Legal Measures: Conclusions

It should also be stressed that the national security trump card may still be deployed on the extra-legal measures model. This may be even more true for the extreme measures such as torture that are envisaged by the model, the disclosure of which may be resisted on the grounds that it could be used against the

[191] Dicey (n 188) 237.
[192] Gross (n 180) 9.
[193] Gross (n 178) 64.

states as a means of recruiting other terrorists.[194] Finally, the extra-legal measures model also appears to be quite narrow in its application, focusing mostly on the debate surrounding the necessity of torture. As a result, it does not displace the need for alternative approaches to emergency powers, eg constitutional or legislative accommodation. Rather, it would appear to be envisaged as being deployed in addition to other less extreme emergency powers. Gross expressly admits this, conceding that: 'It [ELM] does not claim to exclude the constitutional models of emergency powers. It is a model for truly extraordinary occasions.'[195] Consequently, even if a state were to utilise the extra-legal measures model, alternative approaches to confronting emergencies would nevertheless have to be confronted, meaning that the Schmittian Challenge can again arise to confront these responses. The extra-legal measures model therefore does not displace the need for constitutions to provide for emergency powers.

While ELM is offered as a means of circumventing the normalcy–emergency dichotomy, Gross's model has been subject to criticism that it is, nevertheless, dependent upon this distinction. ELM hypothesises extreme scenarios in which the law is breached by an official, thus evoking a threat that lies at the 'core' of the meaning of emergency.[196] It ratchets the severity of the threat envisaged to such an 'extreme' that the official acting extra-legally feels that he has 'no choice' but to act as he has.

Conclusions

Constitutions that do not provide for emergency powers are, nevertheless, prone to extreme crises doing fundamental and permanent damage to their legal orders. By not demarcating clearly between normalcy and emergency, they lose the 'shielding effect' of emergency powers, quarantining them to exceptional situations. Ultimately, they may become vulnerable to the Schmittian Challenge by stretching the concept of legality so broadly as to legitimise anything, thus validating Schmitt. Relatedly, states that resort to confronting emergencies through legislation also face the possibility of permanent states of emergency through abandonment of an ex-ante constitutionally declared state of emergency and the hyper-scrutiny that should accompany such a declaration. Instead, such measures appear more banal by embedding them more deeply in the legal order and removing the stigma attached to a constitutional declaration. Finally, the extra-legal measures do not offer a solution to the Schmittian Challenge due to difficulties

[194] See Laura K Donohue, 'The Shadow of State Secrets' (2010) 159 *University of Pennsylvania Law Review* 77.

[195] Gross (n 3) 1134.

[196] See text to n 147 in ch 1 regarding the 'core' and 'penumbra' of emergency.

surrounding the nature of the authority of the individual to act extra-legally, and the authority ex-post facto ratifying this. Such measures range in their impact on the legal order from being circumscribed by law to creating legal black holes, to potentially pleading to a zone beyond law.

Ultimately, therefore, constitutions should provide for emergency powers; however, this is not to succumb to the first limb of Schmitt's challenge—that sovereign is he who decides as to the existence of a state of exception. Rather, the key to responding to the Schmittian Challenge is, as argued in chapter three, ensuring the temporariness of an emergency is a legal question, and this can only be done if the decision to declare a state of emergency is amenable to judicial review. There is a potential for this argument to apply even in constitutional orders where Parliament is sovereign due to the ambiguous location of constituent power in the UK, for example. As will be argued in the following chapter, however, this should not be the only control on emergency powers.

7

Resisting the Permanent State of Emergency

Introduction

As noted in chapter one, while similar elements making up the emergency paradigm can be identified in many constitutions, there are, nevertheless, substantial differences from state to state in the scope and control of such emergency powers. This chapter will conclude, therefore, with an analysis of the 'ideal' emergency constitution with a view to suggesting what checks and balances constitutions should put in place on emergency powers. In a similar vein, Clinton Rossiter's famous study of constitutional dictatorship concluded with eleven criteria for assessing whether an emergency is constitutional or not; however, he then qualified these by stating that: '[W]hatever the theory, in moments of extreme national emergency, the facts have always been with … John Locke.'[1] In so doing, Rossiter reduces his criteria to merely discretionary suggestions which can potentially be discarded. Faith thus rests on the republican fortitude of those to whom emergency power is entrusted, a course of events that Andrew Arato argues would horrify the US founding fathers.[2] In contrast, throughout this book I have stressed that judicial review of the decision to declare a state of emergency is not some constitutional nicety that can be jettisoned at the first sign of trouble on the horizon. It *must* be provided for in order to ensure that the decision to declare an emergency is one that is done through law and thus that the Schmittian Challenge is resisted.

That stated, judicial review of the decision to declare a state of emergency should not be the only constraint on emergency powers. Moreover, its inclusion may impact upon other checks and balances that constitutions provide for. This chapter will therefore conclude by contextualising judicial review of the decision to declare a state of emergency within these broader constitutional provisions. In addition, pragmatic concerns still remain with regards to *how* judges actually

[1] Clinton Rossiter, *Constitutional Dictatorship: Crisis Government in the Modern Democracies* (Transaction Publishers, 2002) 219.

[2] Andrew Arato, 'The Bush Tribunals and the Specter of Dictatorship' (2002) 9 *Constellations* 457, 457.

exercise this review. These difficulties will also be addressed. Ultimately, as has been the theme throughout this book, in this chapter, I seek to evoke the spirit of constitutional fortitude and a fundamental belief in the rule of law.

Reviewing the Existence of a State of Emergency

I have sought in this book to provide a robust constitutional justification for why judges should have the capacity to review the existence of a state of emergency. This argument centres on addressing the Schmittian Challenge and ensuring that all state power is exercised through law by preserving Hans Kelsen's Identity Thesis.[3] Moreover, concerns were highlighted and addressed in chapter five regarding the rigour with which the judiciary may carry out this function and the risk that an overly deferential approach to this question could provide a 'thin veil of legality' that would legitimise the emergency measures in question.[4] Thus, I argued that the normative risks of recognising a zone beyond law outweighs the risks of creating a legal grey hole. Moreover, by demonstrating the capacity of a permanent state of emergency to invalidate constitutional norms through the process of desuetude and the implications this has for constituent power, I have sought to give judges a strong constitutional justification for conducting review.[5] Nevertheless, fundamental prudential challenges remain regarding how the judiciary should carry out this constitutionally mandated function. To recount from chapter four, concerns abound regarding the efficacy of judicial review in reviewing matters of national security; matters that the judiciary lack democratic legitimacy, expertise, or the practicalities to decide.[6] Chapter four addressed the issue of democratic legitimacy, rejecting this concern due to it being outweighed by more pressing challenges in ensuring all state power is circumscribed by law.[7] Nevertheless, the pragmatic anxieties as to the efficacy of judicial review of emergency powers remain.

Ensuring Robust Review

I have not argued in this book that the judiciary should have the authority either to declare a state of emergency ex ante or review the decision to declare a state of emergency before it has been made. Rather, I emphasised the importance of judicial review once the emergency has been declared. Permanent emergencies

[3] See ch 3.
[4] See text to nn 9–17 in ch 5.
[5] See ch 3.
[6] See text to nn 36–60 in ch 4.
[7] See text to n 120 in ch 4.

are not merely caused by the initial declaration but by this declaration's continued existence, be it by express affirmation or acquiescence. This therefore provides an answer to the concern that judges make decisions too slowly for an emergency: judges would be reviewing the existence of a state of emergency that has already been declared with the resultant measures that are claimed to be necessary already in place. Consequently, the risk of delaying an effective response is mitigated. Nevertheless, when reviewing this question, there may be highly sensitive information that the executive contends it cannot disclose for national security reasons. The judiciary may defer to the executive on this issue and many argue that this is the correct constitutional approach for judges to take.[8] However, it is also the case that the executive simply plays the national security trump card far too frequently, and high-profile instances demonstrate that the executive has damaged this trust. As noted in chapter five, the farce surrounding the Iraq war in the UK and government claims regarding evidence pertaining to Saddam Hussein's supposed stockpile of weapons of mass destruction may be a key reason behind Lord Hoffmann's radically different approach to national security issues in *Belmarsh* when compared with the earlier case of *Rehman*.[9] The legacy of Iraq also looms large over the British Parliament, as evident by the government defeat on whether to authorise military action against the Assad regime in Syria in September 2013.[10]

Similar trump cards may also be played by the executive in the context of emergencies not related to national security. In an economic state of emergency, for example, the executive may claim to be privy to commercially sensitive information regarding the capital needs for banks of systemic importance.[11] Much like a national security emergency, such claims may cause legislatures to defer to the executive's assessment as to what is needed to confront the crisis at hand. Relatedly, such matters are areas of policy-making in which judges are prima facie reluctant to get involved due to the polycentric nature of the disputes involved.[12] However, this polycentricism also reveals why responses to economic crises fall far short of the idea of being 'necessary', established in chapter one as a fundamental

[8] See Eric Posner and Adrian Vermeule, *Terror in the Balance: Security, Liberty and The Courts* (Oxford University Press, 2007). Cora Chan describes as this as the 'dilution approach' from the UK judiciary to national security issues. Cora Chan, 'Business as Usual: Deference in Counter-Terrorism Judicial Review' in Fergal F Davis and Fiona de Londras, *Critical Debates on Counter-Terrorism Judicial Review* (Cambridge University Press, 2014) 228.

[9] *SSHD v Rehman* [2001] UKHL 47; [2002] 1 all er 122; See text to n 137 in ch 5.

[10] Parliament did ultimately approve military action in Syria in November 2015; however, this was to be directed against ISIS rather than the Assad regime who would have been the targets of the proposed September 2013 campaign. See Elizabeth Piper and Kylie MacKellan, 'British Parliament Votes to Bomb Islamic State in Syria' *Reuters* (2 December 2015) <www.reuters.com/article/us-mideast-crisis-syria-britain-idUSKBN0TL00M20151202> accessed 15 August 2017; see also Colin RG Murray and Aoife O'Donoghue, 'Towards Unilateralism? House of Commons Oversight of the Use of Force' (2016) 65 *ICL* 305.

[11] A Greene, 'Questioning Executive Supremacy in an Economic State of Emergency' (2015) 35 *LS* 594, 610–13.

[12] ibid, 614–15.

component of the emergency paradigm.[13] 'Necessity' implies the idea of a constraint in choice with governments arguing that they 'have no other choice' and legislatures accepting this. However, responses to economic crises are much more polarised than national security crises. The left and right often take mutually exclusive positions on economic problems, meaning that a convergence of opinion on what ought to be done can never be achieved.[14]

In light of questionable claims of necessity made by executives in the past, I agree with David Dyzenhaus's contention that judges, and, indeed, the other branches of government, should be given a good reason to defer. Judges do not and should not have a monopoly on reviewing this assessment. Key to what Dyzenhaus terms a 'culture of justification' is that 'there should be a duty to give reasons when officials make decisions that affect important interests of the individual and that judges must avert to those reasons on review'.[15] However, judges are not the only branch of government tasked with this duty. Dyzenhaus argues that members of the legislature should also be conceptualised as legal officials each tasked with an obligation of fidelity to the law.[16] This obligation requires them to be provided with good reasons by the executive before deferring, rather than merely rubber-stamping the wishes of the executive. The legislature, nevertheless, also faces similar problems as that faced by the judiciary regarding access to sensitive material pertaining to national security. However, this may not be the case for emergencies triggered by other phenomena. Thus, claims by the executive that it is privy to sensitive information regarding an economic state of emergency should be particularly resisted by the legislature due, firstly, to the publicly available information that markets are supposed to be based upon; and secondly, to the highly subjective nature of the correct response to take to an economic crisis and the often-permanent impact of such decisions.[17]

A potential solution to both legislative and judicial access to sensitive information would be for this material to be disclosed in a private hearing or secret session. Parliaments and courts could then evaluate the material with the risk of public disclosure of sensitive information mitigated to an extent. In *Belmarsh*, for example, the SIAC at first instance did see confidential material in a closed session; however, the House of Lords did not request to see this material, satisfying itself with the SIAC's conclusion.[18] In turn, the ECtHR expressed that it was satisfied that an emergency existed under Article 15 because the House of Lords was satisfied, thus compounding the deferential effect. The British Parliament has also sat in secret due, again, to the risk of disclosing sensitive information—eg on

[13] See text to nn 173–175 in ch 1.
[14] Greene (n 11) 614–15.
[15] David Dyzenhaus, 'Deference, Security and Human Rights' in Benjamin J Goold and Liora Lazarus (eds), *Security and Human Rights* (Hart Publishing, 2007) 125, 139.
[16] ibid, 143.
[17] Greene (n 11) 620.
[18] Dyzenhaus (n 15) 129.

17 September 1940 during the Battle of Britain.[19] The Australian Parliament took also took similar steps during World War II.[20] In more recent times, Parliament held private sessions on the passing of the Anti-Terrorism Crime and Security Act 2001, again to avoid disclosing sensitive material.[21] The status of leaders of the opposition as members of the Privy Council has also been used by governments in the past to share confidential information 'on Privy Council terms'.[22]

Such approaches are, however, as inherently antithetical to the normative values of many constitutional orders as the state of emergency that they would be scrutinising. As noted in chapter six, closed material procedures and the rise of the use of special advocates in the UK, for example, is a disturbing trend, expanding from their original use in specific counter-terrorist cases regarding detention without trial into other areas, including their use in civil procedures.[23] Secret parliamentary hearings are also inimical to the legislative process where public debate, scrutiny and accountability are fundamental to the normative legitimacy of the legislature as the correct constitutional forum for political disagreement. Moreover, if the judiciary were to defer to a legislative assessment as to the existence of a state of emergency without seeing the material the legislature has seen in a closed session, this would merely shift blind deference to the executive to blind deference to the legislature and would not foster a culture of justification as the reasons for the decision would still be withheld from the public.

Closed parliamentary and judicial hearings are therefore far from ideal. That stated, much debate in many parliamentary systems arguably already takes place behind closed doors in parliamentary party meetings, even in periods of normalcy. The motivations behind such debates are not to protect sensitive information pertaining to national security but to ensure dissent is ironed out in private with members subsequently emerging united in public and voting with the party whip. In this manner, the executive can dominate all parliamentary debate, not just those pertaining to national security. This, of course, is not an argument in favour of legislative deference; rather, it is mentioned here to illustrate that the decline of parliaments and the rise of the executive is much more prevalent than just in the context of national security decisions. Thus, the use of the word 'culture' in 'culture of justification' demonstrates that it would require a root-and-branch buy-in to the idea.

[19] 'Secret Session Parliament in the Air Raids: A Statement to the House of Commons' (17 September 1940) <www.parliament.uk/about/living-heritage/transformingsociety/private-lives/yourcountry/collections/churchillexhibition/churchill-and-ww2/secret-session/> accessed 23 August 2017.

[20] 'Parliament's Secret Session Ends' *The Mail* (21 February 1942) <http://trove.nla.gov.au/newspaper/article/55769308> accessed 23 August 2017.

[21] Julian Glover, 'Lib Dems and Tories Ambush Government on Terror Bill' *The Guardian* (5 December 2001) <www.theguardian.com/politics/2001/dec/05/houseofcommons.uk> accessed 23 August 2017.

[22] Jon Lunn, Louisa Brooke-Holland and Clare Mills, 'The UK National Security Council', House of Commons Briefing Paper No 7456 (11 January 2016) 10–11.

[23] See text to nn 65–66 in ch 6.

Independent Reviewers in a Culture of Justification

To foster this culture of justification, innovative measures of accountability and scrutiny may instead have to be developed. The UK Independent Reviewer of Terrorism Legislation (Independent Reviewer), for example, is one such innovation. Lacking a single statutory footing, the Independent Reviewer is instead tasked to review the operation of various counter-terrorist powers in the UK.[24] The importance of review is compounded by the fact that such legislation was often enacted with scant scrutiny due to the perceived crisis that often precipitated and expedited their enactment.[25] This mechanism has been copied by Australia in the form of the Independent National Security Legislation Monitor, albeit the latter's function is established by a specific statute.[26]

The lack of a formal mandate enables the UK Independent Reviewer to construct a broad or narrow interpretation of their terms of reference. Thus, the first Independent Reviewer, Lord Carlile, interpreted his remit narrowly, stating that he would not question the necessity of anti-terrorism legislation as adjunct to and strengthening of the ordinary criminal law.[27] As a result, Jessie Blackbourn is critical of the manner in which Lord Carlile carried out his function, particularly in the context of control orders where his independence was questionable due to his closeness with the government.[28] In contrast, his successor, David Anderson, stated that: '[A]ny assessment of whether they [counter-terrorist powers in general] are necessary … must be conducted with an eye both to the current nature and extent of the terrorist threat in the United Kingdom.'[29] Consequently, this ultimately means that the functioning of the office is dependent upon the person appointed.[30] Rather than being a mechanism of accountability, independent review could instead become a further reason for other branches to defer to the executive, thus further increasing their legitimacy and propensity to become permanent.

Despite these difficulties, Independent Reviewers may, nevertheless, provide assistance in confronting the practical difficulties regarding the assessment of the existence of a state of emergency and the fragmented approach to the impact of counter-terrorist legislation that courts and legislatures often take. Independent review provides an opportunity to view the UK's counter-terrorist landscape through a hyperopic or 'big-picture' lens and in this regard the Independent Reviewer has a key advantage over the courts. Courts are restricted to addressing

[24] Jessie Blackbourn, 'Independent Reviewers as Alternative: An Empirical Study from Australia and the United Kingdom' in Davis and de Londras (n 8) 161, 164–66.

[25] Jessie Blackbourn, 'The Independent National Security Legislation Monitor's First Term: An Appraisal' (2016) 39 *UNSW Law Journal* 975, 976.

[26] ibid, 978–79; Independent National Security Legislation Monitor Act 2010.

[27] Blackbourn (n 24) 169–70.

[28] ibid, 174–75.

[29] ibid, 171.

[30] ibid.

only the statutes and subsections of such statutes that are relevant to the case before them and, as a result, their approach to counter-terrorism is myopic, or narrow. In addition, as argued in chapter five, thicker, substantive conceptions of the rule of law, particularly those that incorporate substantive values such as human rights may, paradoxically, encourage a constitutionally 'minimalist' approach to judicial review as concepts such as proportionality inevitably come into play.[31]

By focusing only on the relevant measures in question in a given case, a court can ignore the cumulative impact of the counter-terrorism measures as a whole. This cumulative impact of the state's counter-terrorist measures may be ultimately disproportionate to the exigencies of the situation; however, the myopic approach of the courts may fail to identify this. Thus, control orders may, in isolation, look like a measured response to a terrorist threat faced by a state. However, when viewed in conjunction with other counter-terrorist measures—expansive stop-and-search powers, increased surveillance powers, tightened border and immigration controls, etc—a different, more accurate and, ultimately, more dystopian picture may emerge.

Generally speaking, for a court to engage in such a hyperopic view of the legislative landscape would amount to a significant departure from the traditional role of the courts and arguably a role they do not have the legitimacy to undertake. It was noted in Chapter 5 that even where there is an opportunity for a legitimate 'hyperopic approach' to be taken by courts—eg when reviewing the existence of a state of emergency following a derogation from the ECHR—the courts have been reluctant to engage in a meaningful review of such an issue.[32] Instead, the first limb of Article 15 ECHR—whether there exists a war or other public emergency threatening the life of the nation—was collapsed into the second limb—whether the measures taken were proportionate to the exigencies of the situation.[33]

While institutional constraints or pragmatic concerns may restrict a court's ability or willingness to engage in a hyperopic review of the legislative landscape, such problems may not afflict the Independent Reviewer. As noted in chapter six, legislatures may also be susceptible to taking a myopic approach to emergency powers, notwithstanding the fact that theoretically it is constitutionally the best place to assess the overall impact of such emergency powers. Debates regarding the sunsetting or renewal of counter-terrorism legislation, for example, focus only on the specific powers in question, rather than the overall cumulative effect of the entire counter-terrorist legislative landscape.

The Independent Reviewer should not be solely capable of assessing whether a state of emergency exists or not. However, should a circumstance arise in future when the UK does derogate from Article 15, a role for the Independent Reviewer could be envisaged where they provide reports regarding the continued existence of an emergency and the proportionality of the state's response. Such reports could

[31] See text to nn 138–140 in ch 5.
[32] See text to nn 44–54 in ch 5.
[33] ibid.

help facilitate a more rigorous debate in Parliament by ensuring individuals are adequately informed of the cumulative effect of these emergency powers. In turn, this would assist with creating what is termed a 'culture of justification', where deference towards the executive by the legislature, and indeed by the judiciary, is earned by the government.[34] Independent Review should therefore complement rather than replace judicial review of the existence to declare a state of emergency or review by other constitutional branches. Innovative institutional designs may provide solutions to these pragmatic concerns. Nevertheless, even if such concerns persist, they cannot oust the constitutional justification for judicial review of the decision to declare a state of emergency.

Engineering Constitutions against Permanent States of Emergency

As argued in chapter six, failing to expressly provide for a state of emergency does not banish the exception from the constitutional order. Rather, existing constitutional norms may be recalibrated downwards in the face of the perceived necessity of a response to the crises. Emergency powers may be provided for instead through legislation. The argument that the constitution is not a suicide pact often wins out.[35] This is not to say, however, that 'necessity hath no law'. Law is very much a product of necessity and therefore law must attempt to construct an emergency order to ensure a modicum of flexibility in times of crisis but also preserve the fortitude of the constitution so that such flexibility remains temporary and self-defeating. What should such a constitution therefore look like?

Legislative Scrutiny of Emergency Powers: Bruce Ackerman's Super-Majoritarian Escalator

We saw in Chapter 4 that democratic concerns tend to stress a minimal, deferential role for judicial review in a period of emergency. Such values should, however, promote a more robust role for the legislature in controlling the executive in a state of emergency. Moreover, as noted above, effective legislative scrutiny of emergency powers is a vital component of a 'culture of justification'. In this regard, Bruce Ackerman has composed a model of legislative control inspired by the South African model of an ever-increasing legislative majority needed in order to extend the duration of a state of emergency.[36] Ackerman is motivated

[34] Dyzenhaus (n 15) 125–56.

[35] *Terminiello v City of Chicago* (1949) 337 US 1, 37 (Jackson J dissenting).

[36] See Bruce Ackerman, *Before the Next Attack: Preserving Civil Liberties in an Age of Terrorism* (Yale University Press, 2006) ch 4.

by scepticism about actions of the executive and judges in emergencies. This scepticism is mostly based on the historical record which, as was discussed in chapter five, is well founded.

Ackerman's 'super-majoritarian escalator' would prevent emergencies becoming entrenched as with the increased duration of emergency, the legislative hurdle to cross would also increase due to the belief that emergencies decay over time and so too would legislative deference to the executive. Ackerman's suggestion is directed towards a presidential system of government, with a strict separation between legislative and executive branches. It does not, however, address a parliamentary system where a parliamentary whip would most likely be employed which could frustrate the effectiveness of the majoritarian escalator.[37] Moreover, the convergence seen on the left and right on issues of national security could also hamper its effectiveness.[38] Legislators may also prefer to 'push back' not on the existence of the emergency and all the emergency powers taken in lieu of the declaration but on particular measures taken by the executive, thus leaving the emergency intact for a much longer period. Nevertheless, Ackerman's super-majoritarian escalator is an innovative suggestion that is certainly worthy of consideration. However, as stressed throughout this book, such legislative scrutiny cannot be used to justify completely ousting judicial review of the existence of a state of emergency. Ultimately, Ackerman concedes this, finding himself, nevertheless, forced to provide a constitutional role for judges.[39] In particular, Ackerman sees the judicial role as being pivotal in the event that the legislature terminates the emergency but the US president refuses to surrender power. Thus, if a constitution were to opt for a super-majoritarian escalator, this should not displace the need for judicial review.

Time-Limits and Sunset Clauses

As discussed in chapters one and six, the inclusion of time-limits or 'sunset clauses' on emergency powers is a frequently used mechanism designed to reinforce the emergency—normalcy dichotomy and ensure emergency powers remain exceptional. Machiavelli considered the six-month limit to the Roman dictator's office as being the most important control on the office.[40] This time limit was, however, closely tied to the working year of the army at a time when fighting was mostly conducted in the summer months. Emergencies today may not be so neatly compartmentalized, meaning a specific 'one-for-all' time-limit cannot be designed. France's Constitution, for example, provides for a time-limit of six months for

[37] For a critique of parliamentary whips in the context of national security, see Fergal F Davis and Fiona de Londras, 'Controlling the Executive in Times of Terrorism: Competing Perspectives on Effective Oversight Mechanisms' (2010) 30 *Oxford Journal of Legal Studies* 19, 34–36 (per de Londras).

[38] ibid.

[39] Ackerman (n 36) 103–04.

[40] See text to n 43 in ch 1.

the duration of a state of emergency; however, the emergency declared following the attacks on Paris in November 2015 was extended for almost two years until 31 October 2017, whereupon many of the emergency powers were re-enacted under permanent legislation.[41] The discussion in chapter six of the use of sunset clauses in legislation in the UK and the US further suggests that that time-limits, in and of themselves, fail to stymie the perpetuation of emergency powers.[42] The responses that were once considered 'special' and 'emergency' eventually over time become normalised or indeed insufficient to deal with a new threat. A 'ratcheting' effect occurs, where each subsequent attack leads to a further, more draconian response by the authorities, gradually eroding civil liberties.[43] Like the exception becoming the rule, the temporary altering of the legislative field becomes permanent. Indeed, parliamentary debates on the renewal of sunsetting of legislation may provide an opportunity for relegitimation rather than expiration. Consequently, sunset clauses may actually perpetuate emergencies rather than constrain them. That stated, no time-limit on a state of emergency would require proactive steps to be taken by the legislature, for example, in order for a debate on its cessation to take place; something members of the legislature may be reluctant to do, again because of the convergence between left and right on national security issues. Having a sunset clause in place at the very least means that a debate on the ending or perpetuation of the emergency must be held. Ultimately, however, the utility of express time-limits on the duration of a state of emergency is ambivalent at best.

'Discrete Conditions': The 'Shielding Effect' of Emergency Powers

As argued in chapter one, constructing a typology of emergency powers based on the phenomenon that triggers them is difficult, given the fact that one emergency may precipitate another.[44] Nevertheless, many constitutions have sought to provide for different emergency regimes depending upon the phenomenon. The idea behind such powers is to increase the 'shielding effect' of the state of emergency by only allowing the exceptional powers when the discrete conditions delineated exist. There is certainly nothing prima facie wrong from a rule of law perspective with trying to narrow the conditions for a valid emergency; however, without

[41] See Samuel Osborne, 'France declares end to state of emergency almost two years after Paris terror attacks' *The Independent* (31 October 2017) <http://www.independent.co.uk/news/world/europe/france-state-of-emergency-end-terror-attacks-paris-isis-terrorism-alerts-warning-risk-reduced-a8029311.html> accessed 31 October 2017; Alan Greene, 'Pouvoirs Anti-Terroristes Permanents au Royaume-Uni: Quelles Leçons pour la France? (2016) 38 *Archives de politique criminelle* 169.

[42] See text to nn 31–66 in ch 6.

[43] See Andrew Ashworth, 'Crime, Community and Creeping Consequentialism' (1996) *Criminal Law Review* 220; Oren Gross, 'Chaos and Rules: Should Responses to Violent Crises Always Be Constitutional?' (2002–03) 112 *Yale Law Journal* 1011, 1090–92.

[44] See text to n 123 in ch 1.

serious scrutiny of this decision, this narrowing will be meaningless. The ECtHR's interpretation of 'a threat to the life of the nation', for example, has reduced what prima facie appears to be a robust threshold for a crisis to cross to a mere procedural hurdle for states.[45] Ireland is also an illustrative example in this regard. As noted in chapter three, Ireland delineates some of the most discrete conditions for when an emergency can be declared—namely a time of war or armed rebellion.[46] Despite this, as noted in chapter four, Ireland experienced a 56-year long entrenched state of emergency dating from the outbreak of World War II in 1939 until the IRA ceasefire in February 1995. This was in large part due to the weak review of this existence by the Oireachtas and the Supreme Court's refusal to find whether or not it had the authority to review this question.[47] Discrete conditions are therefore only discrete if they are accompanied by effective review.

Limited Emergency Powers

It is rare for constitutions to provide for emergency powers that can potentially make every provision of the constitution subject to suspension.[48] As seen in chapter one, a common strategy for providing for constitutional emergency powers is to enumerate specific constitutional clauses that may be affected by a state of emergency.[49] A similar approach may also be to list the constitutional clauses that are non-derogable, in a manner similar to international human rights treaties. Often, the constitutional provisions in question pertain to human rights. However, this approach has risks. To recall from chapter five, this was the approach taken by the Weimar Constitution to emergencies, listing only certain rights that could be

[45] See text to nn 40–42 in ch 5; A Greene, 'Separating Normalcy from Emergency: The Jurisprudence of Article 15 of the European Convention on Human Rights' (2011) 12 *German Law Journal* 1764, 1783.

[46] The narrowness of such conditions were used to justify two subsequent amendments to Art 28.3.3 such that it now reads: 'Nothing in this Constitution other than Article 15.5.2° shall be invoked to invalidate any law enacted by the Oireachtas which is expressed to be for the purpose of securing the public safety and the preservation of the State in time of war or armed rebellion, or to nullify any act done or purporting to be done in time of war or armed rebellion in pursuance of any such law. In this sub-section "time of war" includes a time when there is taking place an armed conflict in which the State is not a participant but in respect of which each of the Houses of the Oireachtas shall have resolved that, arising out of such armed conflict, a national emergency exists affecting the vital interests of the State and "time of war or armed rebellion" includes such time after the termination of any war, or of any such armed conflict as aforesaid, or of an armed rebellion, as may elapse until each of the Houses of the Oireachtas shall have resolved that the national emergency occasioned by such war, armed conflict, or armed rebellion has ceased to exist.' See Alan Greene, 'The Historical Evolution of Article 28.3.3° of the Irish Constitution' (2012) 47 *Irish Jurist* 117.

[47] See text to n 120 in ch 4.

[48] Prior to the Twenty First Amendment of the Constitution Act 2001 which precludes the introduction of the death penalty, Art 28.3.3° of the Irish Constitution did potentially enable the suspension of every provision of the Irish Constitution. See, however, text to n 121 in ch 4 on whether Art 28.3.3° can be amended using emergency powers so as to circumvent this prohibition of the death penalty. See also Greene (n 46) 140–41.

[49] See text to n 135 in ch 1.

infringed upon. It was also noted that this failed to curtail the scope of Article 48, with Carl Schmitt arguing that a number of other constitutional provisions—eg those delimiting the federal versus the state power—were also infringed.[50] This is the difficulty in trying to list only specific rights provisions that may be suspended in a state of emergency as emergencies invariably impact upon other constitutional provisions, eg those pertaining to the separation of powers. This is not to say, however, that such strategies are doomed to failure; rather it is to emphasise that enumerating a limited emergency power alone will not suffice to curtail such power when the exigencies of the situation are represented as necessitating it. Such powers will only be limited if there are institutional checks to ensure this remains the case.

Proportionality as a Controlling Factor

A common measure for constitutions to take to limit emergency powers is to insist that they are proportionate to the threat at hand. As argued in Chapter 4, the inclusion of a proviso that the emergency measures taken be proportionate to the exigencies of the situation has led the ECtHR to focus only on this issue, essentially neglecting to assess whether an emergency exists or not. This was further compounded by the decision in *Belmarsh* where the ECtHR expressly stated that nowhere in Article 15 does it suggest that an emergency be temporary.[51] The ECtHR in *Belmarsh* further damages this shielding effect by eliminating the exceptional nature that phenomena must constitute to trigger a state of emergency, by declaring that emergency under Article 15 does not necessarily have to be temporary.[52] Instead, 'duration' becomes merely another factor in determining whether the measures undertaken were proportionate to the exigencies of the situation.[53] This fundamentally uproots Article 15 as a representation of the normalcy—emergency dichotomy, as the goal of restoring the latter is abandoned by the ECtHR.

Providing that the measures taken in lieu of a declaration of a state of emergency be proportionate to the exigencies of the situation should therefore operate as a 'second limb' to controlling emergency powers. It should not act as a replacement for the criterion that there exists a state of emergency. Attempting to control emergencies solely through the doctrine of proportionality is, in effect, a 'business as usual' approach and this lacks the quarantining or 'shielding effect' that a state of emergency can provide. However, if the approach of the ECtHR is also followed and the existence of a state of emergency question glossed over in favour of the

[50] See text to nn 158–69 in ch 5.

[51] *A v Secretary of State for the Home Department* [2005] 2 WLR 87; *A and Others v United Kingdom*, Judgment of 19 February 2009, [2009] ECHR 3455/05, [96].

[52] ibid, [178].

[53] ibid.

proportionality question, or collapsed into the proportionality question, this also damages the shielding effect.

What is fundamental to the requirement of proportionality and, indeed, express limitations on what constitutional provisions may be infringed in a state of emergency, is that they clearly demonstrate that the decision to declare a state of emergency is a constituted power as distinct from the constituent power. It should therefore corroborate judicial review of the decision to declare a state of emergency, not act as a scapegoat for a 'rule by law' review of this decision and subsequent focus only on the proportionality requirement. Proportionality should therefore complement not overrule the first question regarding the existence of a state of emergency.

The Transformative Nature of Permanent States of Emergency

One of the key themes highlighted throughout this book has been a sceptical approach to executive claims as to the existence of a state of emergency. This scepticism is, I believe, well founded. Indeed, it is this scepticism that drives many controls on emergency powers and the rejection of the emergency paradigm by 'business as usual' constitutional orders.[54] The language of emergency can be manipulated to mobilise popular support around measures antithetical to the constitutional order and no branch of government is more capable of doing this or has more historical experience of doing so than the executive.

It must not be forgotten that the normative value of the state of emergency is inherently bound to the constitutional order it is designed to protect. It is for this reason that chapter one stressed the link between phenomenon and response, with the state of emergency being designed to protect these constitutional values through their temporary suspension rather than render them ineffective in perpetuity. Of course, constitutions are human creations and humans are fallible. Consequently, even the best-engineered constitution may buckle under extreme stress. Chapter four, for example, noted how institutional design is fundamental in ensuring that the judiciary can carry out its function independently.[55] This assumption also underpins much of my argument pertaining to the importance of judicial review of the decision to declare a state of emergency and distinguishing this assessment as a legal, rather than a political question. It is often these checks, however, that come under pressure during a state of emergency where the motivations behind its declaration are, for want of a better word, questionable.

[54] See text to nn 1–26 in ch 6 of this book.

[55] See text to n 40 in ch 4; Joseph Raz, *The Authority of Law*, 2nd edn (Oxford University Press, 2009) 216–17.

For example, on 21 July 2016, Turkey declared a state of emergency following the failed military coup aimed at ousting President Recep Tayyip Erdoğan.[56] This was immediately followed by a large-scale purging of public servants, including the judiciary. It would be difficult, therefore, to see what merit, if any, judicial review of the decision to declare a state of emergency would have from the perspective of the rule of law, given its fundamental link to the independence of the judiciary.[57]

In a constitutional environment such as Turkey, where 2,700 judges were removed following the coup, it may fall on international courts to vindicate the rule of law. There is a strong case to be made that the ECtHR should narrow the margin of appreciation afforded to Turkey when assessing its decision to declare a state of emergency, in line with that afforded the Greek military junta in the *Greek Case*.[58] There, the lack of democratic legitimacy was fundamental to the European Commission finding that no state of emergency existed in Greece and instead, the emergency was fabricated in order to justify the crackdown on the communist opposition. While Turkish President Erdoğan was democratically elected, according a wide margin of appreciation on this basis would constitute a particularly narrow conception of democracy. Moreover, because a state's government has been elected, it does not follow that it will protect human rights. As noted in Chapter 2, this is particularly acute in a time of emergency when the democratic pressures for an emasculated government may be to clamp down on human rights and to show a fearful public that it is 'doing something', whether that something is effective or not.[59] Emergencies, therefore, are the very conditions when human rights are needed most. In overtly political emergencies, such as the coup facing Turkey, this concern for human rights is even more pressing. That stated, at the time of writing, the signals have not been promising. The ECtHR appears to be utilising avoidance mechanisms to side-step reviewing the emergency measures taken by Turkey.[60] However, the language coming from the Council of Europe has been much more forceful and critical, thus demonstrating the highly politicised nature of the issue and the legitimacy challenges currently facing the ECtHR as an international human rights court.

Turkey's declaration of a state of emergency was subsequently followed by a successful referendum on fundamental constitutional reforms, radically altering the constitutional order of Turkey by enhancing the powers of the president.

[56] Kareem Shaheen and Owen Bowcott, 'Turkey MPs Approve State of Emergency Bill Allowing Rule by Decree' *The Guardian* (21 July 2016) <www.theguardian.com/world/2016/jul/21/turkey-parliament-expected-to-pass-erdogan-emergency-measures> accessed 21 August 2017.

[57] Raz (n 55).

[58] *Denmark, Norway, Sweden and the Netherlands v Greece* App No 3221.67, European Commission of Human Rights, 5 November 1969.

[59] See text to nn 129–38 in ch 2; see also Cass Sunstein, *Laws of Fear: Beyond the Precautionary Principle* (Cambridge University Press, 2005).

[60] See *Çatal v Turkey* App No 2873/17, 10 March 2017, where the Court ruled inadmissible on the grounds of a failure to exhaust domestic remedies the case of a Turkish judge who was arrested, placed in police custody and then subsequently dismissed by the Turkish Supreme Council of Judges.

While this referendum was not directly connected to the official declaration of a state of emergency, many constitutions, nevertheless, contain provisions precluding the amendment of the constitution during a state of emergency.[61] This is done in order to prevent heightened public emotions being manipulated to effect radical change antithetical to the constitutional order ex ante.

Permanent States of Emergency and Constitutional Moments

Turkey is a particularly visceral example of the transformative potential of emergency powers. However, one must not be blind-sided by more banal permanent states of emergency. Throughout this book, I have sought to highlight the paradox of permanent states of emergency by stressing that emergency powers should negate their own existence by defeating the crisis that necessitates their enactment. A corollary, and equally paradoxical, consequence of this is the very idea of a crisis as extreme as that evoked by a state of emergency being one that a state can face perpetually. As noted in Chapter 2, a key driver of this is the application of the emergency paradigm to more banal phenomena than in the past. However, this banality must not cause us to let our guard down as the transformative capacity of the banal is no less potent than that of the more tumultuous emergency.

As emergencies shift from being temporary disruptors of the status quo to quotidian, more banal crises, the threat is conceptualised as one that needs to be managed rather than defeated.[62] Somewhat ironically, however, this managerialism is itself dependent upon certain aspects of the normalcy—emergency dichotomy. Risk assessment requires broad actuarial decisions to be made that are often based upon oversimplistic prejudices. Consequently, risk management may rely on many of the crude and racist distinctions utilised to distinguish friend from enemy as discussed in chapter two.[63] 'Moralising and managerialism therefore need each other badly.'[64] By operating on a macro-level, risk assessment and management makes broad assumptions about environments and about individuals. This shift towards managerialism and risk management is fundamentally transformative to the constitutional order of the state and the norms it espouses to represent. This transformative nature, however, is much more clandestine than that of, for example, Schmitt's sovereign dictatorship or the communist dictatorship of the proletariat.[65] The transformative nature of Schmitt's sovereign dictatorship and the communist dictatorship of the proletariat is express. It is this transformative aspect that gives these dictatorships their legitimacy in the eyes of their followers—it is their raison d'être. The status quo ex ante *is* the emergency that

[61] See text to n 138 in ch 1.

[62] See Oren Gross, 'Chaos and Rules: Should Responses to Violent Crises always be Constitutional?' (2002) 112 *Yale Law Journal* 112, 1069–95.

[63] See text to n 21 in ch 2.

[64] Lucia Zedner, 'Dangers of Dystopia in Legal Theory' (2002) 22 *OJLS* 341, 358.

[65] See text to n 123 in ch 3.

must be responded to. However, even in the context of the communist dictatorship of the proletariat, the inherent illegitimacy of this was acknowledged. Hence, the dictatorship of the proletariat, like the Roman dictatorship, would only be a temporary necessity; however, unlike the Roman dictatorship, it was transformative, envisaged as lasting until the state withered away, rather than until the status quo ex ante could be restored. In contrast, the Schmittian sovereign dictatorship embraces both its permanent and transformative qualities. Permanent states of emergency today, however, are potentially transformative but this transformative dimension is never expressly acknowledged. It is this clandestine dimension that that makes them so dangerous. Relatedly, so-called de facto states of emergency—situations in which a state conceptualises and responds to a threat as if a state of emergency exists but does not, de jure, declare one—are also pernicious.

Bruce Ackerman describes the transformative nature that certain events have on constitutions as 'constitutional moments'.[66] Talking specifically about the US context, Ackerman argues that Article 5 of the US Constitution does not exhaust the amendment process. Rather, amendments can take place through unenumerated means in this critical period of the constitutional moment. In such moments, politics shifts from the everyday normal to more intense, higher-law-making processes where conflict is over much more fundamental political questions usually involving the legitimacy of permanently entrenched norms.[67] Ackerman breaks down the constitutional moment into four steps: (i) a branch of government claims a mandate from the people to effect constitutional change; (ii) a proposal is put forward for such a change; (iii) this proposal faces resistance from another branch of government, with Ackerman highlighting the US Supreme Court's resistance to Roosevelt's New Deal; and (iv) a 'critical election' takes place in which the people demonstrate 'broad and deep' popular support for constitutional change, resulting in the opposing branch of government being forced to reappraise its position.[68]

Key to Ackerman's constitutional moment is the role of the people. Ackerman stresses the dualist nature of the US constitution envisaged by its founding fathers: a distinction between ordinary law-making and higher or constitutional law-making.[69] Ackerman argues that everyday ordinary law-making does not actually represent 'the people'. Rather, elites have contrived to keep ordinary people out of the process of law-making. Constitutional moments are periods whereby the people break through the ordinary system of politics to affirm or reject the proposed constitutional changes.

Attempts to conceptualise presidential elections post 9/11 as 'a critical election' under Ackerman's conception have been made, with Oren Gross noting the argument of John Yoo, author of the infamous torture memos, that the people

[66] See Bruce Ackerman, *We the People*, vol 2: *Transformation* (Belknap Press, 1998).

[67] ibid, ch 2; Sujuit Choudhry, 'Ackerman's Higher Lawmaking in Comparative Constitutional Perspective: Constitutional Moments as Constitutional Failures?' (2008) 6 ICON 193, 199–204.

[68] Ackerman (n 66) 20–21, 279–312.

[69] ibid, ch1.

had their say on these measures in the 2004 US presidential election.[70] Gross, however, rejects this argument on the merits, stating that torture was not on the agenda during the presidential campaign.[71] Relatedly, this clandestine nature of permanent states of emergency distinguishes them from what Ackerman terms a 'constitutional moment'. As noted in Chapter 2, economic states of emergency may amount to a constitutional moment; however, this is because they expressly repudiate the status quo ex ante, rather than justifying the measures taken as necessary to restore this status quo.[72] This is clearly seen Naomi Klein's famous exposition of the use of emergency powers and coups d'état in South America to usher in profound and radical transformations in economic policy and constitutional orders in states.[73] Hence, I have argued in greater detail elsewhere against conceptualising economic crises as states of emergency.

Through this pivotal role of the people, one can see the contrast between a permanent state of emergency and a constitutional moment. Constitutional moments and the branch of government trying to effect constitutional change are express in their motivations. The desire for change, the fundamental nature of this change, and the repudiation of the status quo ex ante is both *express* and *embraced*. Permanent states of emergency are, in contrast, the anthesis of the constitutional moment. The status quo ex ante is not repudiated; rather, it is held up as the standard to be restored. It is thus not a constitutional moment but instead the perpetual suspension of the moment of judgment by the people that affirms the constitutional moment. Yet it is no less transformative than a constitutional moment. It is a clandestine claim to higher-law-making power masquerading as everyday normal politics.

Final Conclusions

The emergency paradigm is not obsolete. Yet its application has deviated dramatically from the ideal-type emergency response as envisaged by theory. These permanent emergencies are, I have argued, not primarily caused by an empirically more dangerous world today, but by the application of the emergency paradigm to phenomena that are more mundane than those traditionally labelled as emergencies and by the inclusion of emergency powers in more banal legal mechanisms, such as legislation, than a separate constitutional state being declared. It is this *broadening* and *deepening* of emergency powers that is a major factor in causing

[70] Oren Gross, 'Extra-Legality and the Ethic of Political Responsibility' in Victor V Ramraj (ed), *Emergencies and the Limits of Legality* (Cambridge University Press, 2008) 60, 67–68.

[71] ibid.

[72] See text to nn 176–177 in ch 2.

[73] See Naomi Klein, *The Shock Doctrine: The Rise of Disaster Capitalism* (Allen Lane, 2008).

the 'permanent emergency'. This broadening and deepening is the result of political decisions and the perception or representation of a threat by political actors, rather than by an inherent objective criterion specific to modern crises that lead to permanent emergencies. Moreover, in utilising emergency responses to deal with increasingly low-level threats the state erodes the 'shielding effect' of a state of emergency. Relatedly, constitutions that fail to provide a mechanism for dealing with emergencies are often recalibrated in a manner that permits such a response but without the 'shielding effect' that accompanies a de jure state of emergency. Emergency powers therefore cannot be ignored.

These banal emergencies or de facto emergencies are, however, are no less transformative than the tumultuous crises that suddenly or violently befall a state. In times of such crises, human rights norms are vulnerable to consequentialist arguments in favour of the greater good. Consequently, so too are arguments in favour of judicial review that are exclusively justified on the grounds that such review best protects human rights. Relatedly, emergencies impact upon constitutional norms beyond human rights. An argument in favour of judicial review in a period of emergency from the perspective of a narrower conception of the rule of law can, I have argued, help to corroborate and fortify human rights norms as such an argument should be more insulated from the criticisms levied at judicial review as politics by other means. Moreover, it can also justify judicial review of other constitutional norms. Judicial review of the decision to declare a state of emergency is necessary in order to prevent a permanent state of emergency remaining 'unchallengeable' in the legal sphere and resulting in the permanent suspension of fundamental constitutional norms. In the absence of such judicial review the political sphere supersedes the legal order. The validity of the decision to declare an emergency that then becomes perpetual in nature cannot be referenced back to the legal norm that initially enabled the declaration. Such an interpretation of the constitution amounts to a claim for the constituent power by the body seeking exclusive authority to declare an emergency and so such an interpretation of the constitution should be rejected by the judiciary.

While states of emergency are an express admission that there are certain conditions in which fundamental constitutional norms can be jettisoned, they are also a pledge that the constitutional order is something worth defending. Ultimately, sacrificing constitutional norms in order to save these very norms can only be justified if the emergency is temporary. The transformative potential of the state of emergency therefore must never be forgotten. It is these constitutional values that the state of emergency is designed to protect and, therefore, the transformative potential of the permanent state of emergency must be resisted.

INDEX

www.ingramcontent.com/pod-product-compliance
Ingram Content Group UK Ltd.
Pitfield, Milton Keynes, MK11 3LW, UK
UKHW020808290926
15470UKWH00003B/1035

9 781509 906154